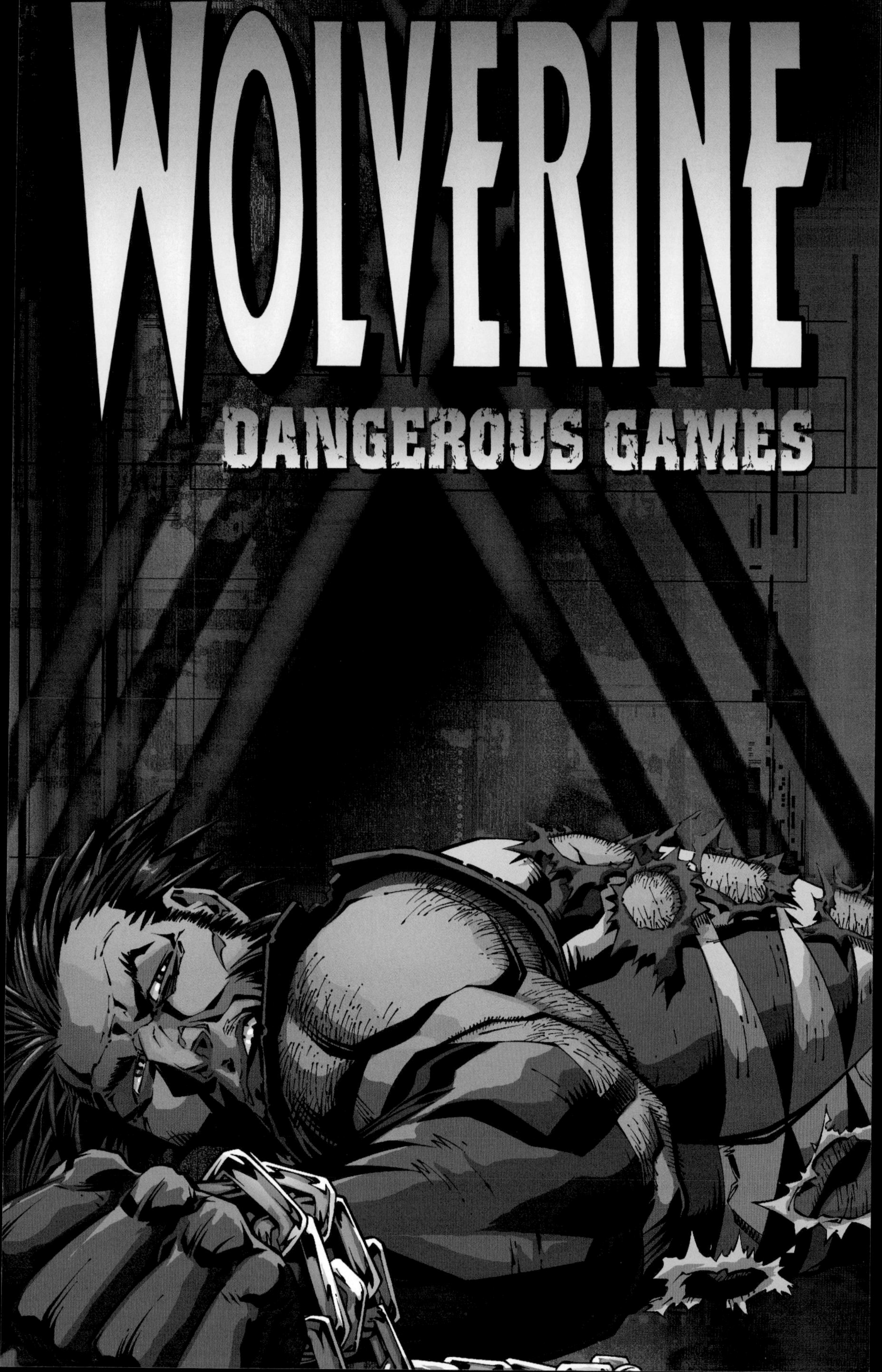
WOLVERINE
DANGEROUS GAMES

WOLVERINE

DANGEROUS GAMES

"The Death Song of J. Patrick Smitty"
Writer: Gregg Hurwitz
Artist: Marcelo Frusin
Letters: Todd Klein
Assistant Editor: Aubrey Sitterson
Editor: Axel Alonso

"Tally Ho!"
Writer: Simon Spurrier
Artist: Ben Oliver
Colors: Nestor Pereyra
Letters: Blambot's Nate Piekos
Editor: Aubrey Sitterson

"Purity"
Writer: Rick Remender
Artist: Jerome Opena
Colors: Michelle Madsen
Letters: Blambot's Nate Piekos
Editor: Aubrey Sitterson

"Killing Wolverine Made Simple"
Writer: Christopher Yost
Penciler: Koi Turnbull
Inker: Sal Regla
Colors: Beth Sotelo
Letters: Virtual Calligraphy's Cory Petit
Assistant Editor: Michael Horwitz
Editor: John Barber

WOLVERINE: DANGEROUS GAMES. Contains material originally published in magazine form as WOLVERINE ANNUAL #1: DEATHSONG, WOLVERINE: DANGEROUS GAMES, WOLVERINE: FIREBREAK and WOLVERINE: KILLIN▮ MADE SIMPLE. First printing 2008. ISBN# 978-0-7851-3471-8. Published by MARVEL PUBLISHING, INC., a subsidiary of MARVEL ENTERTAINMENT, INC. OFFICE OF PUBLICATION: 417 5th Avenue, New York, NY 1001▮ Copyright © 2007 and 2008 Marvel Characters, Inc. All rights reserved. $24.99 per copy in the U.S. and $26.50 in Canada (GST #R127032852); Canadian Agreement #40668537. All characters featured in this issu▮ and the distinctive names and likenesses thereof, and all related indicia are trademarks of Marvel Characters, Inc. No similarity between any of the names, characters, persons, and/or institutions in this magazine wi▮ those of any living or dead person or institution is intended, and any such similarity which may exist is purely coincidental. **Printed in the U.S.A**. ALAN FINE, CEO Marvel Toys & Publishing Divisions and CMO Marve▮ Characters, Inc.; DAVID GABRIEL, SVP of Publishing Sales & Circulation; DAVID BOGART, SVP of Business Affairs & Talent Management; MICHAEL PASCIULLO, VP of Merchandising & Communications; JIM O'KEEFE, V▮ of Operations & Logistics; DAN CARR, Executive Director of Publishing Technology; JUSTIN F. GABRIE, Director of Editorial Operations; SUSAN CRESPI, Editorial Operations Manager; STAN LEE, Chairman Emeritus. F▮ information regarding advertising in Marvel Comics or on Marvel.com, please contact Mitch Dane, Advertising Director, at mdane@marvel.com. For Marvel subscription inquiries, please call 800-217-9158.

10 9 8 7 6 5 4 3 2 1

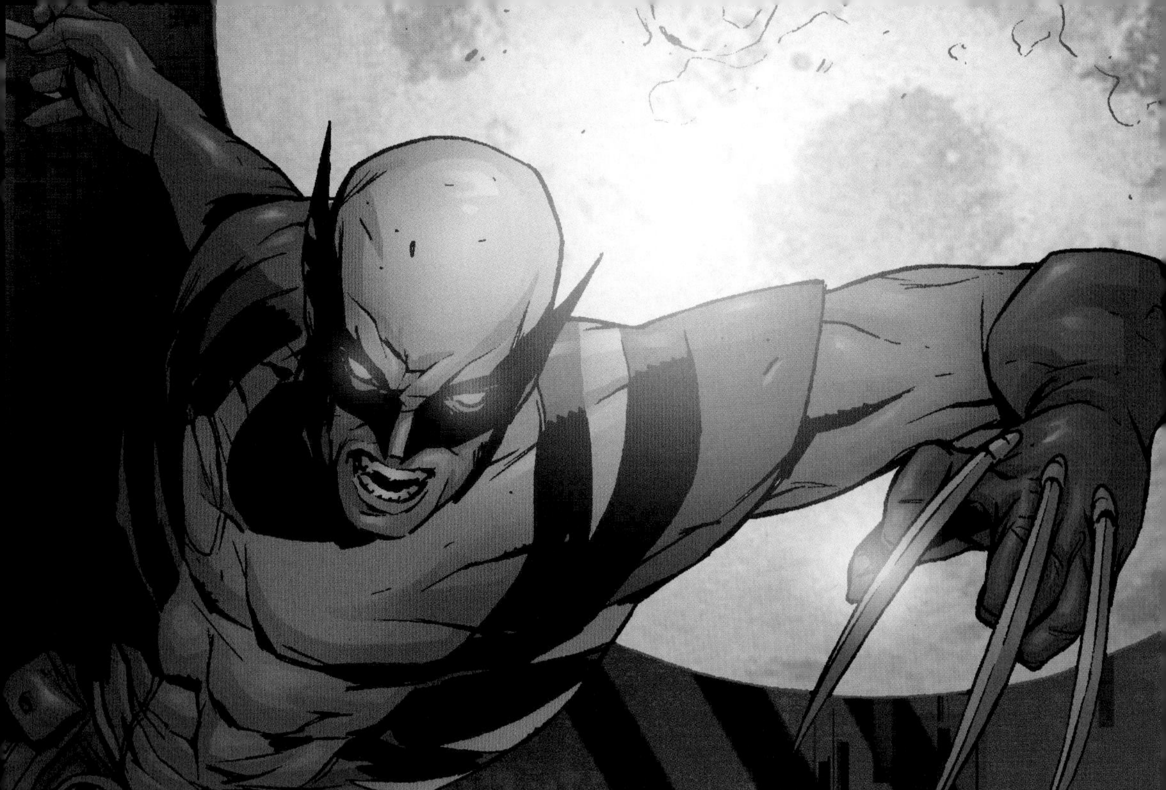

"DISTURBING CONSEQUENCES"
WRITER: TODD DEZAGO
PENCILER: STEVE KURTH
INKER: SERGE LAPOINTE
COLORS: JOEL SEGUIN
LETTERS: VIRTUAL CALLIGRAPHY'S CORY PETIT
ASSISTANT EDITOR: MICHAEL HORWITZ
EDITOR: JOHN BARBER

"FIREBREAK"
WRITER: MIKE CAREY
PENCILER: SCOTT KOLINS
COLORS: MOOSE BAUMANN
LETTERS: TROY PETERI
EDITOR: AUBREY SITTERSON

"LITTLE WHITE LIES"
WRITER: MACON BLAIR
ARTIST: VASILIS LOLOS
COLORS: NESTOR PEREYRA
LETTERS: TROY PETERI
EDITOR: AUBREY SITTERSON

COVER ARTISTS: MARCELO FRUSIN, BOO COOK,
STEPHEN SEGOVIA & SCOTT KOLINS

COLLECTION EDITOR: CORY LEVINE
EDITORIAL ASSISTANT: ALEX STARBUCK
ASSISTANT EDITOR: JOHN DENNING
EDITORS, SPECIAL PROJECTS: JENNIFER GRÜNWALD
& MARK D. BEAZLEY
SENIOR EDITOR, SPECIAL PROJECTS: JEFF YOUNGQUIST
SENIOR VICE PRESIDENT OF SALES: DAVID GABRIEL
PRODUCTION: JERRY KALINOWSKI & CARRIE BEADLE
EDITOR IN CHIEF: JOE QUESADA
PUBLISHER: DAN BUCKLEY

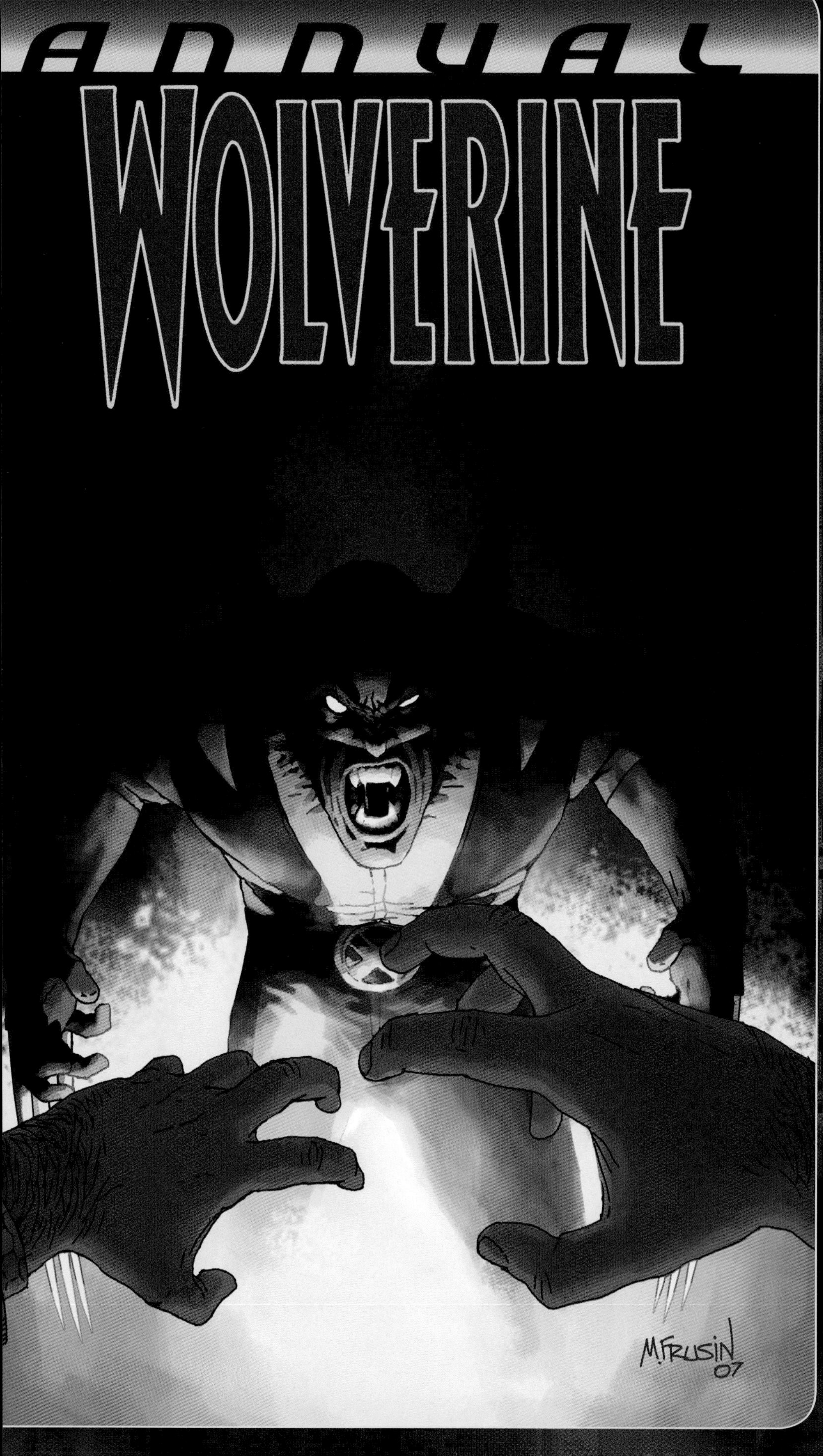
ANNUAL
WOLVERINE
M.FRUSIN
07

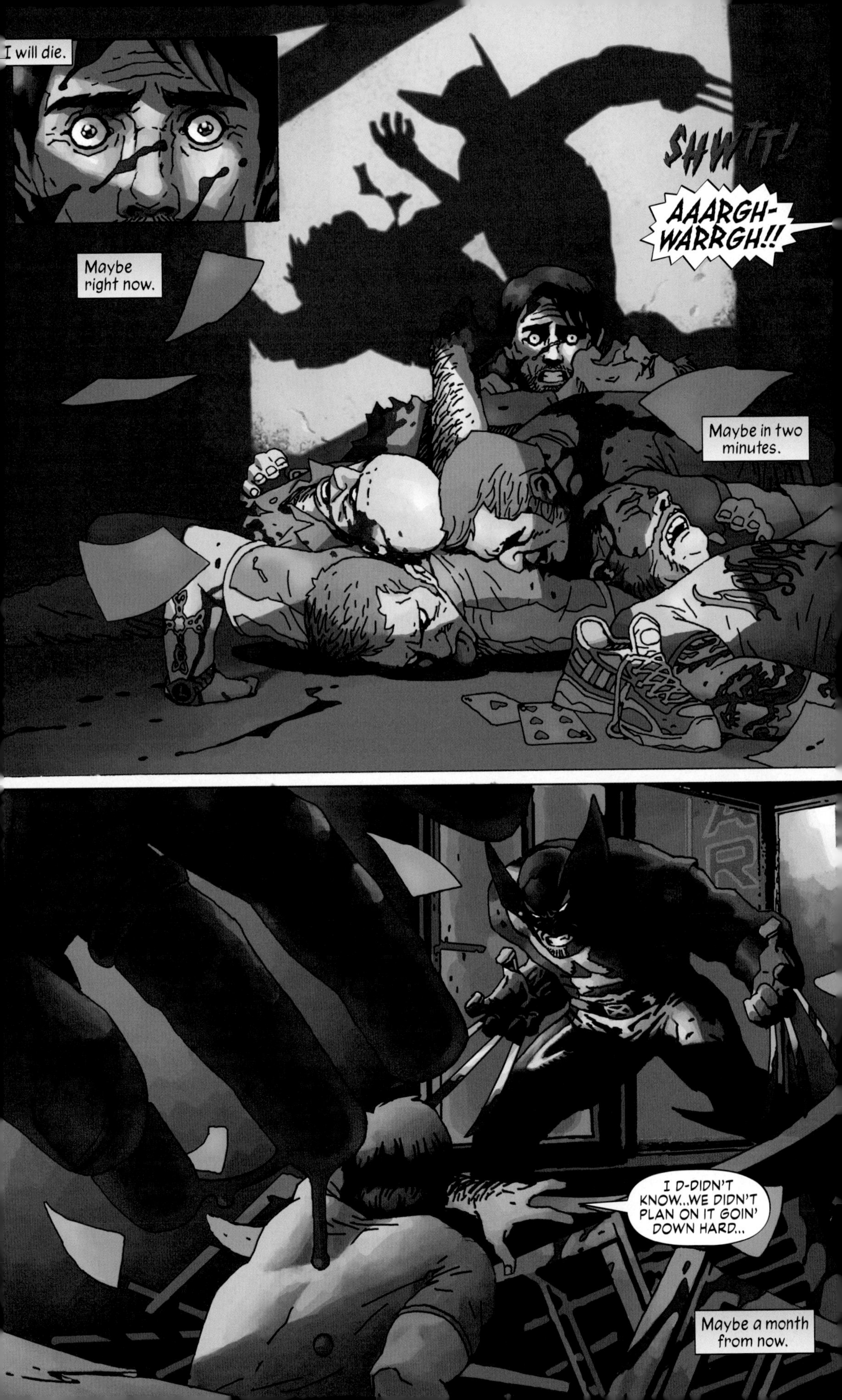

I will die.
Maybe right now.
AAARGH-WARRGH!!
Maybe in two minutes.
I D-DIDN'T KNOW...WE DIDN'T PLAN ON IT GOIN' DOWN HARD...
Maybe a month from now.

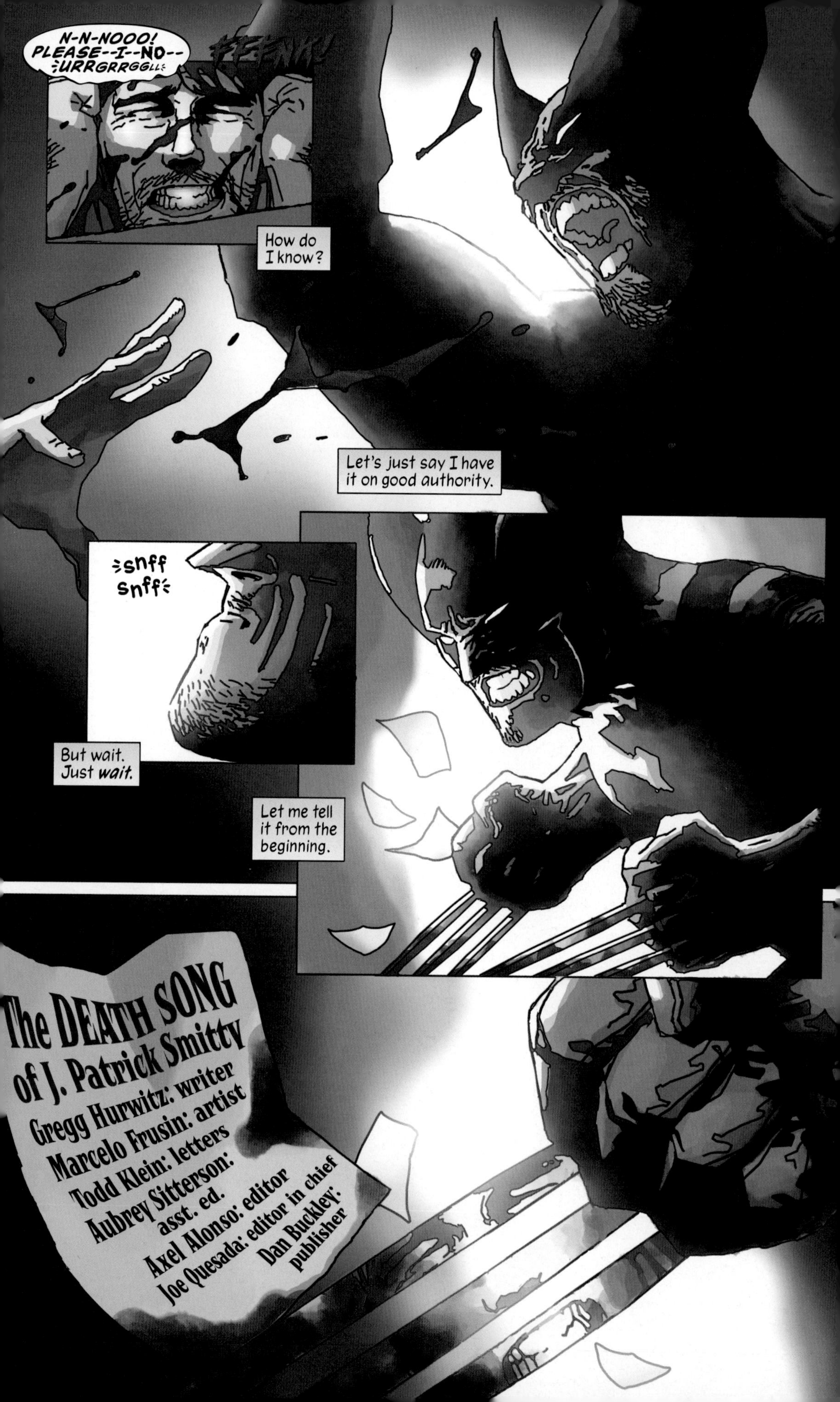

N-N-NOOO! PLEASE--I--NO-- URRGRRGGLL
How do I know?
Let's just say I have it on good authority.
snff snff
But wait. Just *wait.*
Let me tell it from the beginning.
The DEATH SONG of J. Patrick Smitty
Gregg Hurwitz: writer
Marcelo Frusin: artist
Todd Klein: letters
Aubrey Sitterson: asst. ed.
Axel Alonso: editor
Joe Quesada: editor in chief
Dan Buckley: publisher

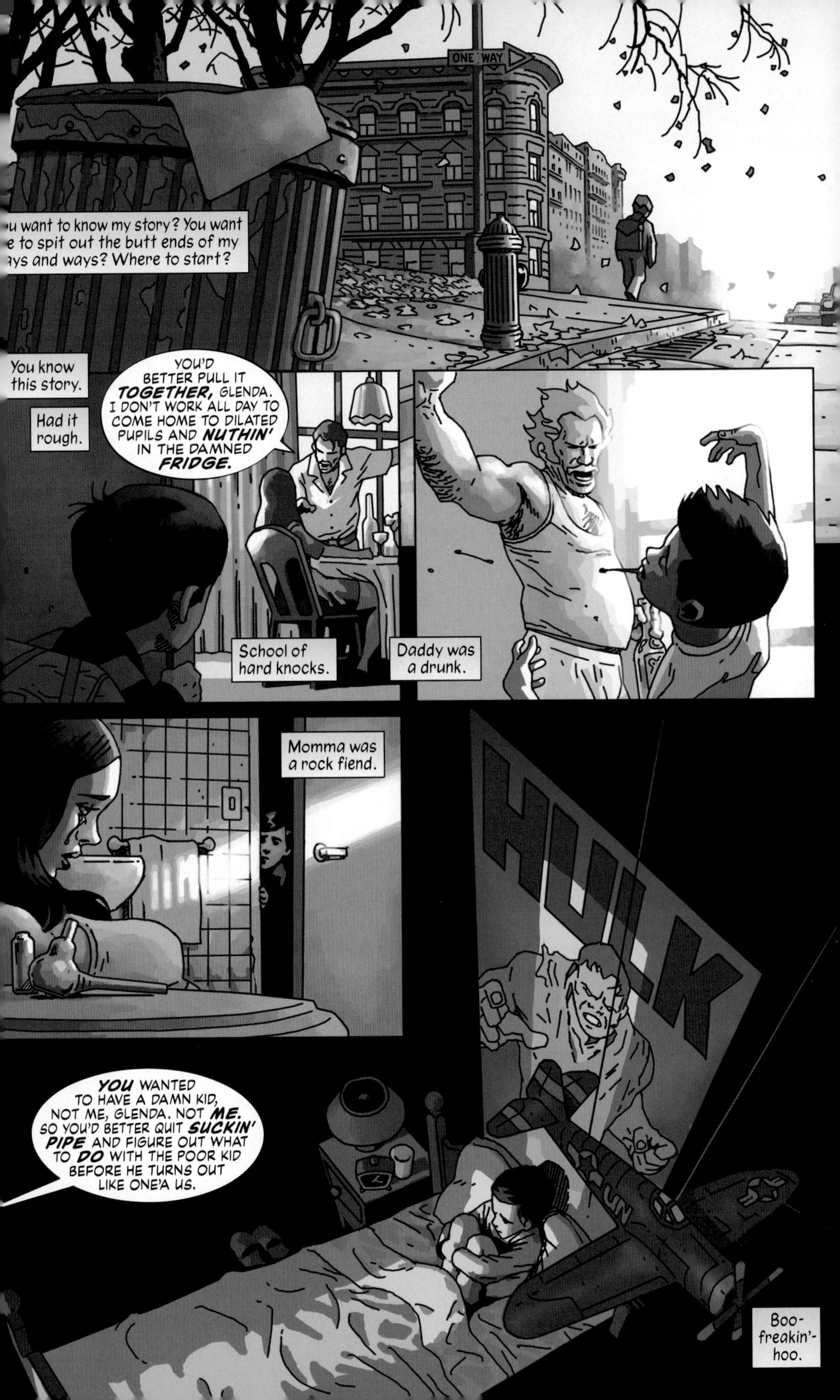

u want to know my story? You want e to spit out the butt ends of my ays and ways? Where to start?
ONE WAY
You know this story.
Had it rough.
YOU'D BETTER PULL IT TOGETHER, GLENDA. I DON'T WORK ALL DAY TO COME HOME TO DILATED PUPILS AND NUTHIN' IN THE DAMNED FRIDGE.
School of hard knocks.
Daddy was a drunk.
Momma was a rock fiend.
HULK
YOU WANTED TO HAVE A DAMN KID, NOT ME, GLENDA. NOT ME. SO YOU'D BETTER QUIT SUCKIN' PIPE AND FIGURE OUT WHAT TO DO WITH THE POOR KID BEFORE HE TURNS OUT LIKE ONE'A US.
Boo-freakin'-hoo.

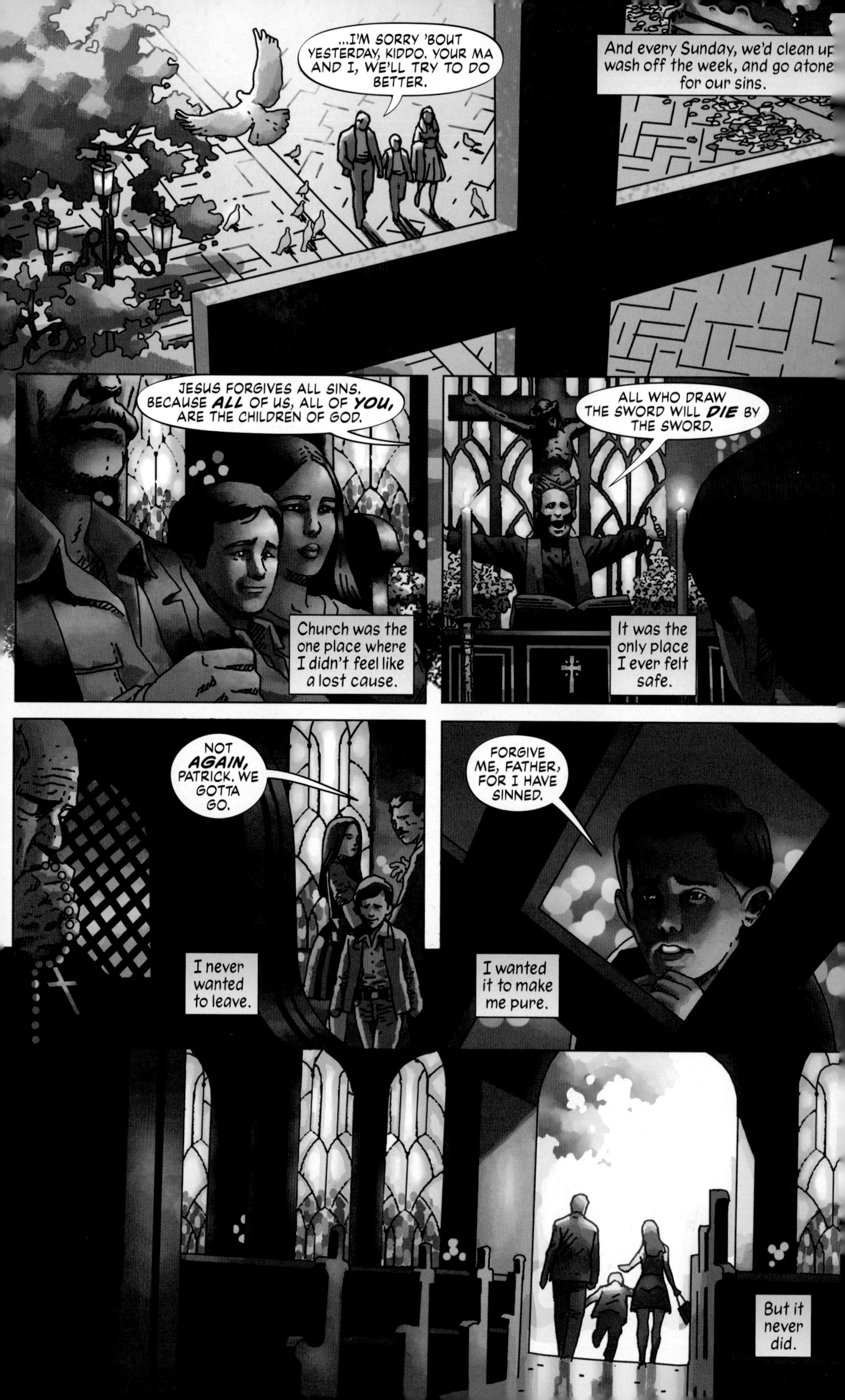
...I'M SORRY 'BOUT YESTERDAY, KIDDO. YOUR MA AND I, WE'LL TRY TO DO BETTER.
And every Sunday, we'd clean up wash off the week, and go atone for our sins.
JESUS FORGIVES ALL SINS. BECAUSE ALL OF US, ALL OF YOU, ARE THE CHILDREN OF GOD.
Church was the one place where I didn't feel like a lost cause.
ALL WHO DRAW THE SWORD WILL DIE BY THE SWORD.
It was the only place I ever felt safe.
NOT AGAIN, PATRICK. WE GOTTA GO.
I never wanted to leave.
FORGIVE ME, FATHER, FOR I HAVE SINNED.
I wanted it to make me pure.
But it never did.

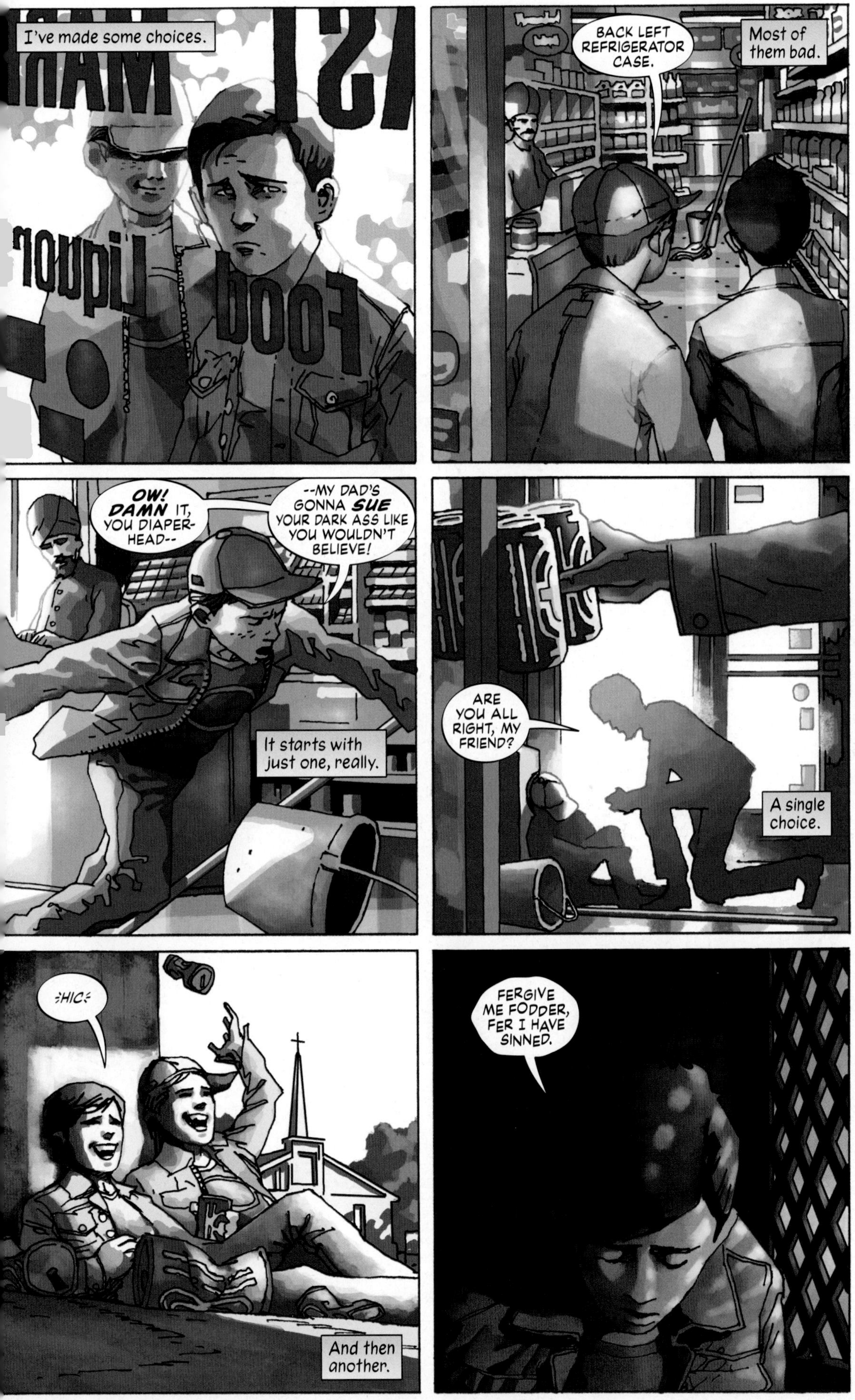

I've made some choices.
BACK LEFT REFRIGERATOR CASE.
Most of them bad.
OW! DAMN IT, YOU DIAPER-HEAD--
--MY DAD'S GONNA SUE YOUR DARK ASS LIKE YOU WOULDN'T BELIEVE!
It starts with just one, really.
ARE YOU ALL RIGHT, MY FRIEND?
A single choice.
HIC
And then another.
FERGIVE ME FODDER, FER I HAVE SINNED.

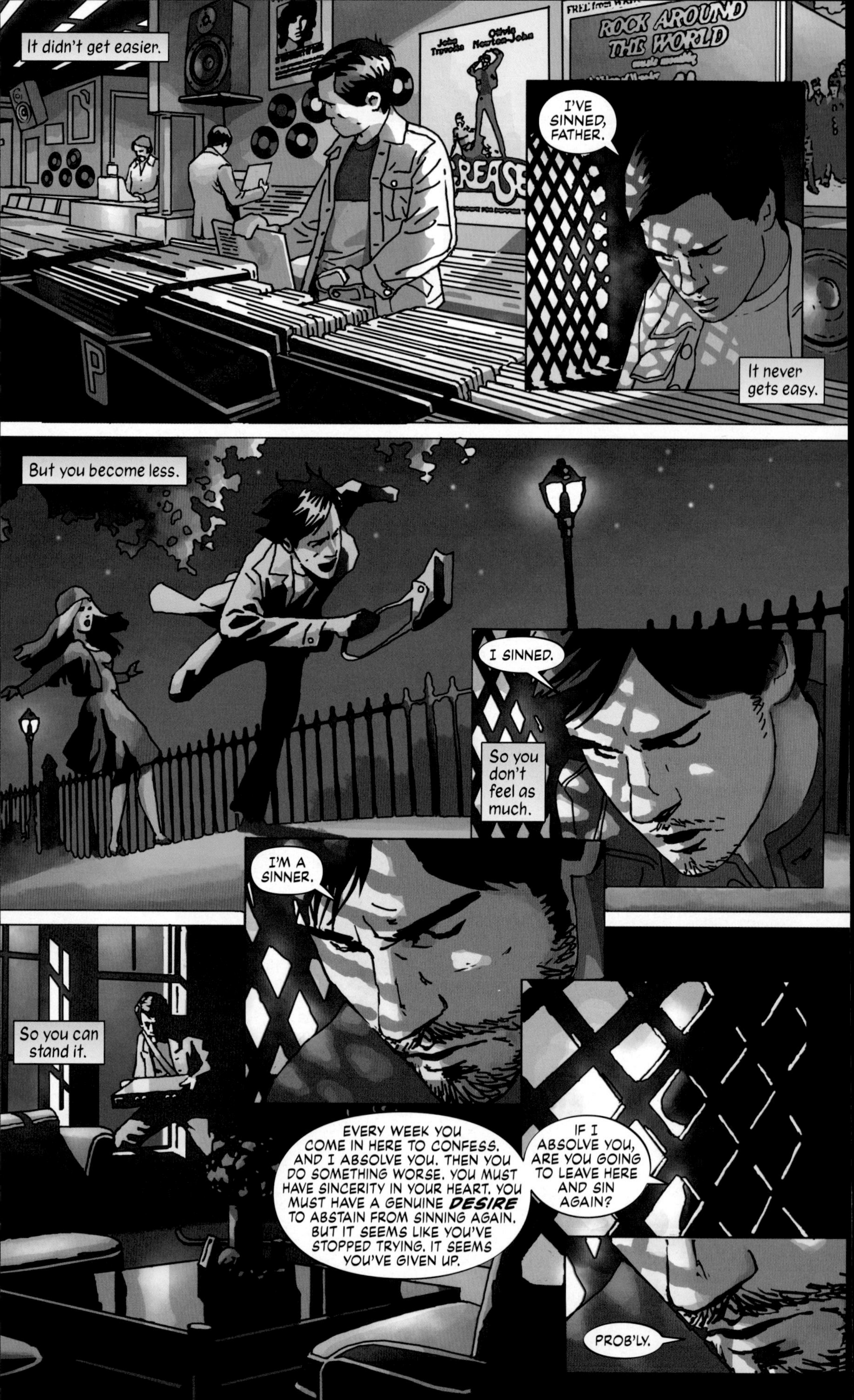

It didn't get easier.
ROCK AROUND THE WORLD
John Travolta
Olivia Newton-John
I'VE SINNED, FATHER.
It never gets easy.
But you become less.
I SINNED.
So you don't feel as much.
I'M A SINNER.
So you can stand it.
EVERY WEEK YOU COME IN HERE TO CONFESS. AND I ABSOLVE YOU. THEN YOU DO SOMETHING WORSE. YOU MUST HAVE SINCERITY IN YOUR HEART. YOU MUST HAVE A GENUINE DESIRE TO ABSTAIN FROM SINNING AGAIN. BUT IT SEEMS LIKE YOU'VE STOPPED TRYING. IT SEEMS YOU'VE GIVEN UP.
IF I ABSOLVE YOU, ARE YOU GOING TO LEAVE HERE AND SIN AGAIN?
PROB'LY.

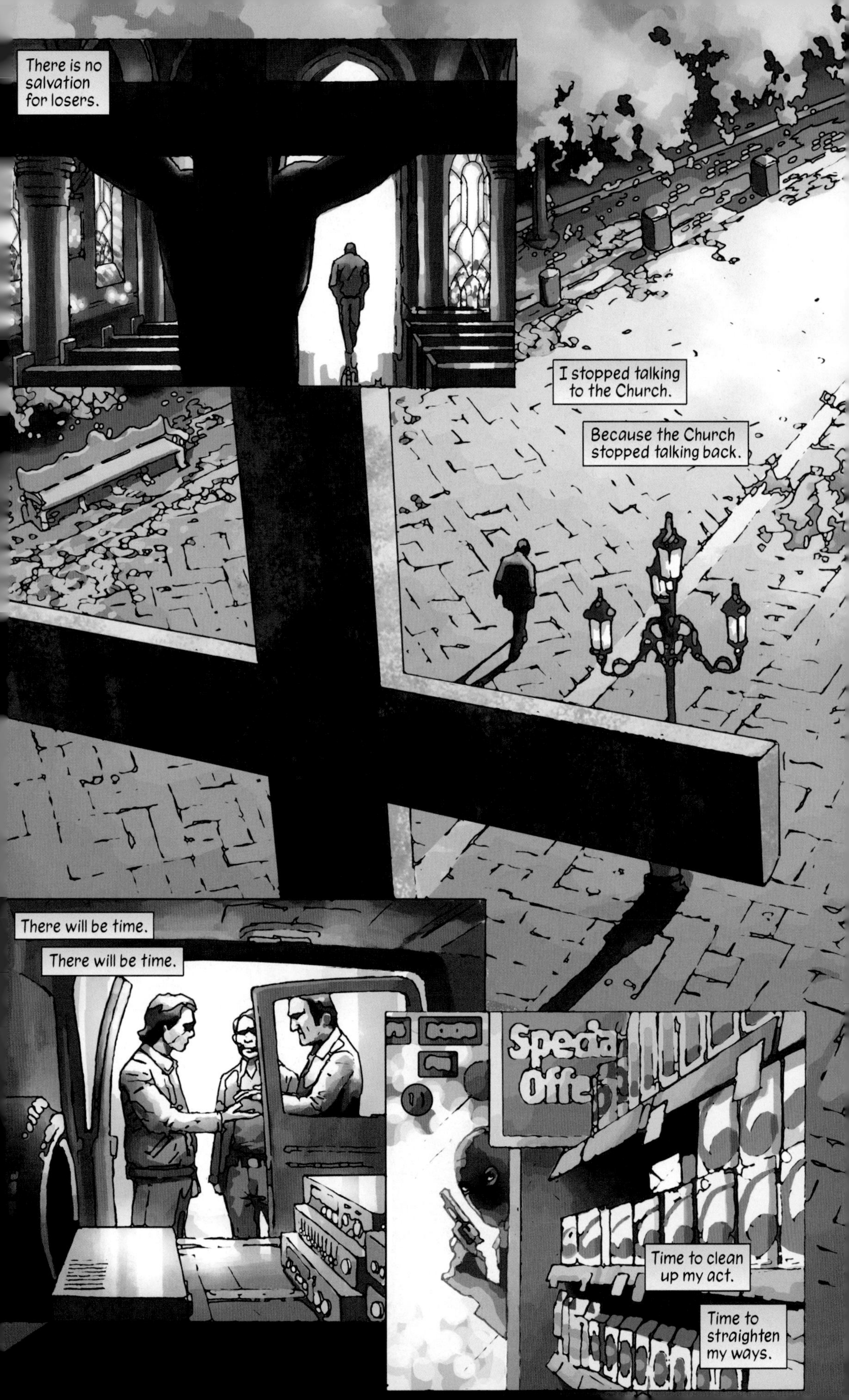
There is no salvation for losers.
I stopped talking to the Church.
Because the Church stopped talking back.
There will be time.
There will be time.
Time to clean up my act.
Time to straighten my ways.

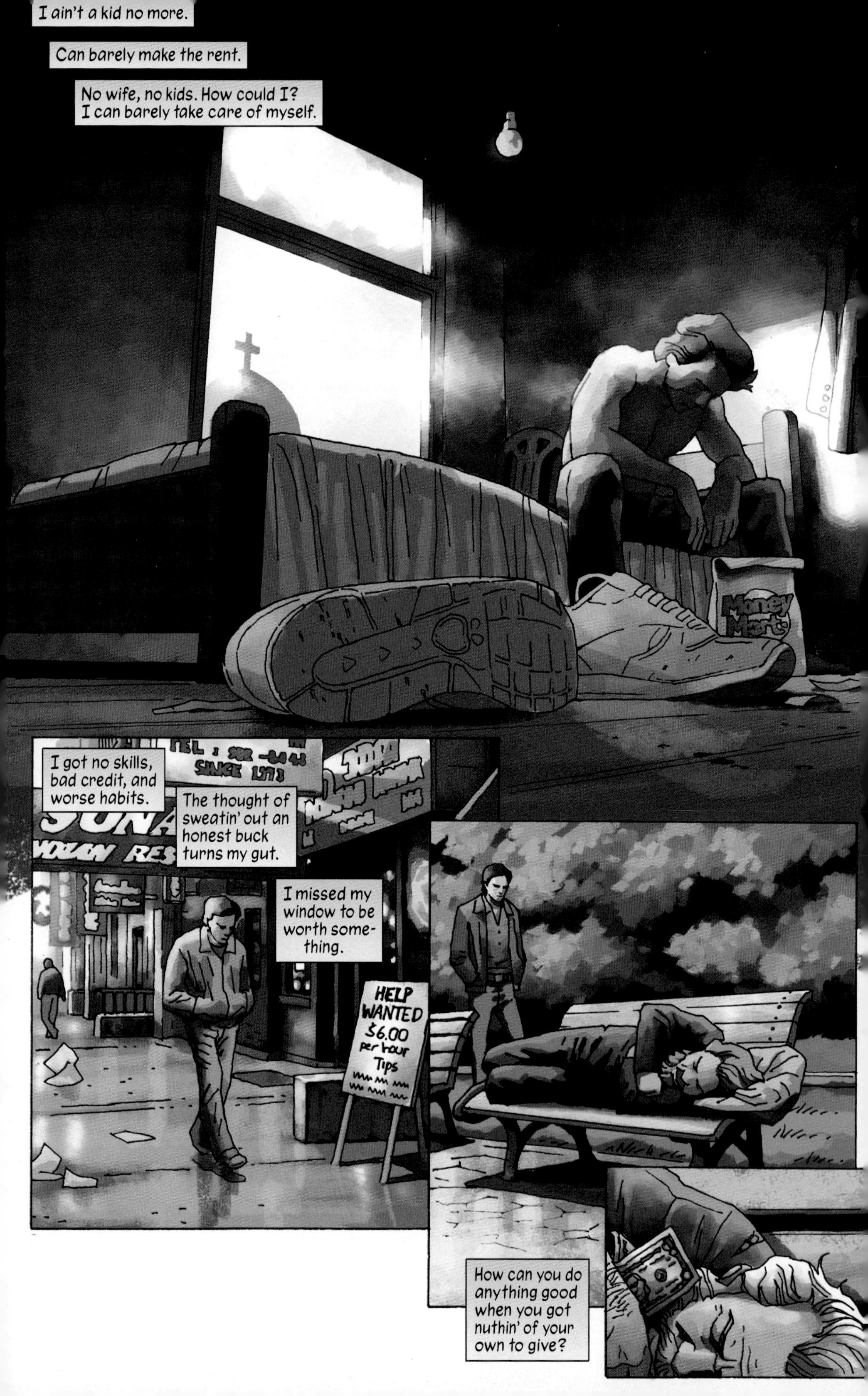
I ain't a kid no more.
Can barely make the rent.
No wife, no kids. How could I? I can barely take care of myself.
Money Mart
TEL
SINCE
I got no skills, bad credit, and worse habits.
The thought of sweatin' out an honest buck turns my gut.
I missed my window to be worth something.
HELP WANTED $6.00 per hour Tips
How can you do anything good when you got nuthin' of your own to give?

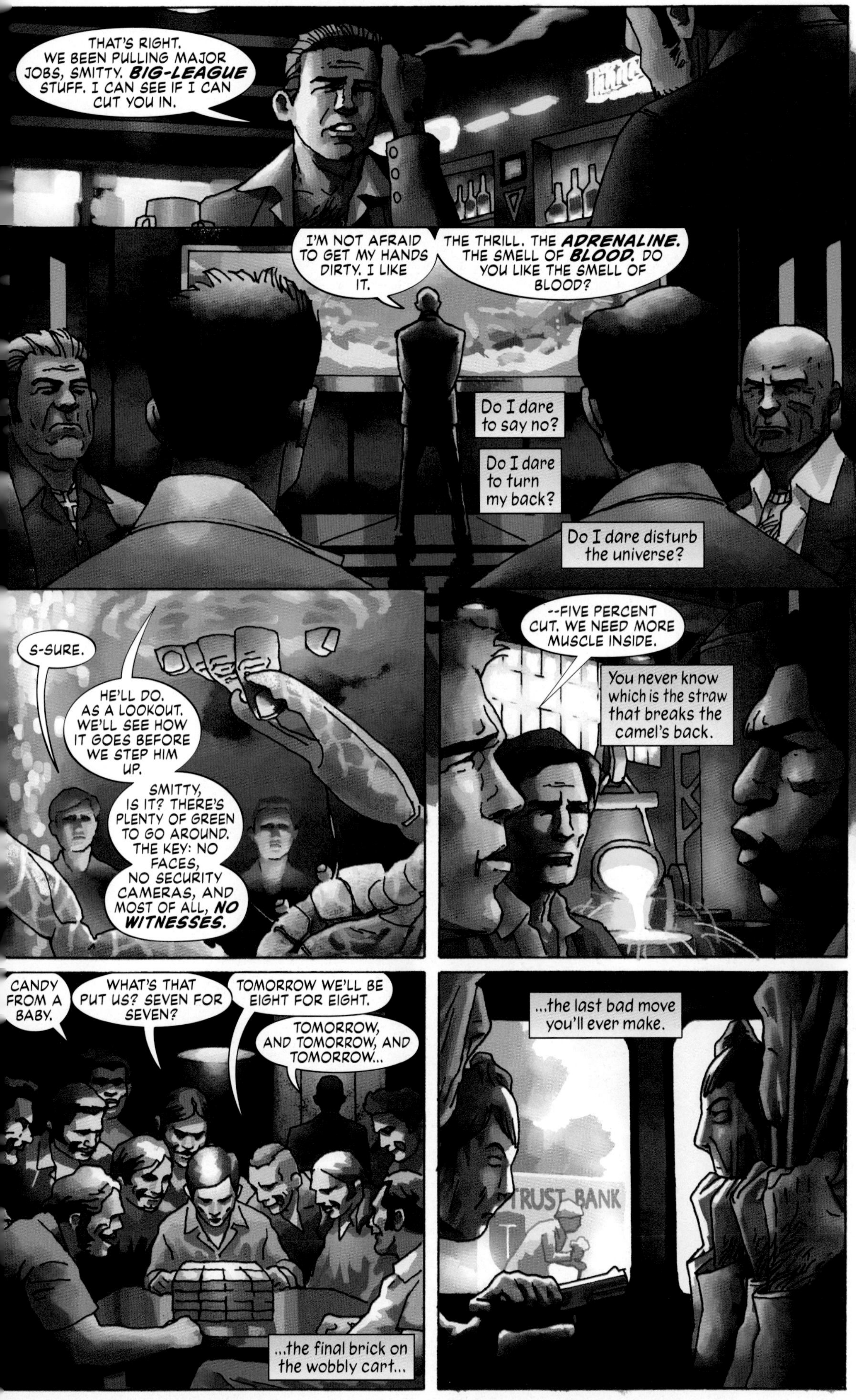
THAT'S RIGHT. WE BEEN PULLING MAJOR JOBS, SMITTY. BIG-LEAGUE STUFF. I CAN SEE IF I CAN CUT YOU IN.
I'M NOT AFRAID TO GET MY HANDS DIRTY. I LIKE IT.
THE THRILL. THE ADRENALINE. THE SMELL OF BLOOD. DO YOU LIKE THE SMELL OF BLOOD?
Do I dare to say no?
Do I dare to turn my back?
Do I dare disturb the universe?
S-SURE.
HE'LL DO. AS A LOOKOUT. WE'LL SEE HOW IT GOES BEFORE WE STEP HIM UP.
SMITTY, IS IT? THERE'S PLENTY OF GREEN TO GO AROUND. THE KEY: NO FACES, NO SECURITY CAMERAS, AND MOST OF ALL, NO WITNESSES.
--FIVE PERCENT CUT. WE NEED MORE MUSCLE INSIDE.
You never know which is the straw that breaks the camel's back.
CANDY FROM A BABY.
WHAT'S THAT PUT US? SEVEN FOR SEVEN?
TOMORROW WE'LL BE EIGHT FOR EIGHT.
TOMORROW, AND TOMORROW, AND TOMORROW...
...the final brick on the wobbly cart...
...the last bad move you'll ever make.
TRUST BANK

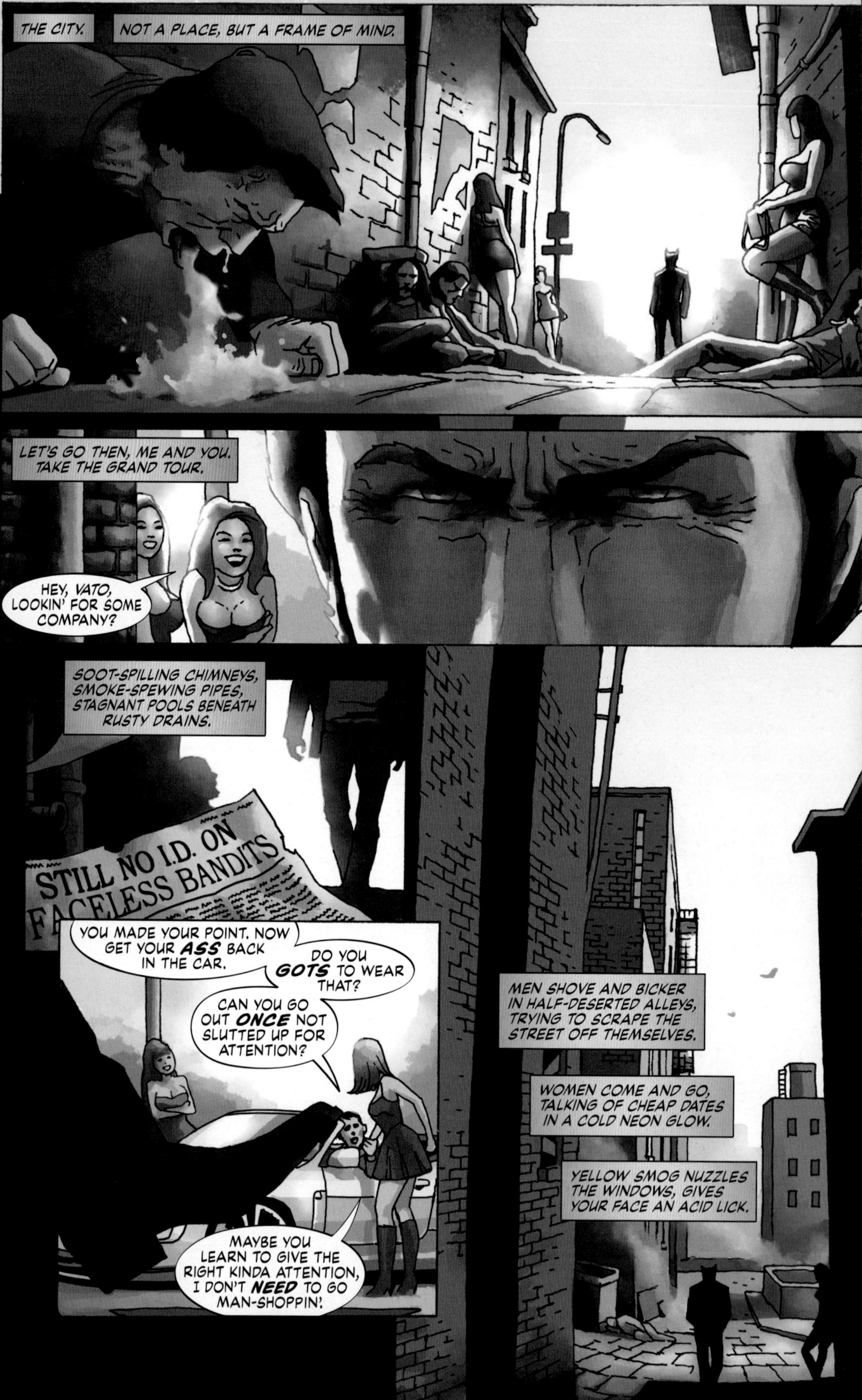
THE CITY.
NOT A PLACE, BUT A FRAME OF MIND.
LET'S GO THEN, ME AND YOU. TAKE THE GRAND TOUR.
HEY, VATO, LOOKIN' FOR SOME COMPANY?
SOOT-SPILLING CHIMNEYS, SMOKE-SPEWING PIPES, STAGNANT POOLS BENEATH RUSTY DRAINS.
STILL NO I.D. ON FACELESS BANDITS
YOU MADE YOUR POINT. NOW GET YOUR ASS BACK IN THE CAR.
DO YOU GOTS TO WEAR THAT?
CAN YOU GO OUT ONCE NOT SLUTTED UP FOR ATTENTION?
MAYBE YOU LEARN TO GIVE THE RIGHT KINDA ATTENTION, I DON'T NEED TO GO MAN-SHOPPIN'.
MEN SHOVE AND BICKER IN HALF-DESERTED ALLEYS, TRYING TO SCRAPE THE STREET OFF THEMSELVES.
WOMEN COME AND GO, TALKING OF CHEAP DATES IN A COLD NEON GLOW.
YELLOW SMOG NUZZLES THE WINDOWS, GIVES YOUR FACE AN ACID LICK.

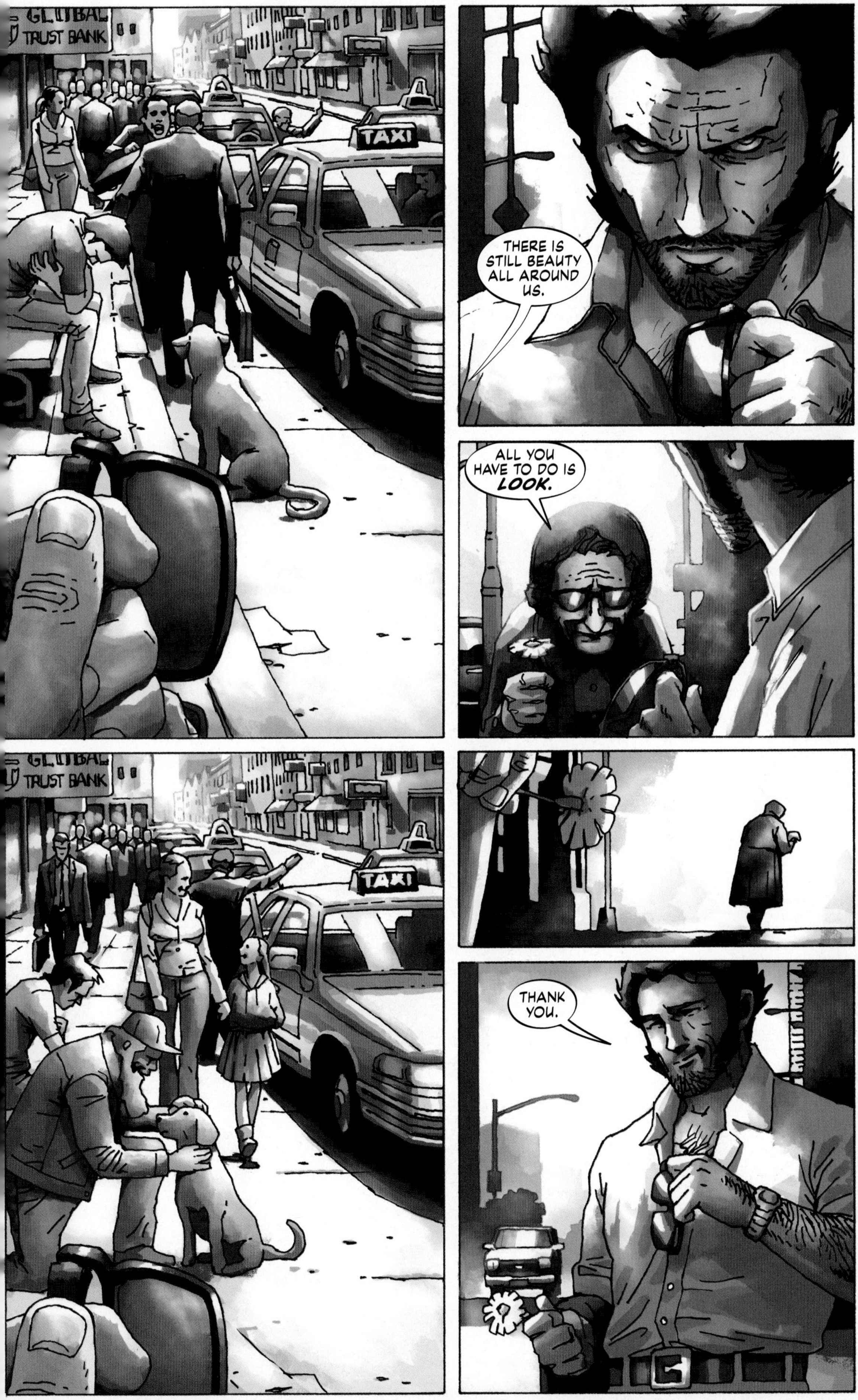
GLOBAL TRUST BANK
TAXI
THERE IS STILL BEAUTY ALL AROUND US.
ALL YOU HAVE TO DO IS *LOOK.*
GLOBAL TRUST BANK
TAXI
THANK YOU.

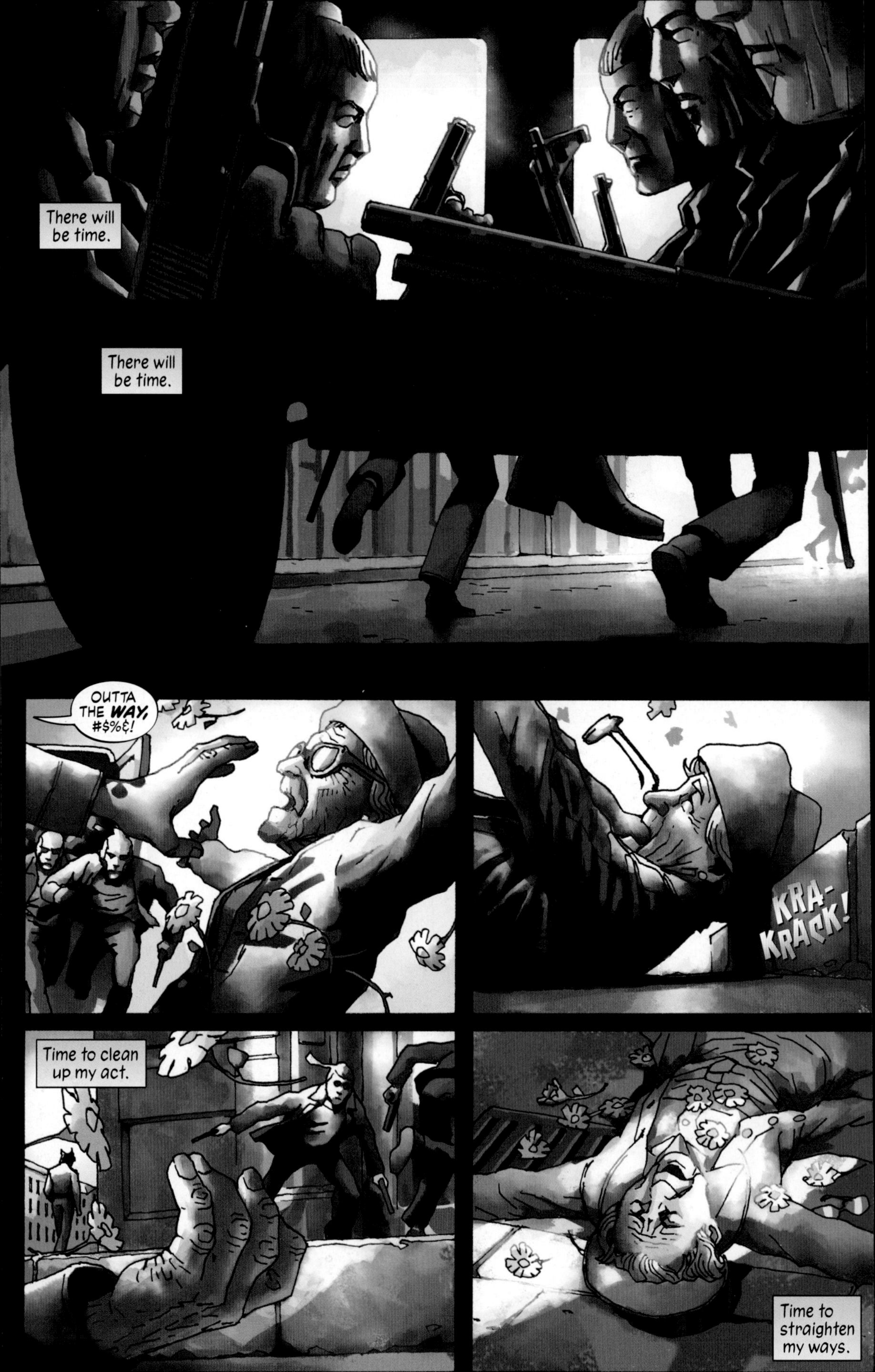
There will be time.
There will be time.
OUTTA THE WAY, #$%&!
KRA-KRACK!
Time to clean up my act.
Time to straighten my ways.

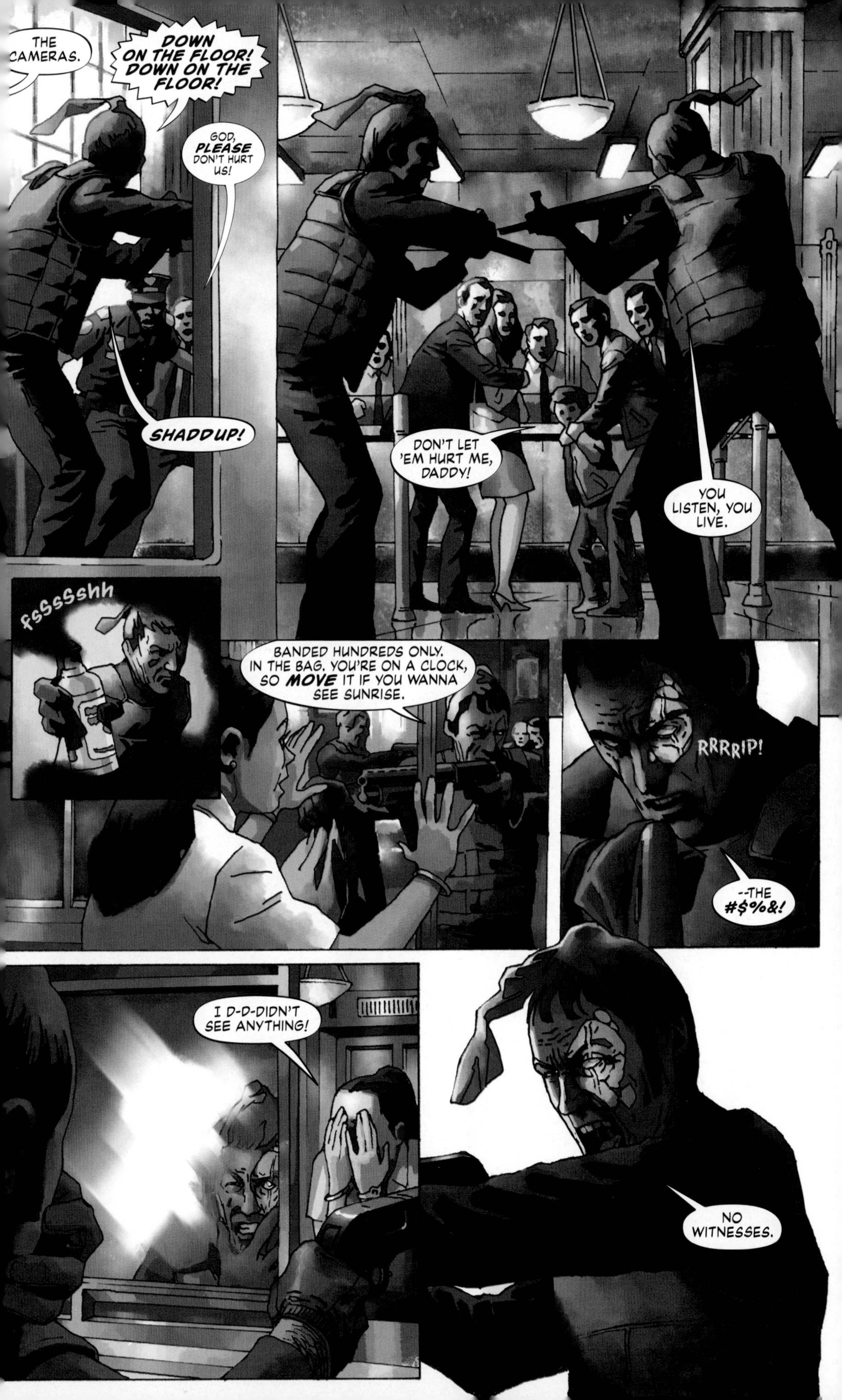
THE CAMERAS.
DOWN ON THE FLOOR! DOWN ON THE FLOOR!
GOD, PLEASE DON'T HURT US!
SHADDUP!
DON'T LET 'EM HURT ME, DADDY!
YOU LISTEN, YOU LIVE.
fsSSSshh
BANDED HUNDREDS ONLY. IN THE BAG. YOU'RE ON A CLOCK, SO MOVE IT IF YOU WANNA SEE SUNRISE.
RRRRIP!
--THE #$%&!
I D-D-DIDN'T SEE ANYTHING!
NO WITNESSES.

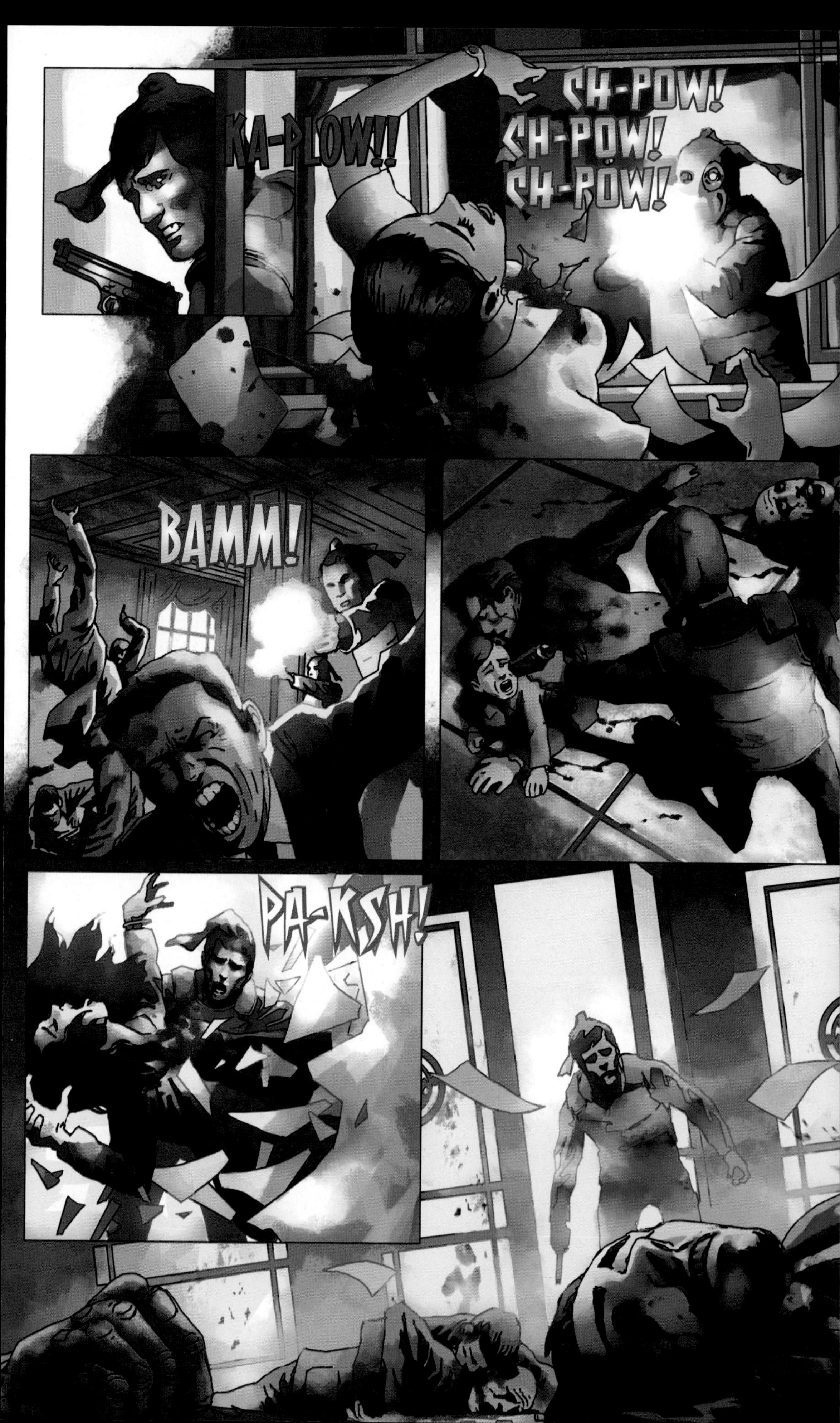
KA-PLOW!!
CH-POW!
CH-POW!
CH-POW!
BAMM!
PA-KSH!

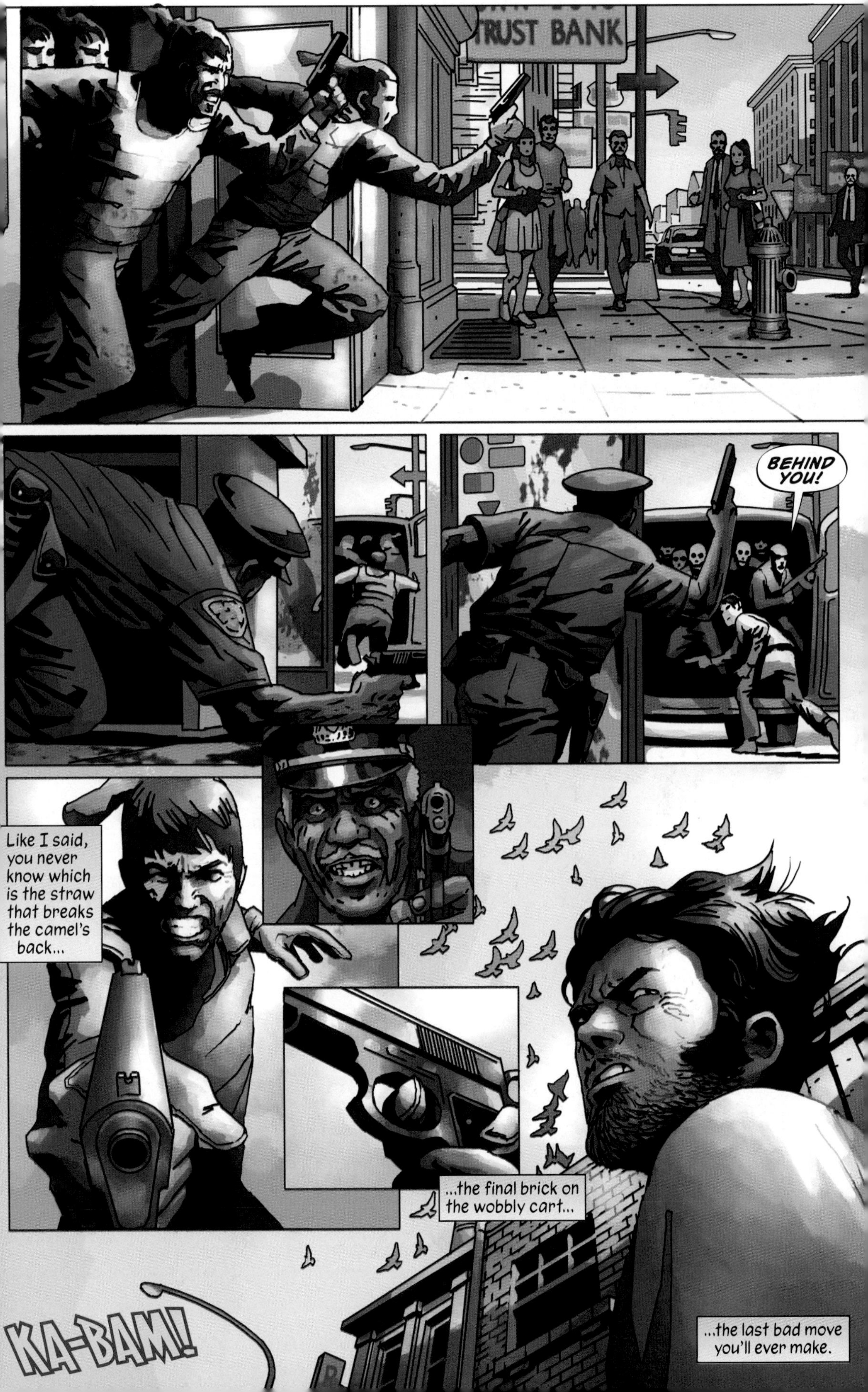
TRUST BANK
BEHIND YOU!
Like I said, you never know which is the straw that breaks the camel's back...
...the final brick on the wobbly cart...
KA-BAM!
...the last bad move you'll ever make.

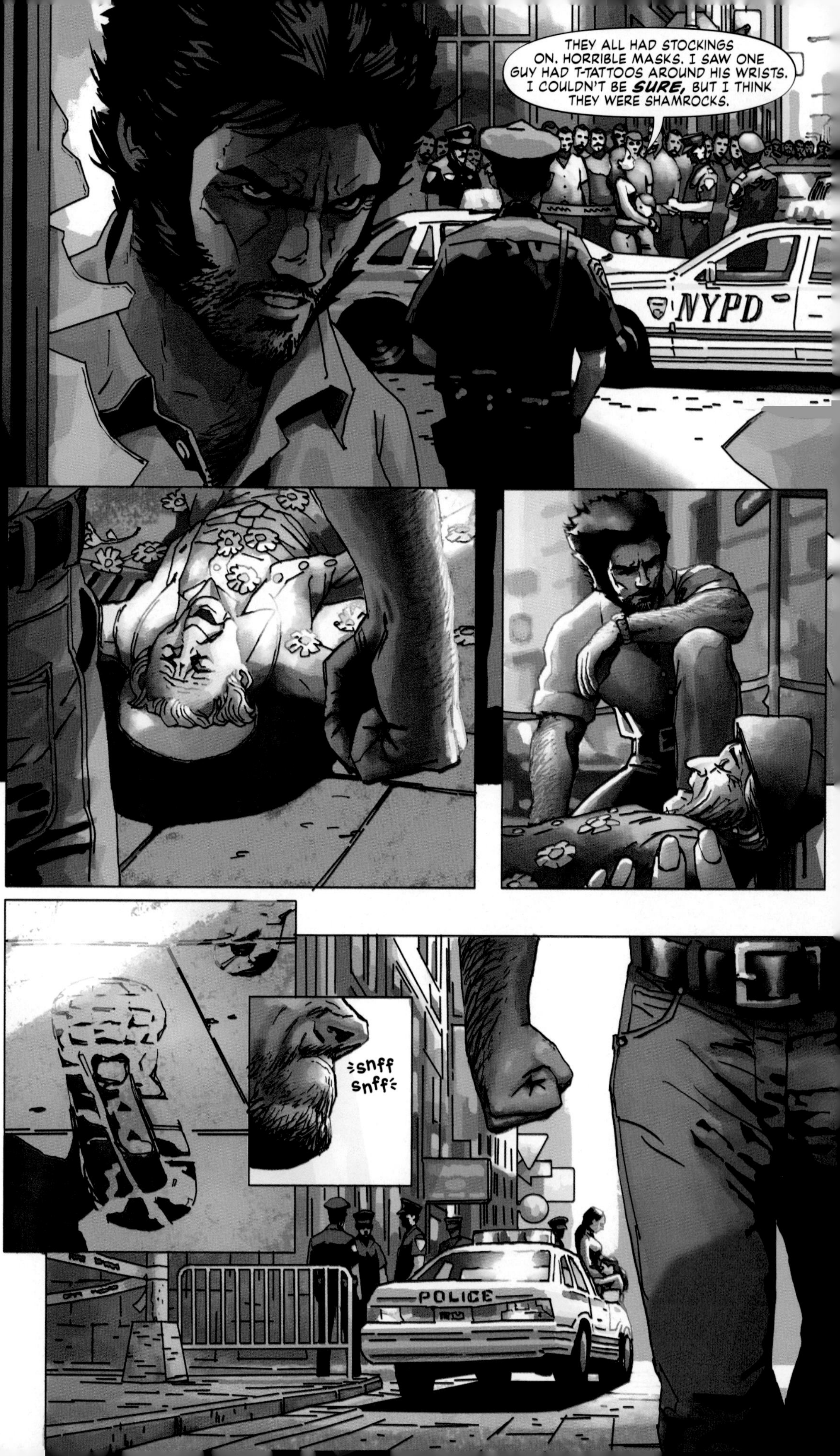
THEY ALL HAD STOCKINGS ON. HORRIBLE MASKS. I SAW ONE GUY HAD T-TATTOOS AROUND HIS WRISTS. I COULDN'T BE SURE, BUT I THINK THEY WERE SHAMROCKS.
NYPD
snff snff
POLICE

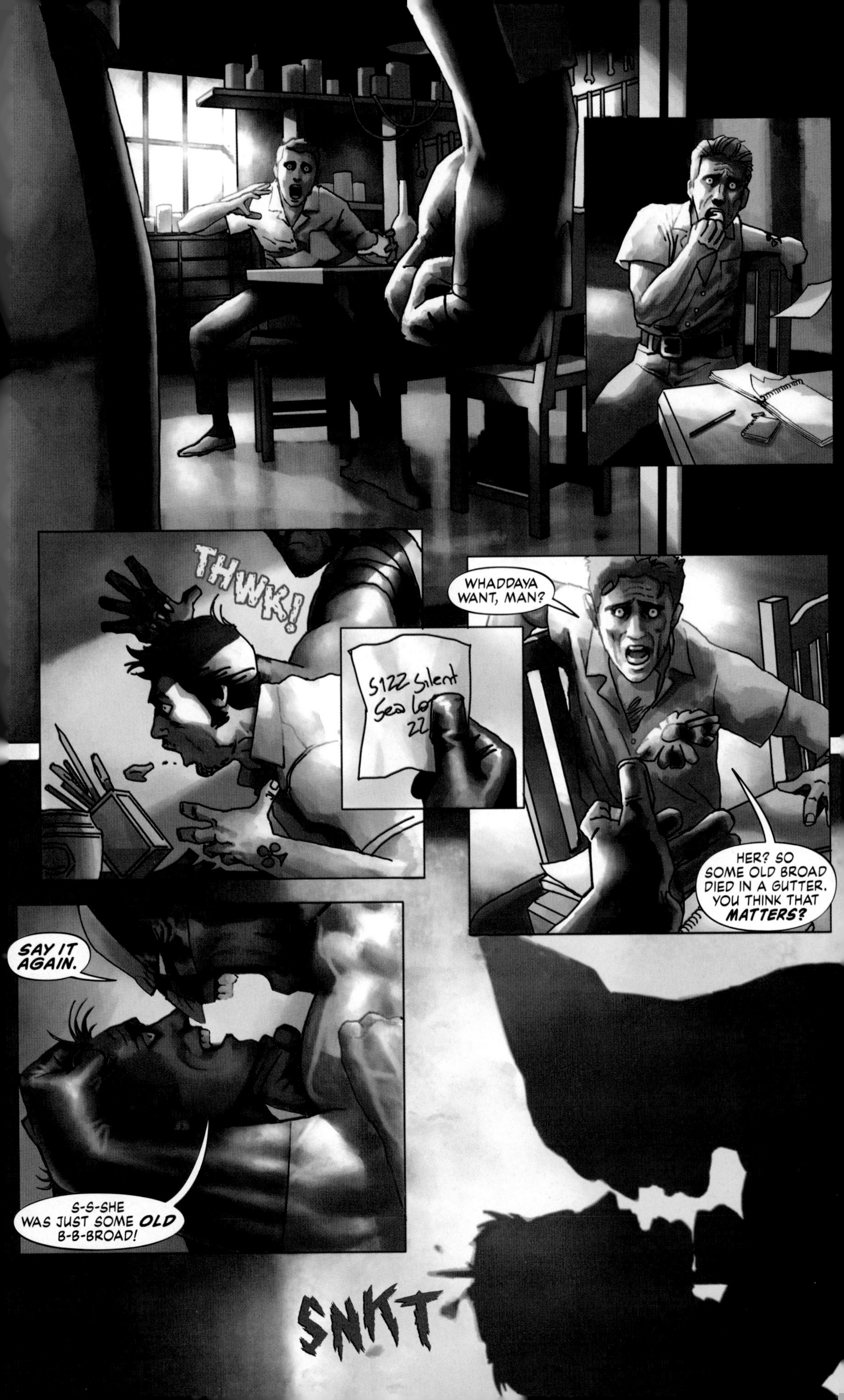
THWK!
5122 Silent Sea Lo 22
WHADDAYA WANT, MAN?
HER? SO SOME OLD BROAD DIED IN A GUTTER. YOU THINK THAT MATTERS?
SAY IT AGAIN.
S-S-SHE WAS JUST SOME OLD B-B-BROAD!
SNKT

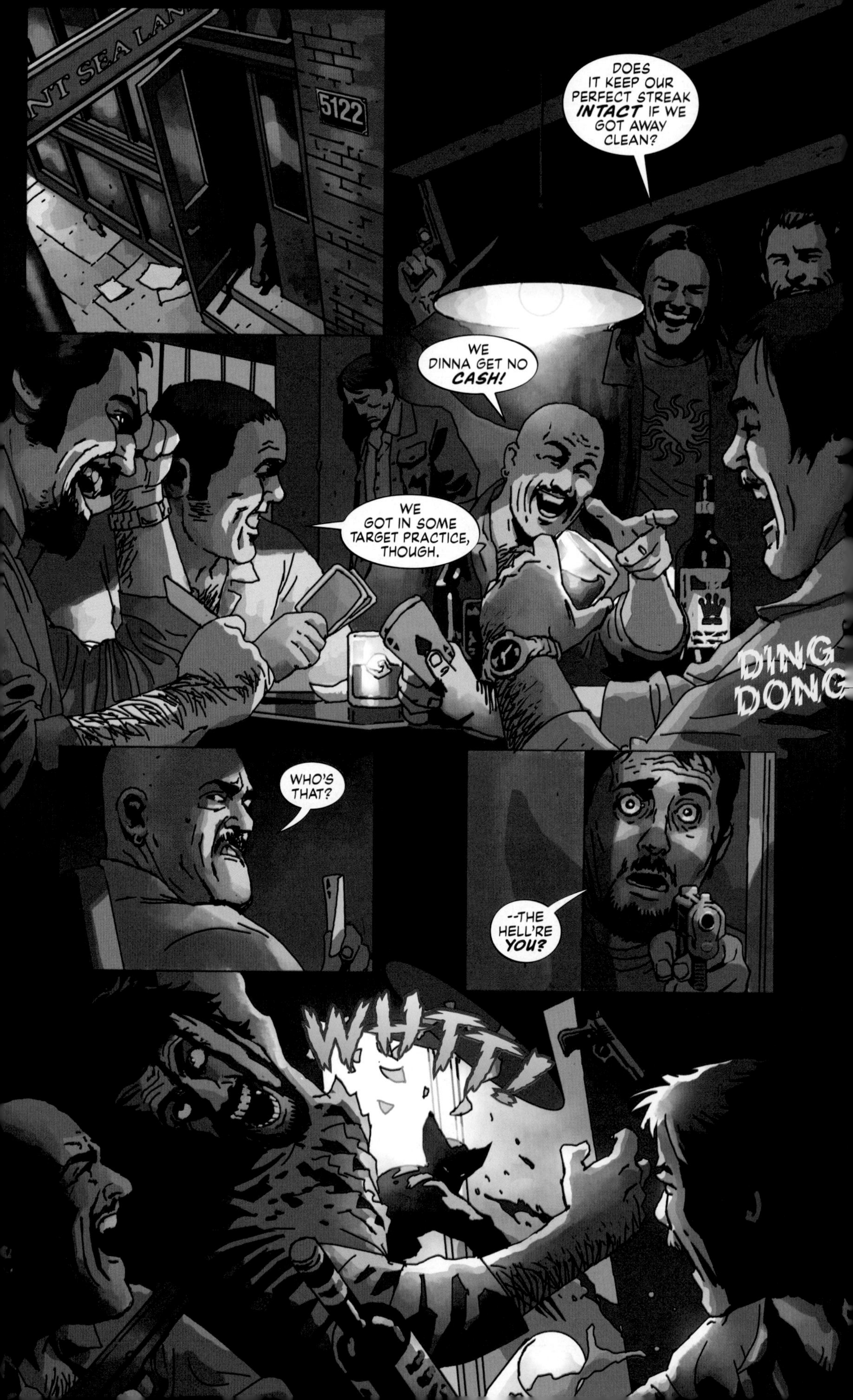

5122
DOES IT KEEP OUR PERFECT STREAK INTACT IF WE GOT AWAY CLEAN?
WE DINNA GET NO CASH!
WE GOT IN SOME TARGET PRACTICE, THOUGH.
DING DONG
WHO'S THAT?
--THE HELL'RE YOU?
WHTT!

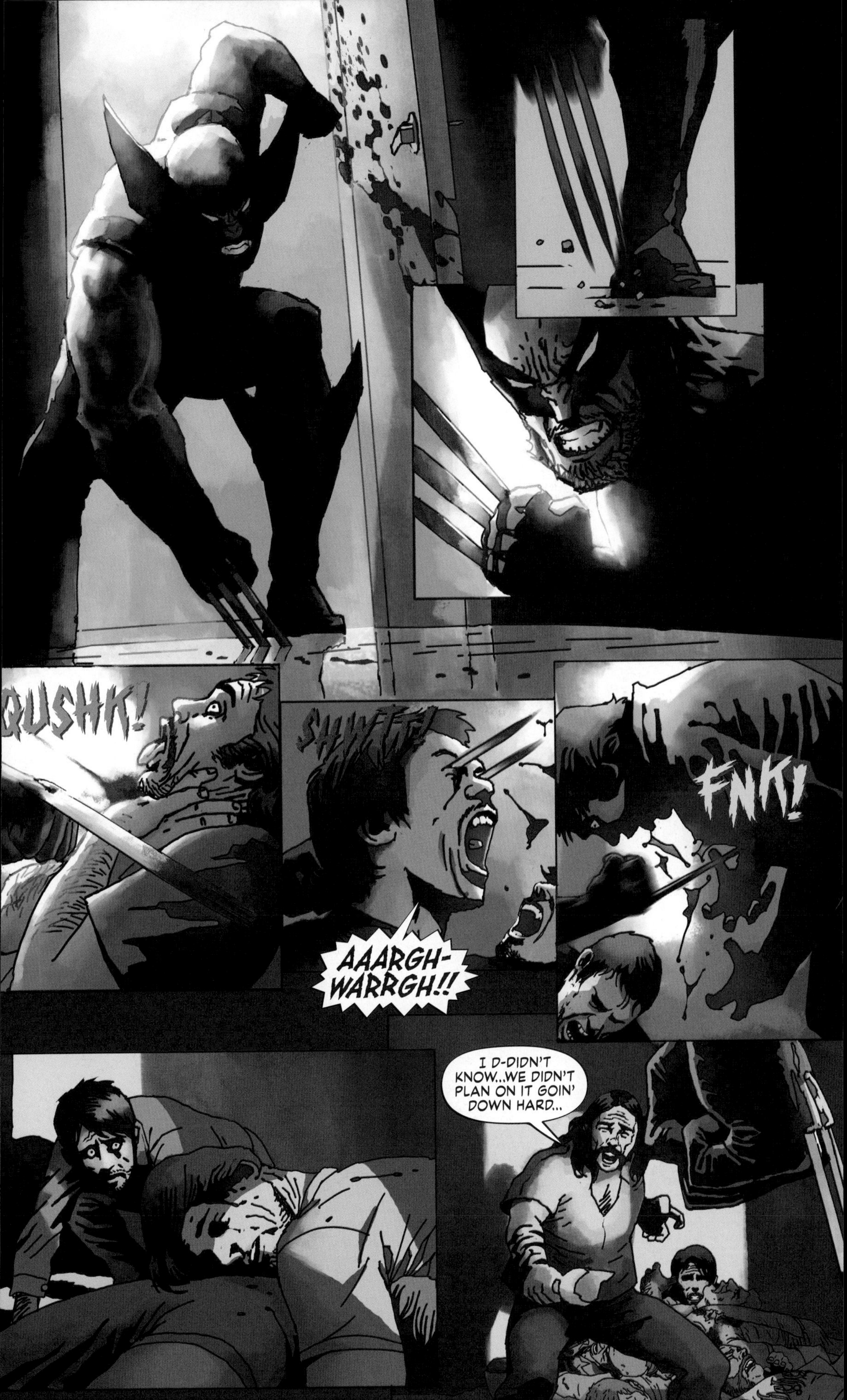
QUSHK!
AAARGH-WARRGH!!
FNK!
I D-DIDN'T KNOW...WE DIDN'T PLAN ON IT GOIN' DOWN HARD...

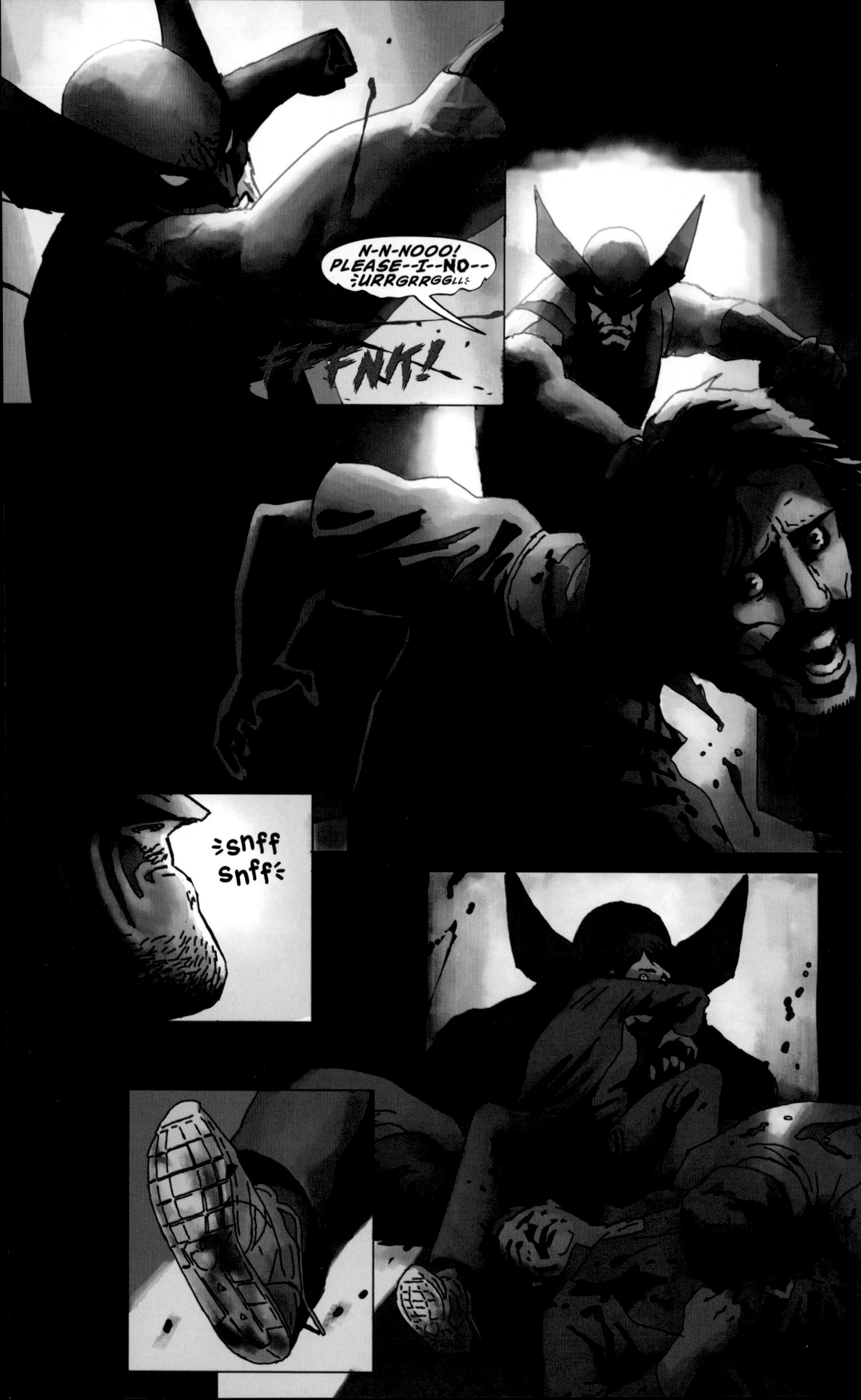
N-N-NOOO! PLEASE--I--NO-- URRGRRGGLL
FFFNK!
snff snff

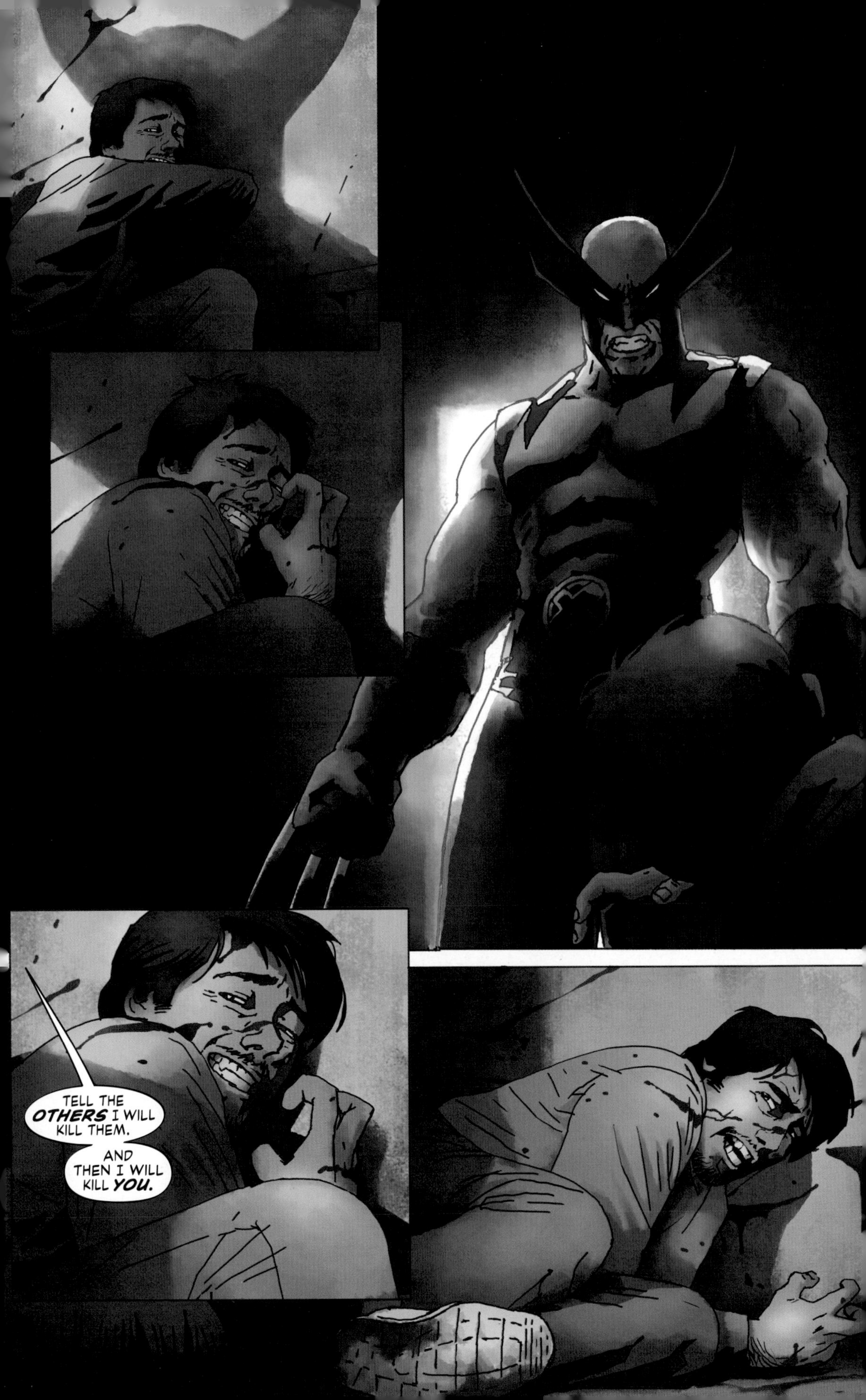
TELL THE OTHERS I WILL KILL THEM.
AND THEN I WILL KILL YOU.

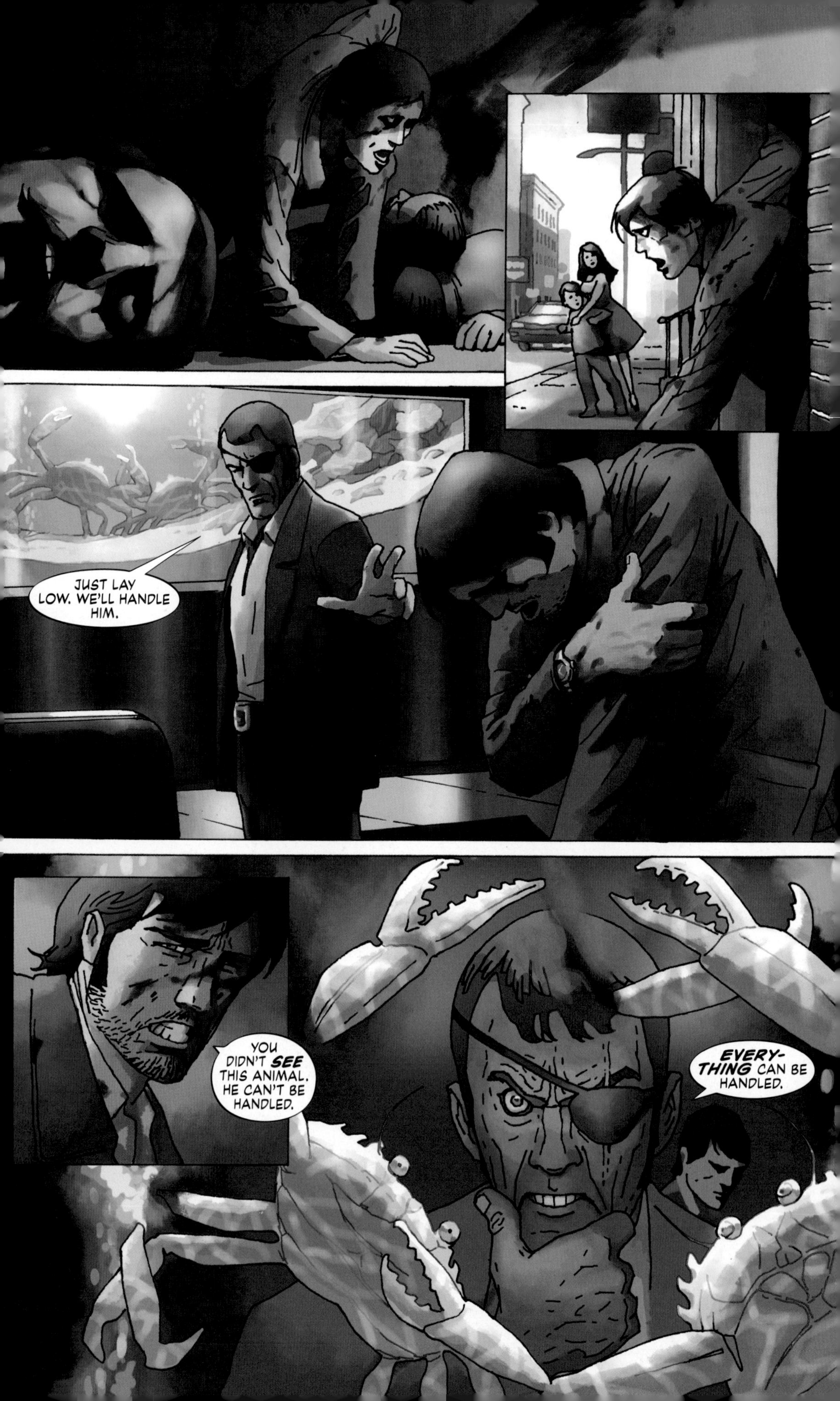
JUST LAY LOW. WE'LL HANDLE HIM.
YOU DIDN'T **SEE** THIS ANIMAL. HE CAN'T BE HANDLED.
EVERY-THING CAN BE HANDLED.

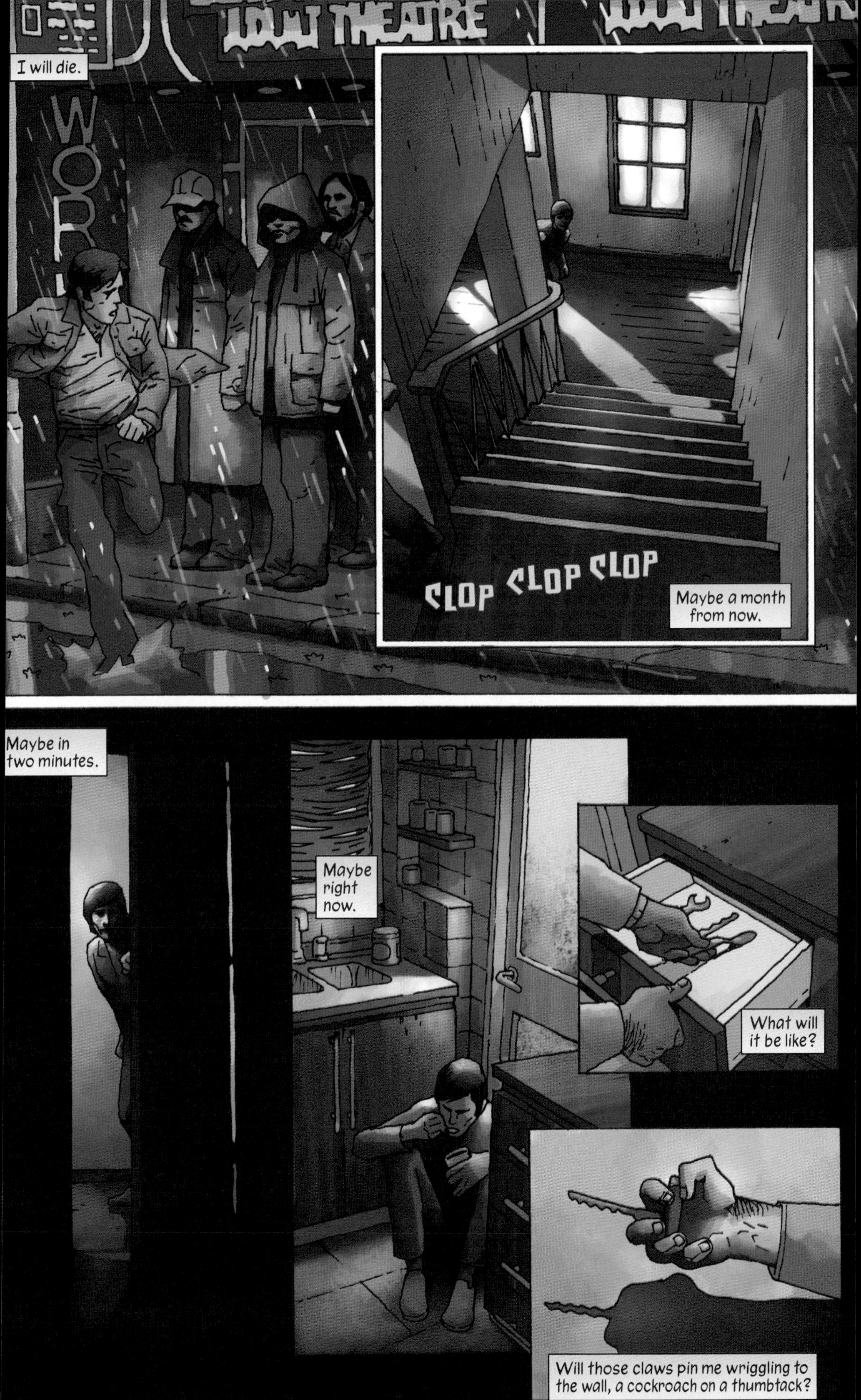

THEATRE
I will die.
WOR
CLOP CLOP CLOP
Maybe a month from now.
Maybe in two minutes.
Maybe right now.
What will it be like?
Will those claws pin me wriggling to the wall, a cockroach on a thumbtack?

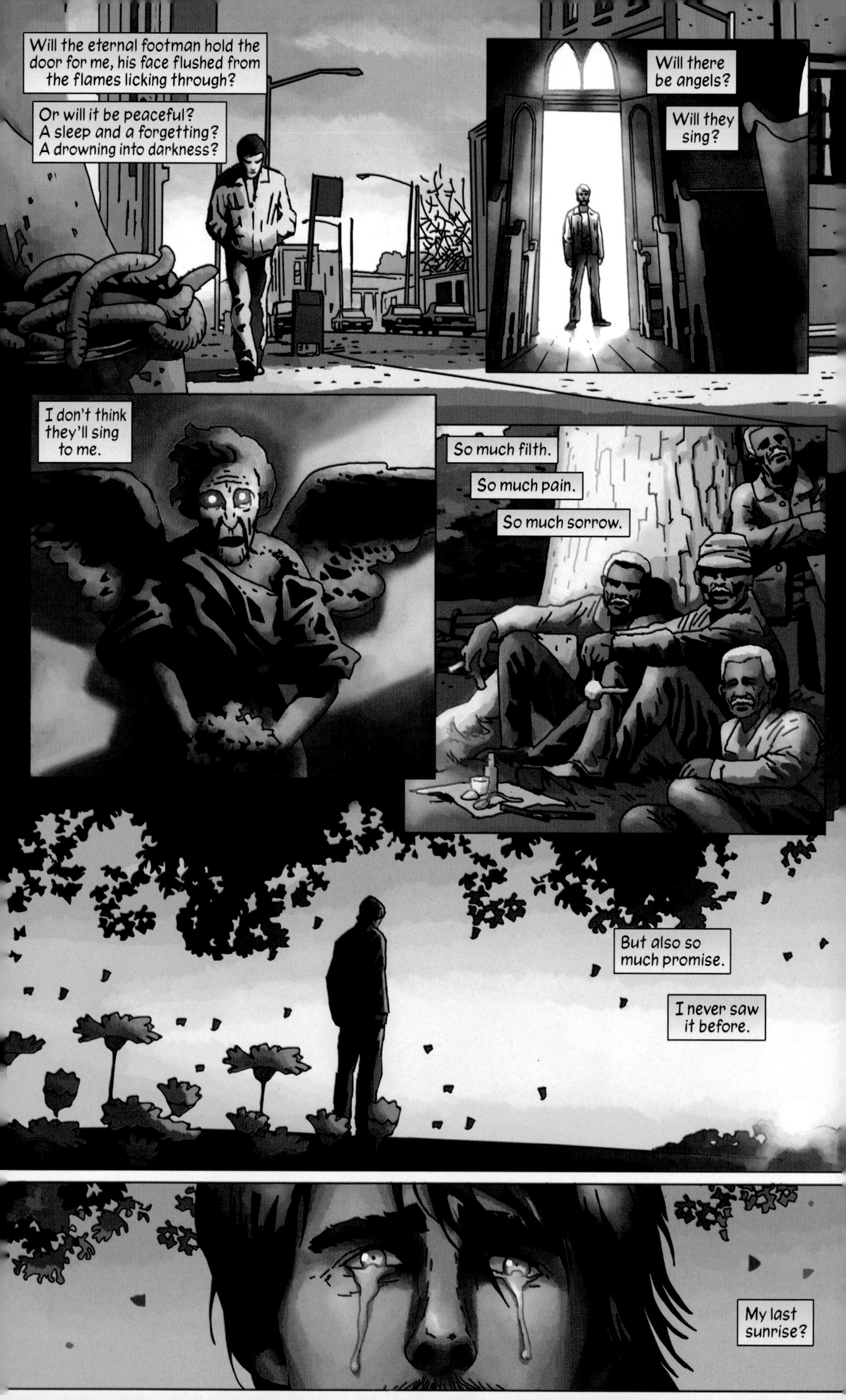
Will the eternal footman hold the door for me, his face flushed from the flames licking through?
Or will it be peaceful? A sleep and a forgetting? A drowning into darkness?
Will there be angels?
Will they sing?
I don't think they'll sing to me.
So much filth.
So much pain.
So much sorrow.
But also so much promise.
I never saw it before.
My last sunrise?

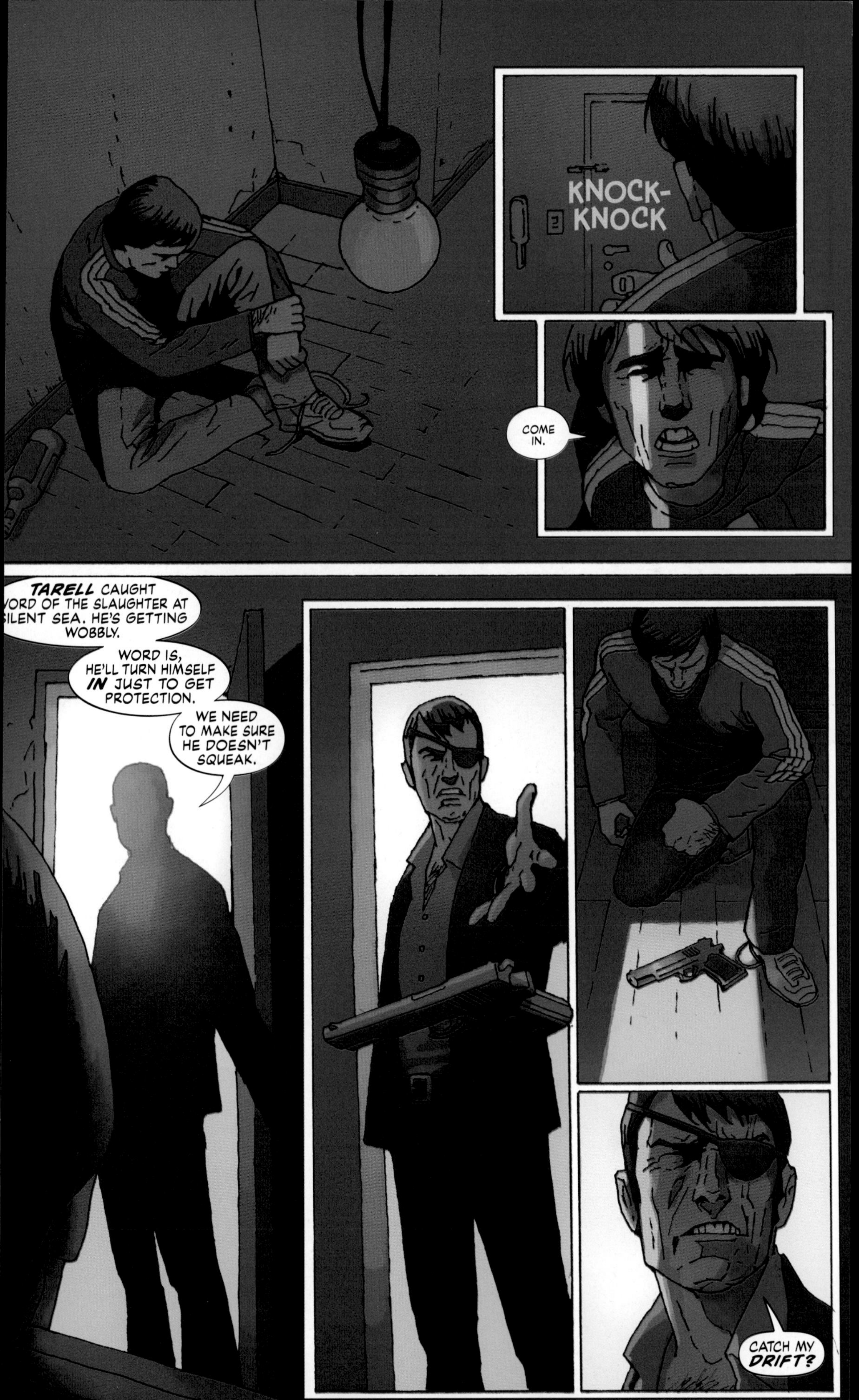
KNOCK-KNOCK
COME IN.
TARELL CAUGHT WORD OF THE SLAUGHTER AT SILENT SEA. HE'S GETTING WOBBLY.
WORD IS, HE'LL TURN HIMSELF IN JUST TO GET PROTECTION.
WE NEED TO MAKE SURE HE DOESN'T SQUEAK.
CATCH MY DRIFT?

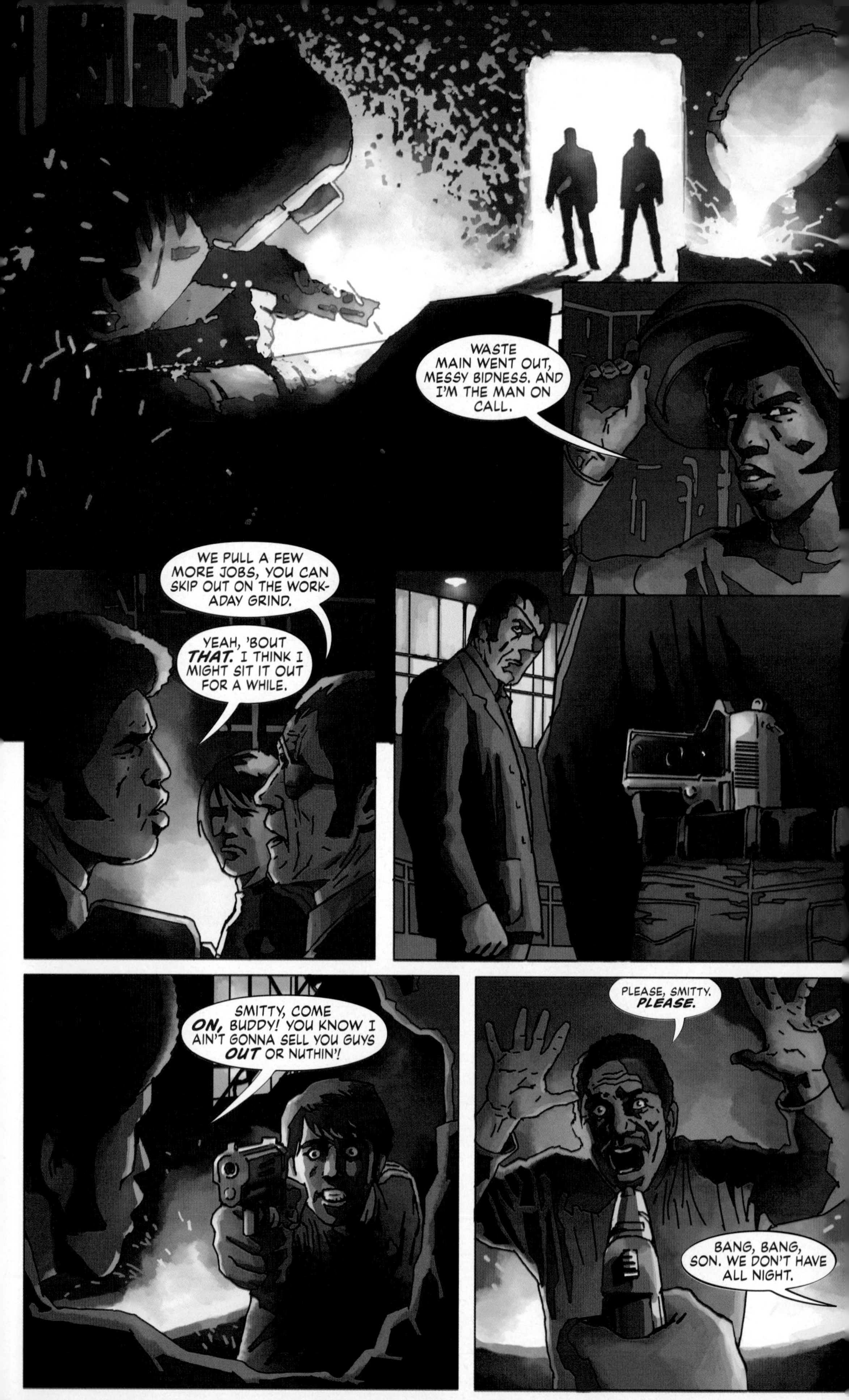

WASTE MAIN WENT OUT, MESSY BIDNESS. AND I'M THE MAN ON CALL.
WE PULL A FEW MORE JOBS, YOU CAN SKIP OUT ON THE WORK-ADAY GRIND.
YEAH, 'BOUT THAT. I THINK I MIGHT SIT IT OUT FOR A WHILE.
SMITTY, COME ON, BUDDY! YOU KNOW I AIN'T GONNA SELL YOU GUYS OUT OR NUTHIN'!
PLEASE, SMITTY. PLEASE.
BANG, BANG, SON. WE DON'T HAVE ALL NIGHT.

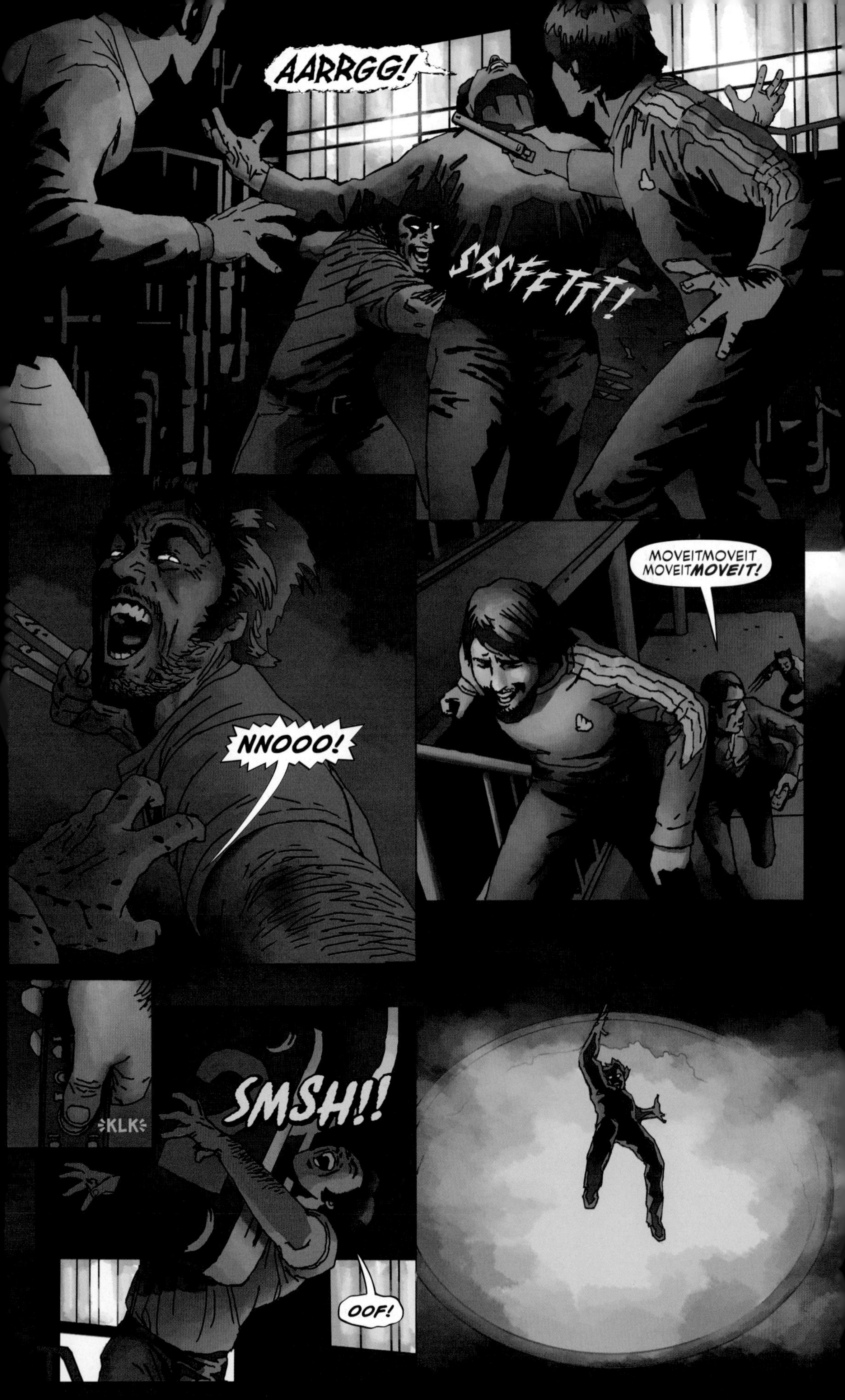
AARRGG!
SSSFFTTT!
NNOOO!
MOVEITMOVEIT
MOVEITMOVEIT!
KLK
SMSH!!
OOF!

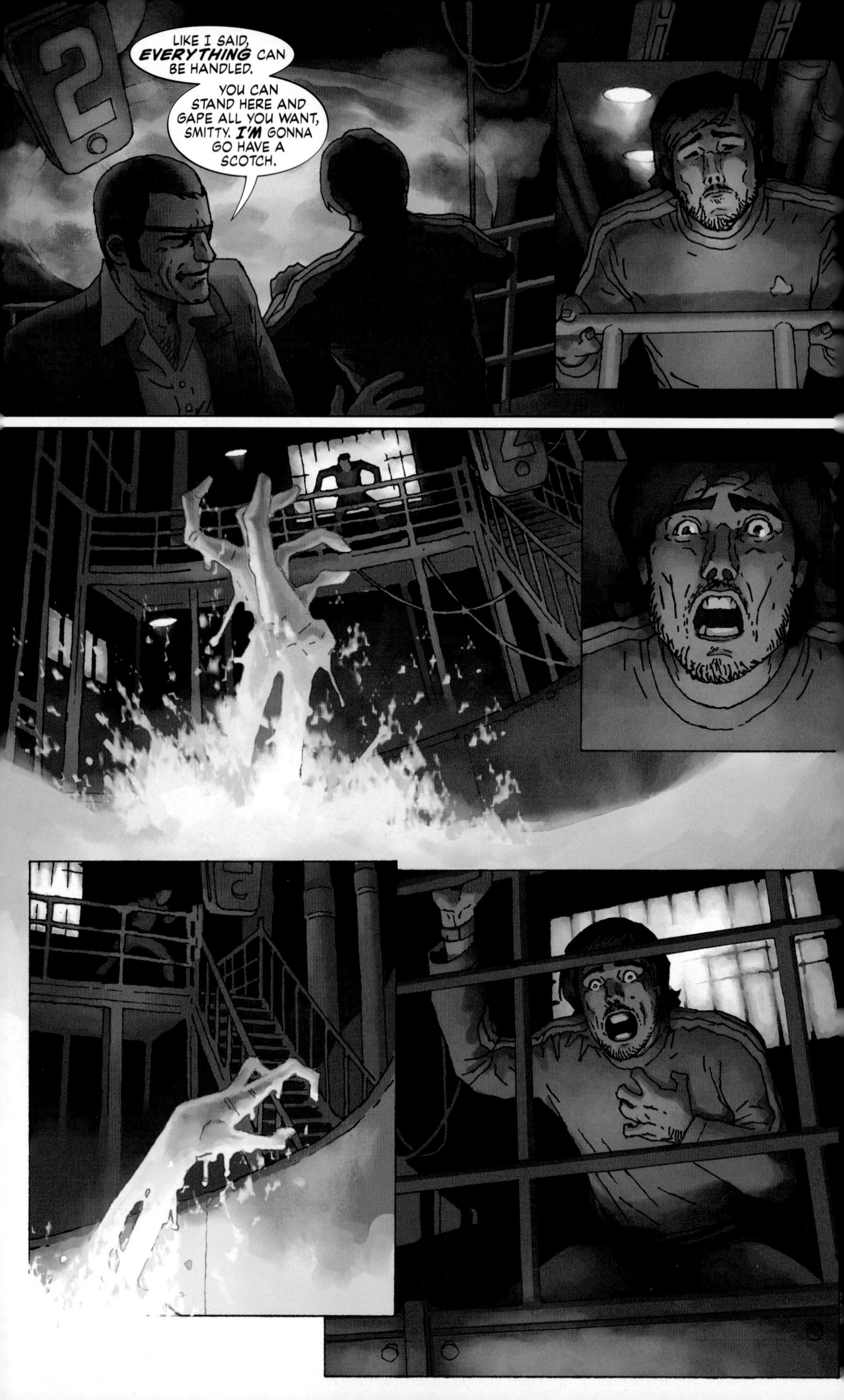
LIKE I SAID, **EVERYTHING** CAN BE HANDLED.
YOU CAN STAND HERE AND GAPE ALL YOU WANT, SMITTY. **I'M** GONNA GO HAVE A SCOTCH.

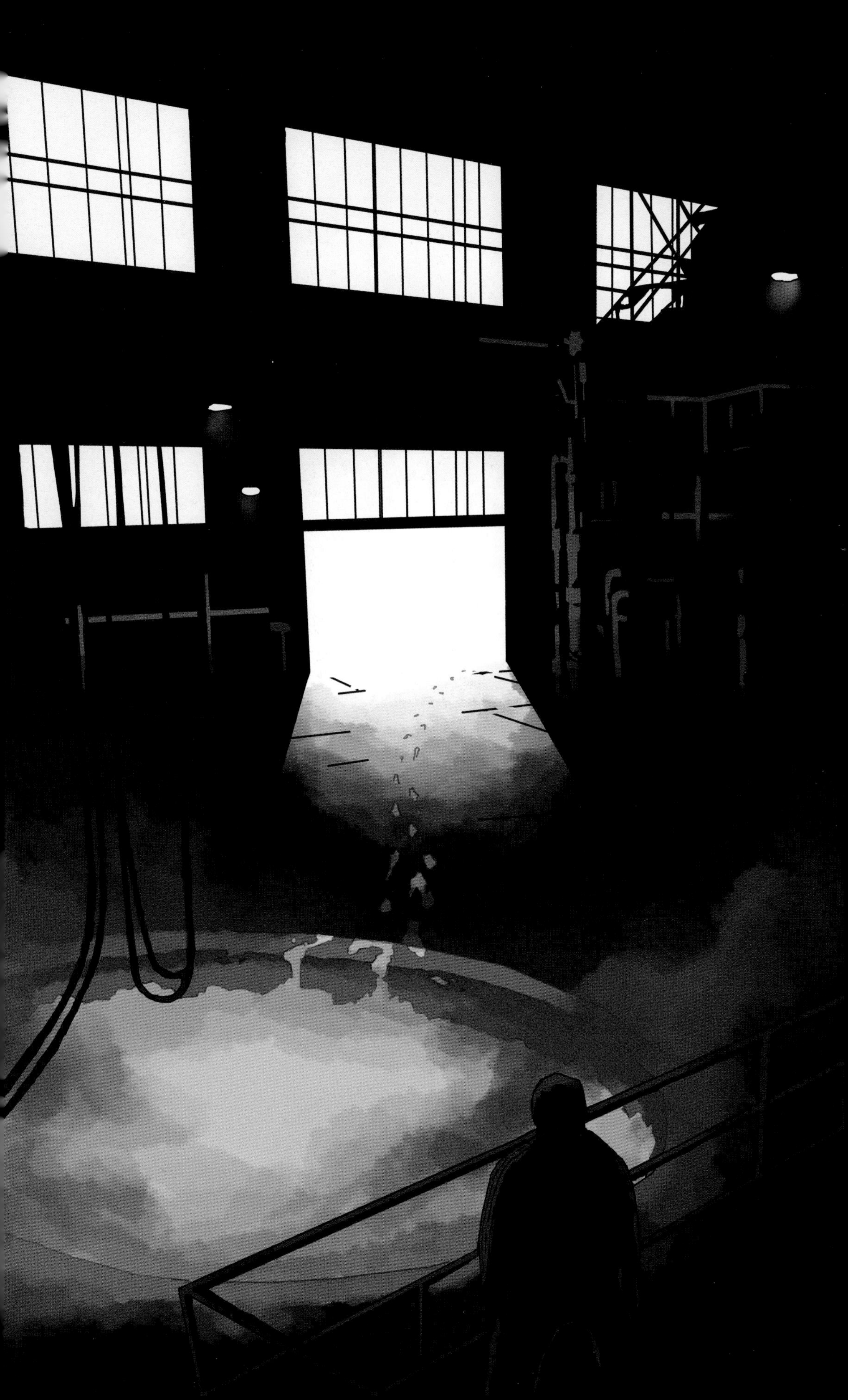

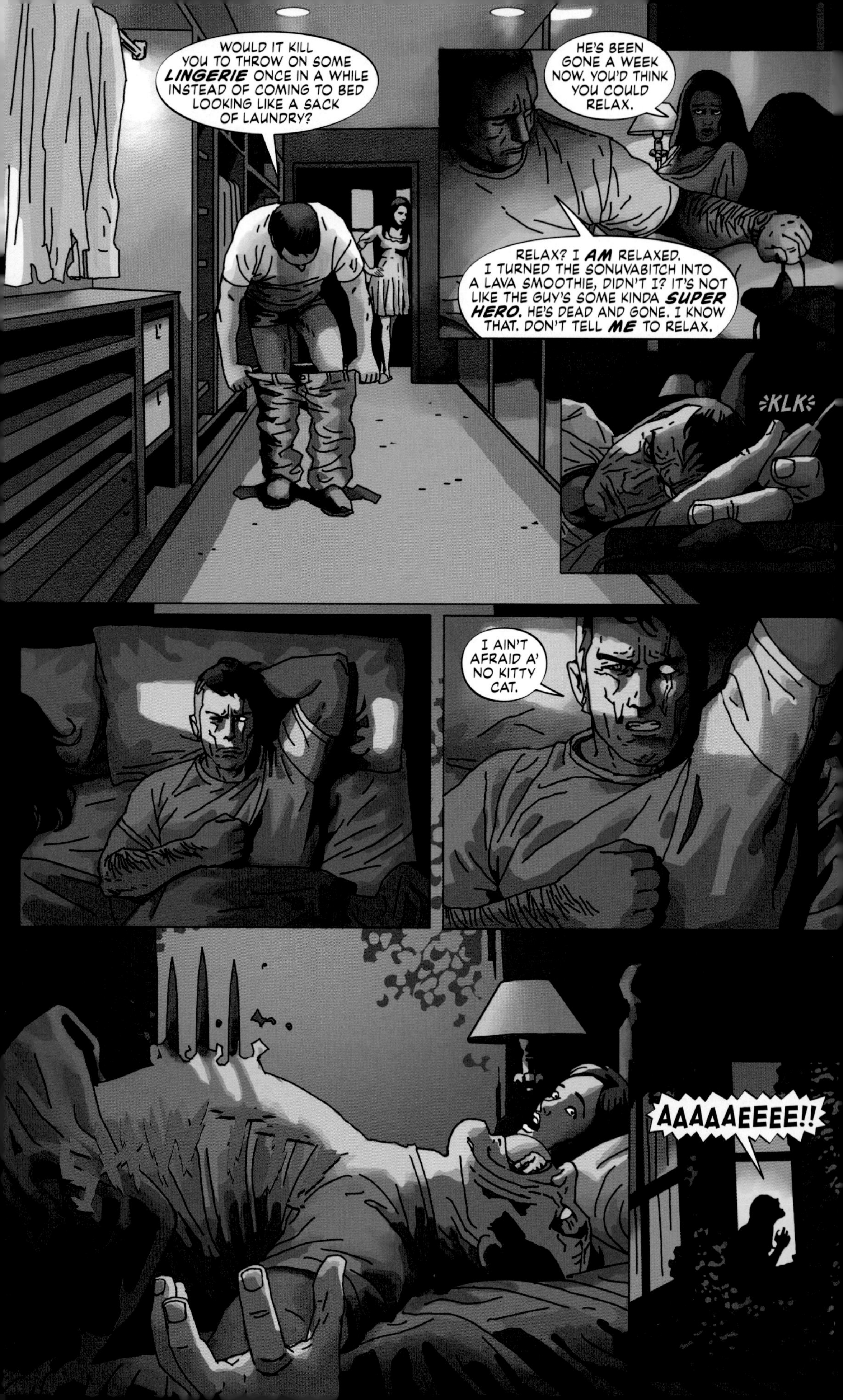
WOULD IT KILL YOU TO THROW ON SOME LINGERIE ONCE IN A WHILE INSTEAD OF COMING TO BED LOOKING LIKE A SACK OF LAUNDRY?
HE'S BEEN GONE A WEEK NOW. YOU'D THINK YOU COULD RELAX.
RELAX? I AM RELAXED. I TURNED THE SONUVABITCH INTO A LAVA SMOOTHIE, DIDN'T I? IT'S NOT LIKE THE GUY'S SOME KINDA SUPER HERO. HE'S DEAD AND GONE. I KNOW THAT. DON'T TELL ME TO RELAX.
KLK
I AIN'T AFRAID A' NO KITTY CAT.
AAAAAEEEE!!

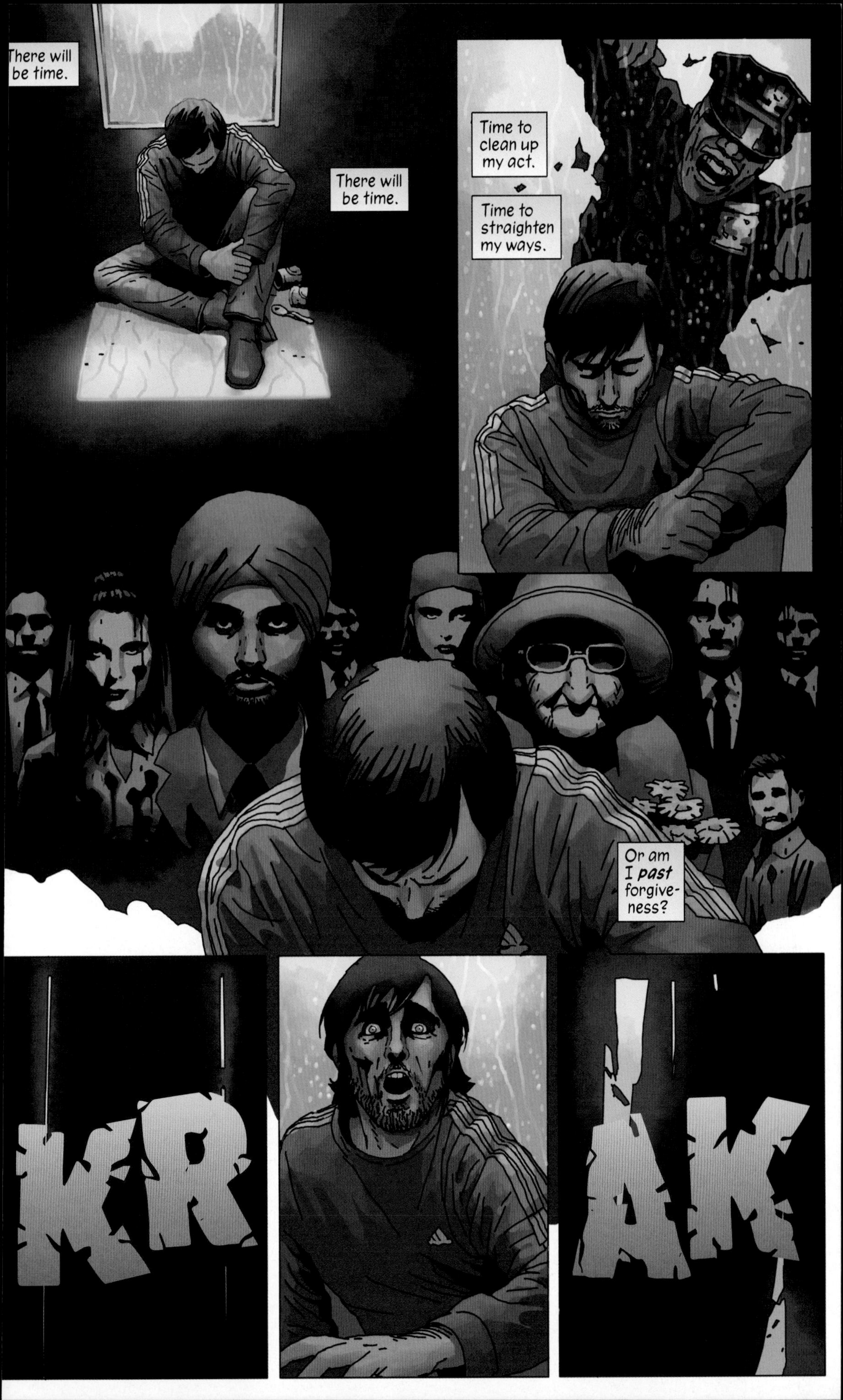
There will be time.
There will be time.
Time to clean up my act.
Time to straighten my ways.
Or am I *past* forgive-ness?
KR
AK

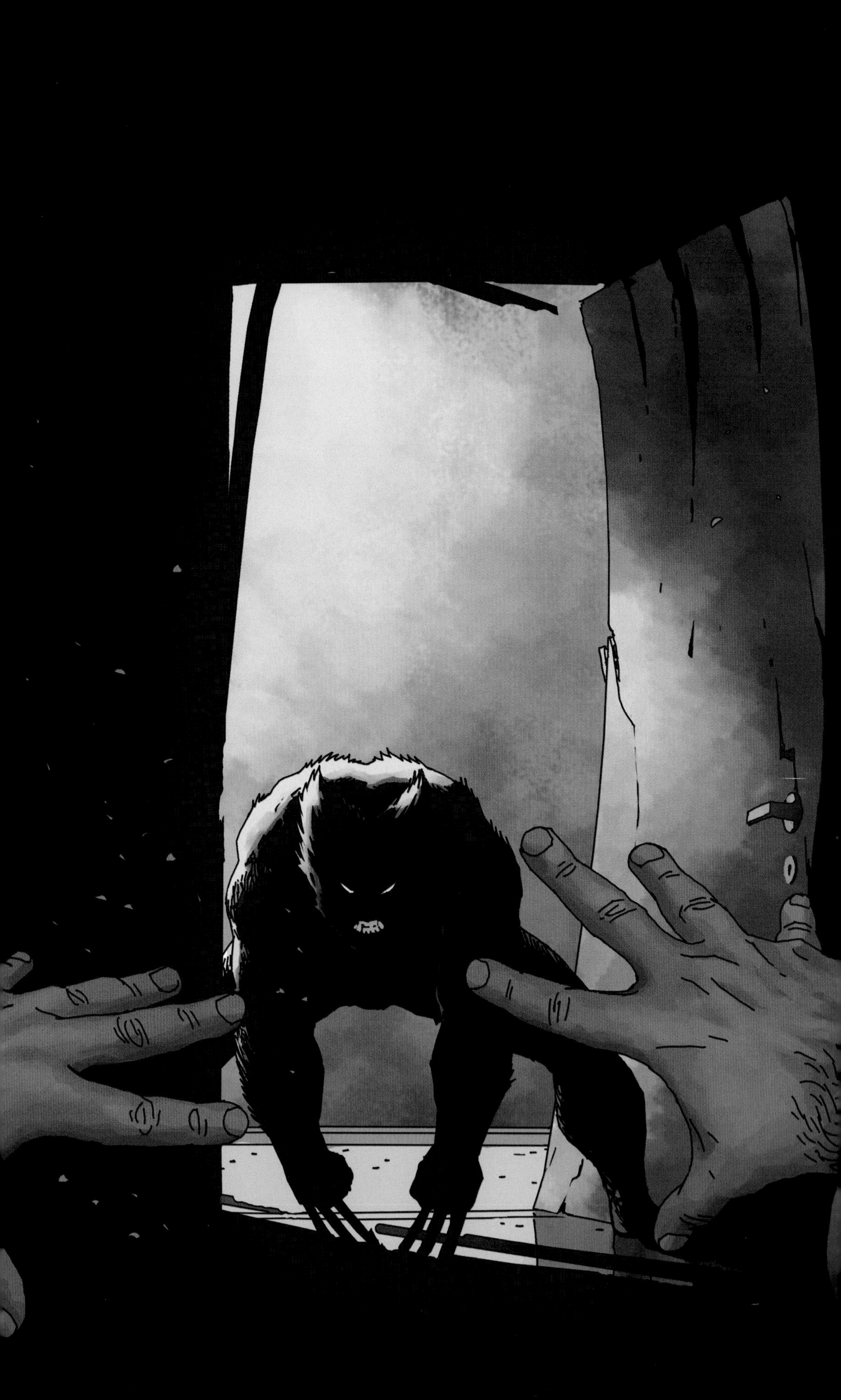

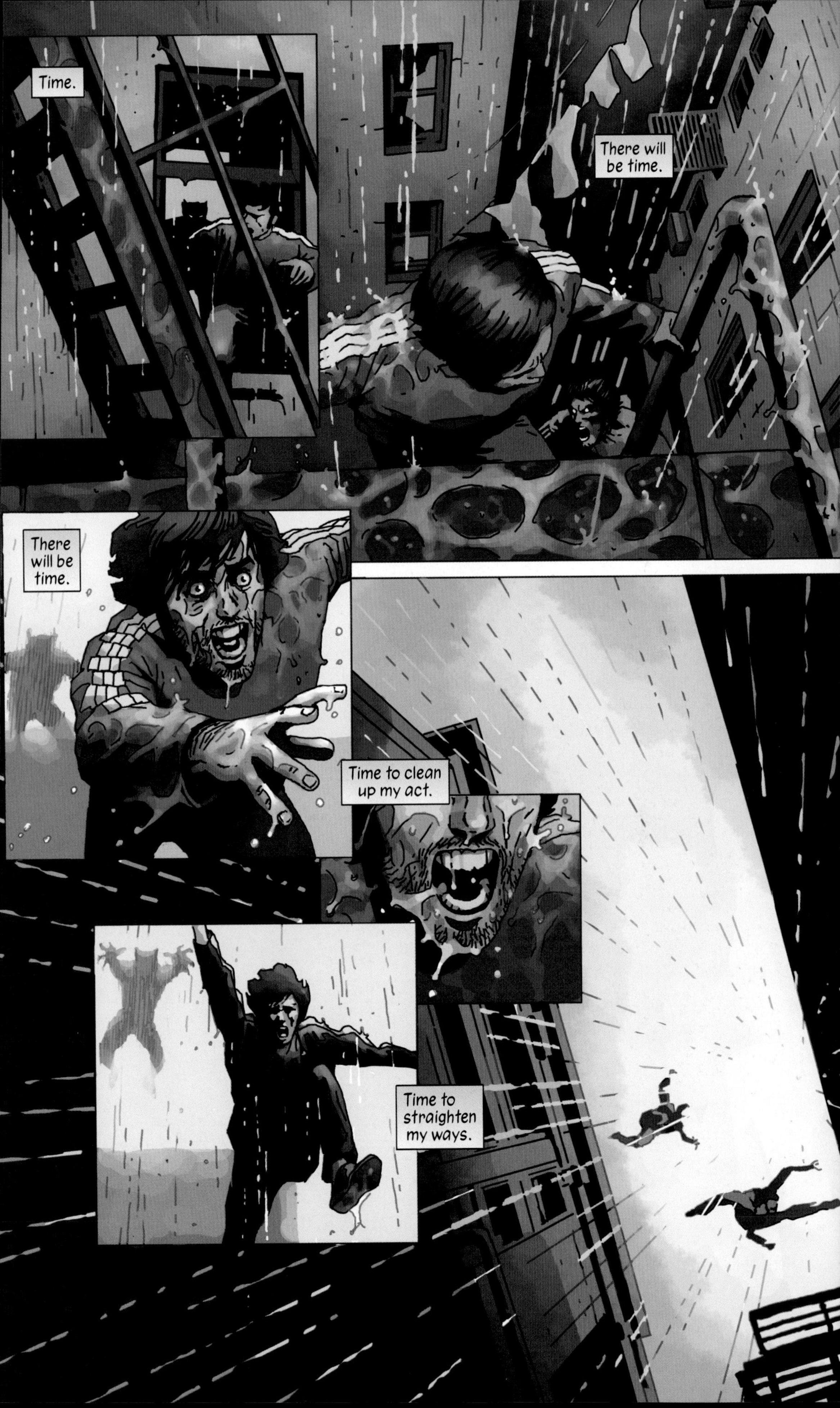
Time.
There will be time.
There will be time.
Time to clean up my act.
Time to straighten my ways.

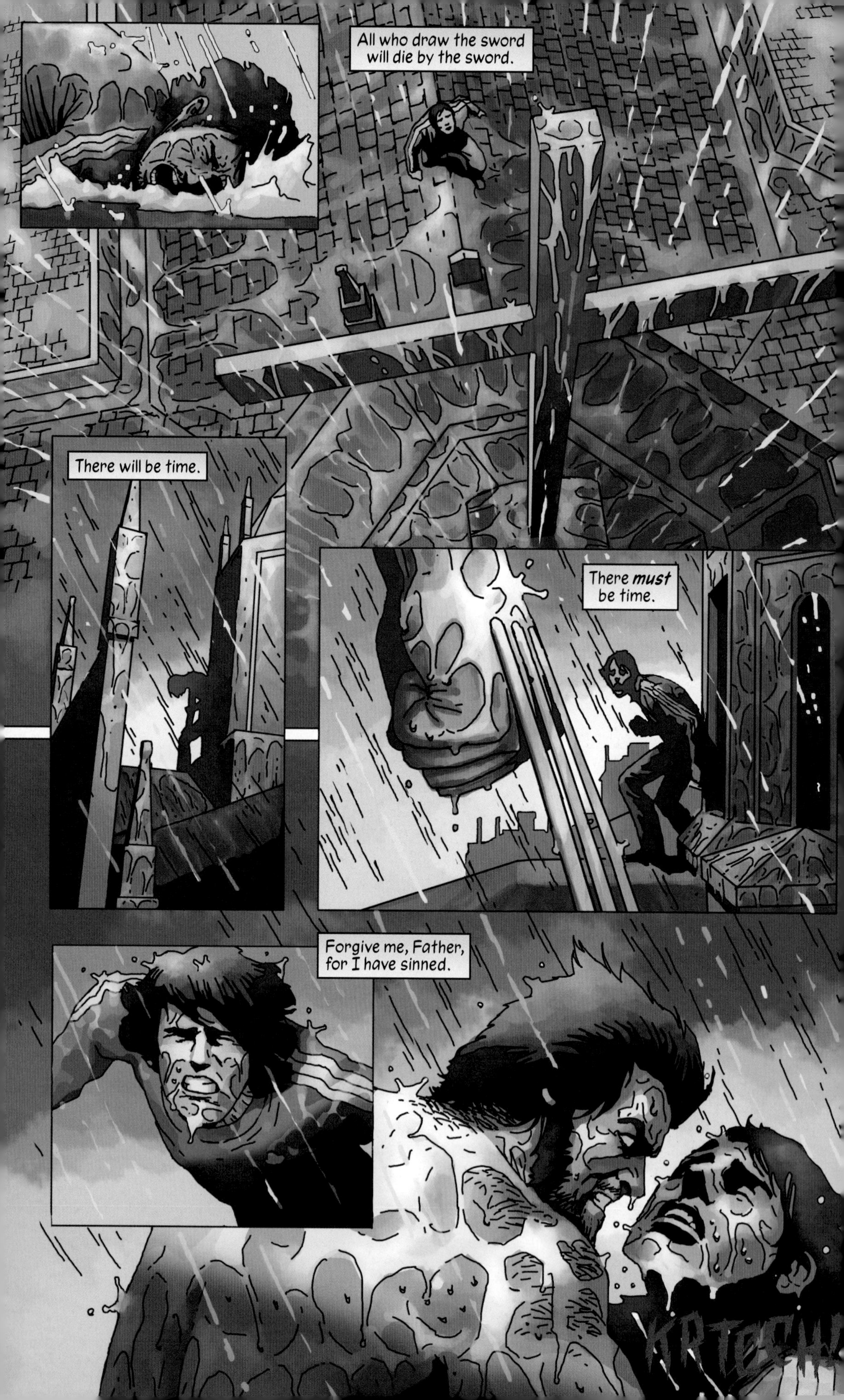
All who draw the sword will die by the sword.
There will be time.
There *must* be time.
Forgive me, Father, for I have sinned.

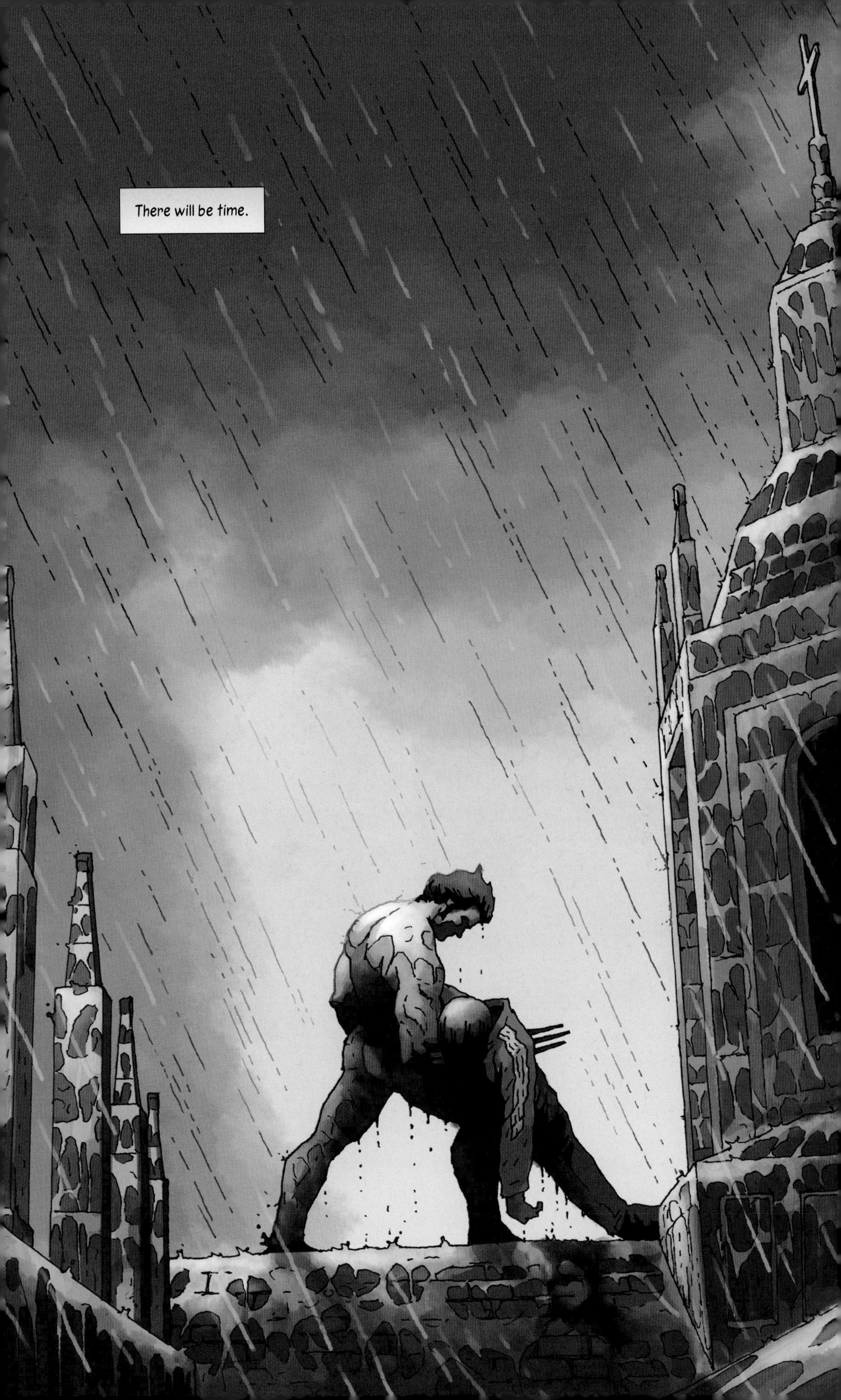
There will be time.

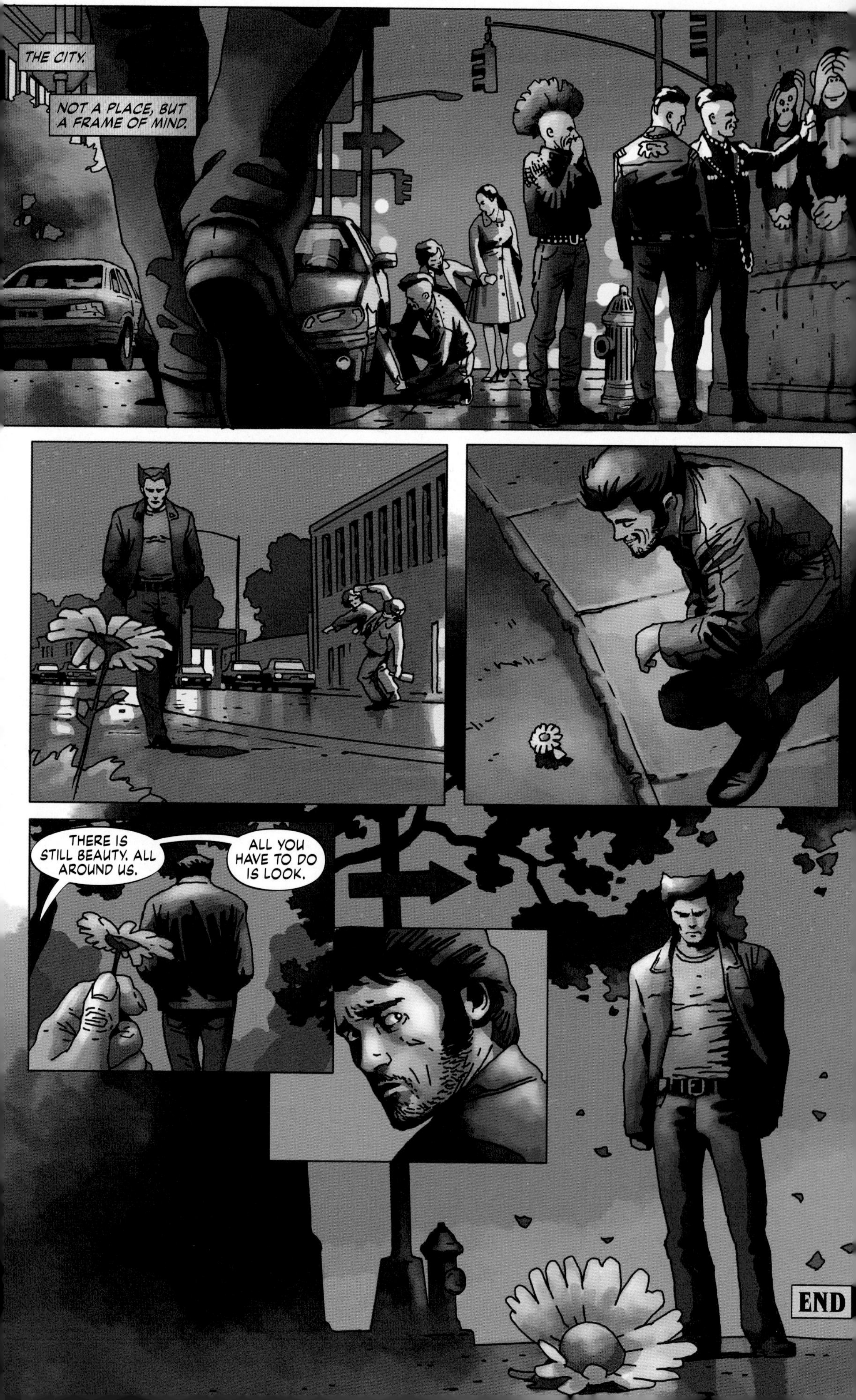

THE CITY.
NOT A PLACE, BUT A FRAME OF MIND.
THERE IS STILL BEAUTY. ALL AROUND US.
ALL YOU HAVE TO DO IS LOOK.
END

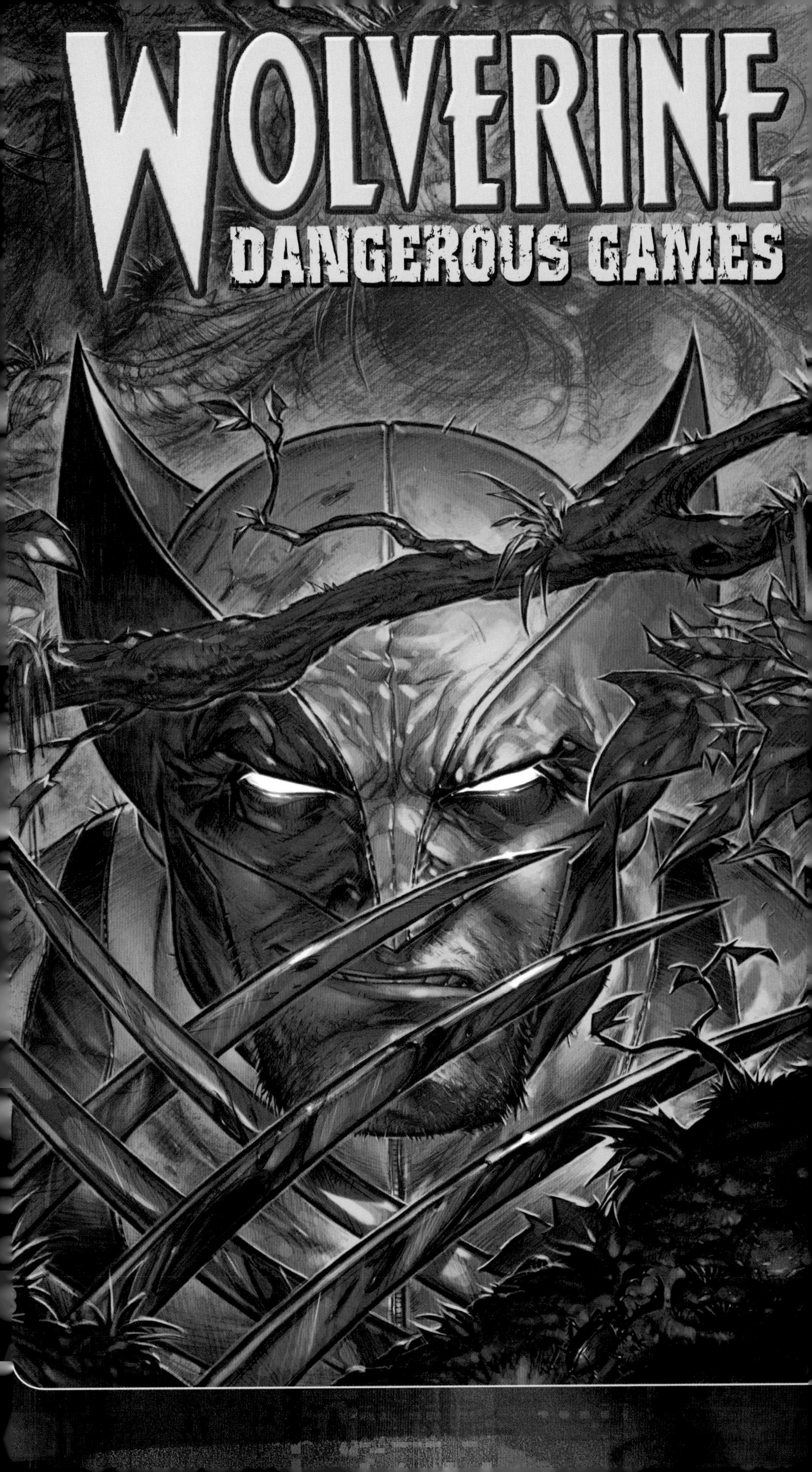
WOLVERINE
DANGEROUS GAMES

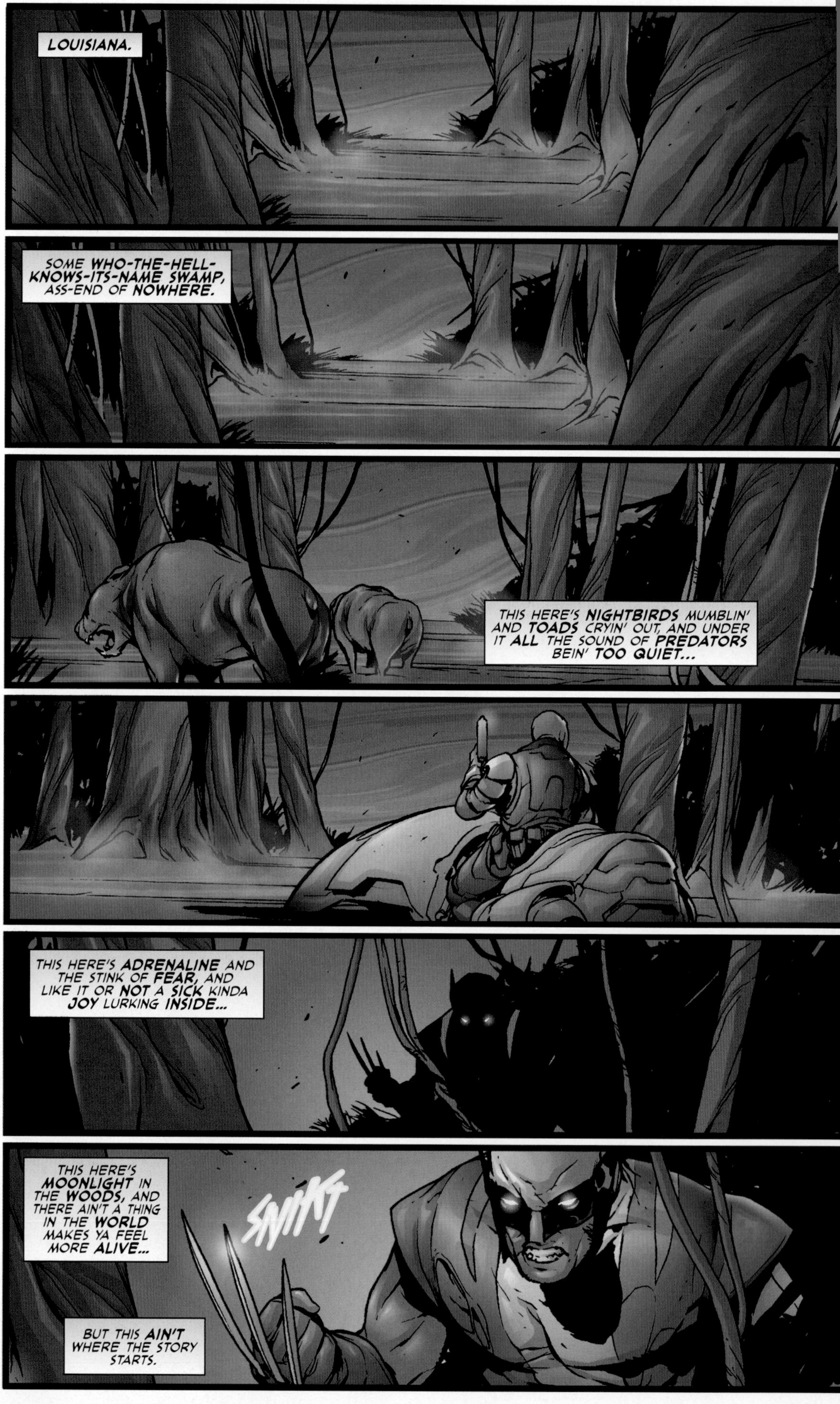
LOUISIANA.
SOME WHO-THE-HELL-KNOWS-ITS-NAME SWAMP, ASS-END OF NOWHERE.
THIS HERE'S NIGHTBIRDS MUMBLIN' AND TOADS CRYIN' OUT, AND UNDER IT ALL THE SOUND OF PREDATORS BEIN' TOO QUIET...
THIS HERE'S ADRENALINE AND THE STINK OF FEAR, AND LIKE IT OR NOT A SICK KINDA JOY LURKING INSIDE...
THIS HERE'S MOONLIGHT IN THE WOODS, AND THERE AIN'T A THING IN THE WORLD MAKES YA FEEL MORE ALIVE...
SNIKT
BUT THIS AIN'T WHERE THE STORY STARTS.

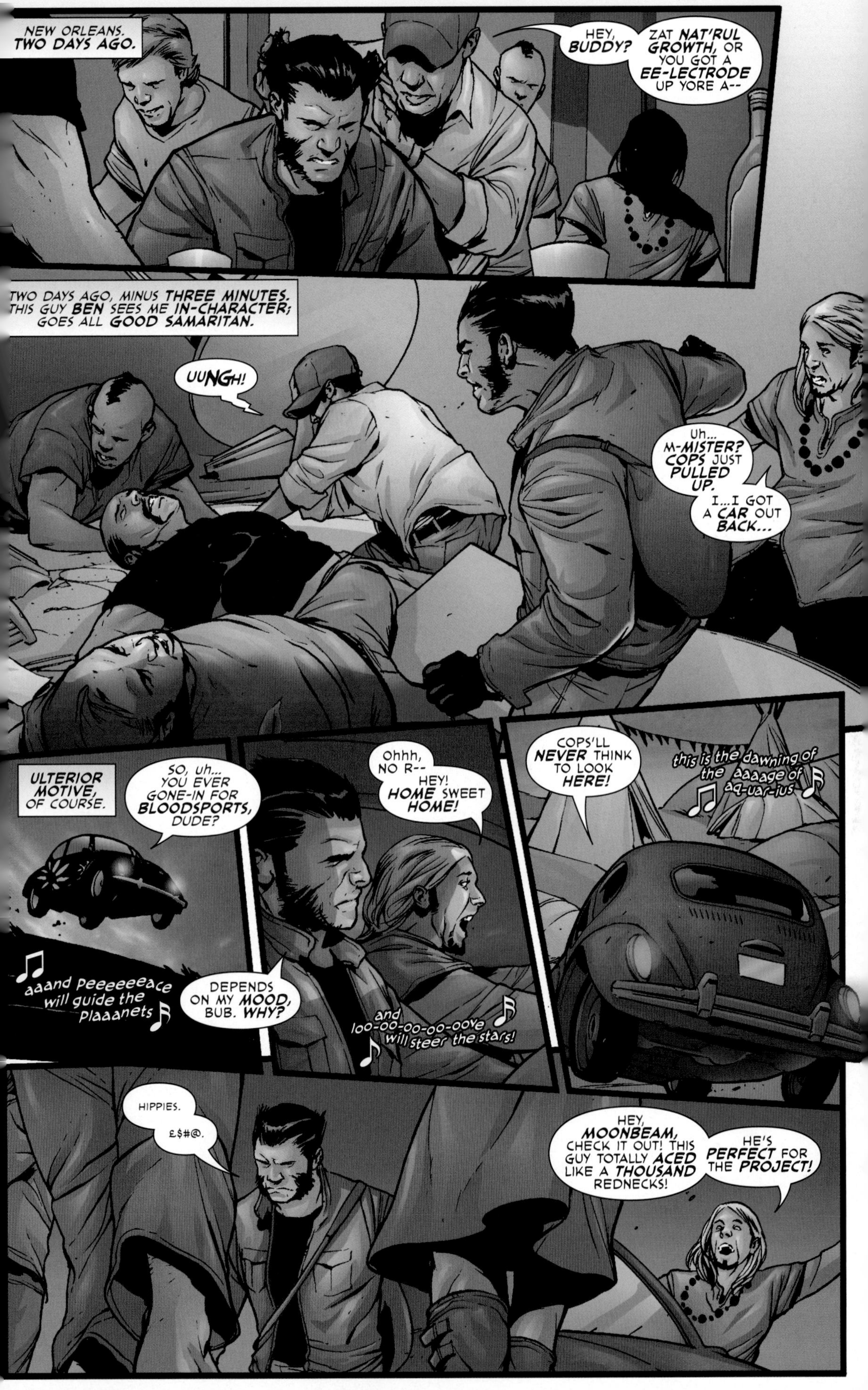

NEW ORLEANS. TWO DAYS AGO.
HEY, BUDDY?
ZAT NAT'RUL GROWTH, OR YOU GOT A EE-LECTRODE UP YORE A--
TWO DAYS AGO, MINUS THREE MINUTES. THIS GUY BEN SEES ME IN-CHARACTER; GOES ALL GOOD SAMARITAN.
UUNGH!
Uh... M-MISTER? COPS JUST PULLED UP.
I...I GOT A CAR OUT BACK...
ULTERIOR MOTIVE, OF COURSE.
SO, uh... YOU EVER GONE-IN FOR BLOODSPORTS, DUDE?
aaand peeeeeeace will guide the plaaanets
DEPENDS ON MY MOOD, BUB. WHY?
Ohhh, NO R--
HEY! HOME SWEET HOME!
and loo-oo-oo-oo-oove will steer the stars!
COPS'LL NEVER THINK TO LOOK HERE!
this is the dawning of the aaaage of aq-uar-ius
HIPPIES.
£$#@.
HEY, MOONBEAM, CHECK IT OUT! THIS GUY TOTALLY ACED LIKE A THOUSAND REDNECKS!
HE'S PERFECT FOR THE PROJECT!

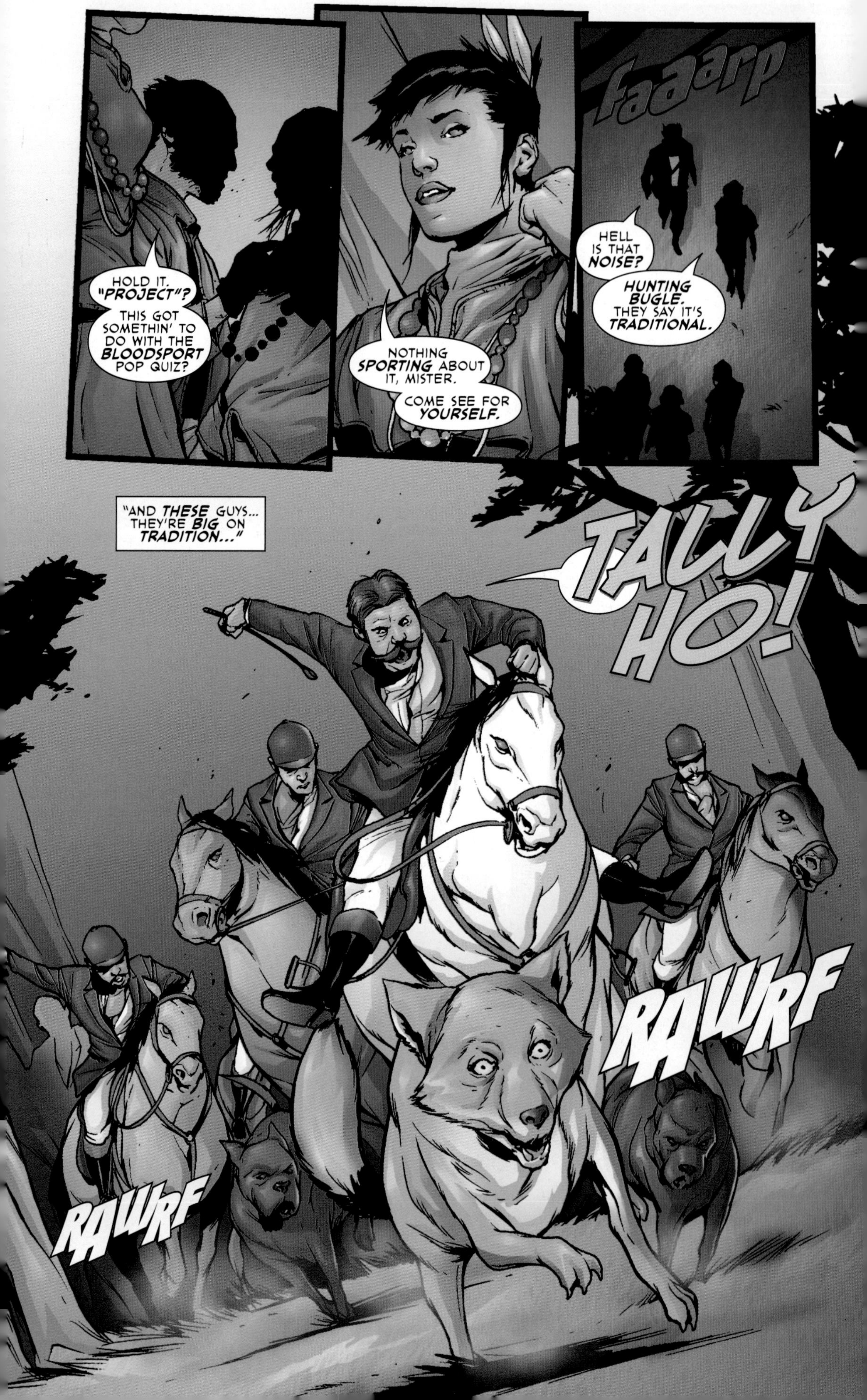
HOLD IT. "PROJECT"? THIS GOT SOMETHIN' TO DO WITH THE BLOODSPORT POP QUIZ?
NOTHING SPORTING ABOUT IT, MISTER.
COME SEE FOR YOURSELF.
faaarp
HELL IS THAT NOISE?
HUNTING BUGLE. THEY SAY IT'S TRADITIONAL.
"AND THESE GUYS... THEY'RE BIG ON TRADITION..."
TALLY HO!
RAWRF
RAWRF

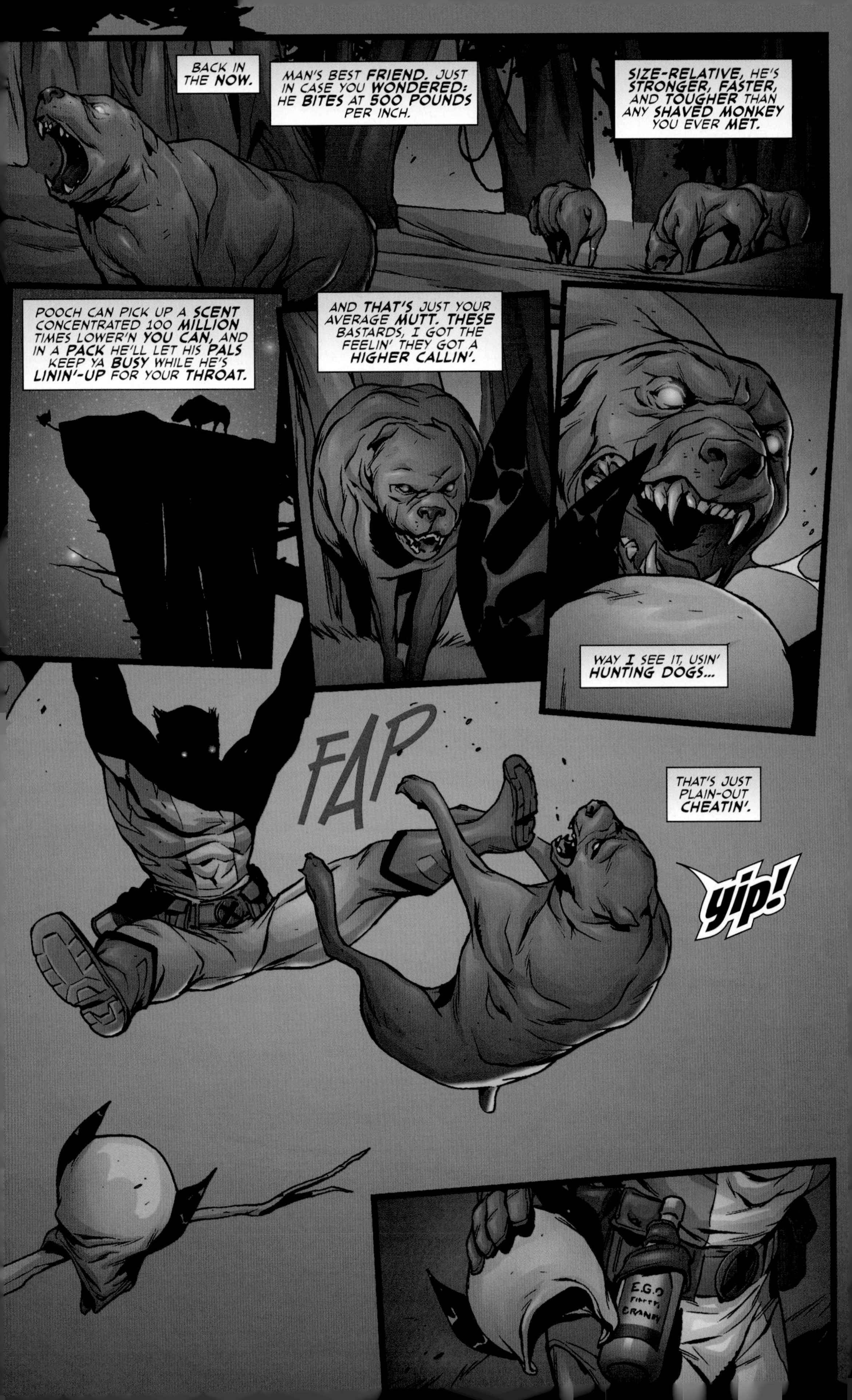
BACK IN THE NOW.
MAN'S BEST FRIEND. JUST IN CASE YOU WONDERED: HE BITES AT 500 POUNDS PER INCH.
SIZE-RELATIVE, HE'S STRONGER, FASTER, AND TOUGHER THAN ANY SHAVED MONKEY YOU EVER MET.
POOCH CAN PICK UP A SCENT CONCENTRATED 100 MILLION TIMES LOWER'N YOU CAN, AND IN A PACK HE'LL LET HIS PALS KEEP YA BUSY WHILE HE'S LININ'-UP FOR YOUR THROAT.
AND THAT'S JUST YOUR AVERAGE MUTT. THESE BASTARDS, I GOT THE FEELIN' THEY GOT A HIGHER CALLIN'.
WAY I SEE IT, USIN' HUNTING DOGS...
FAP
THAT'S JUST PLAIN-OUT CHEATIN'.
yip!

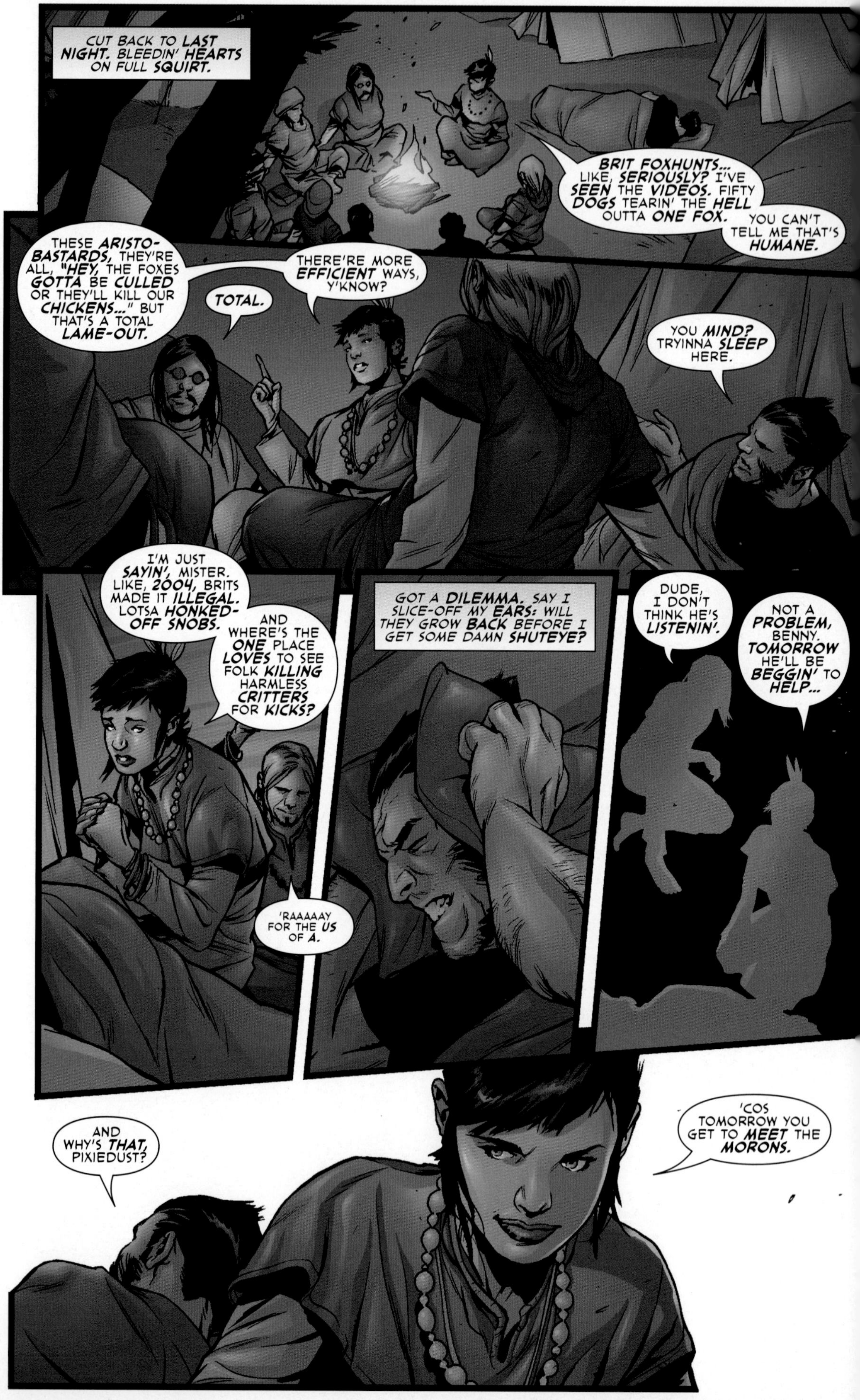
CUT BACK TO LAST NIGHT. BLEEDIN' HEARTS ON FULL SQUIRT.
BRIT FOXHUNTS... LIKE, SERIOUSLY? I'VE SEEN THE VIDEOS. FIFTY DOGS TEARIN' THE HELL OUTTA ONE FOX.
YOU CAN'T TELL ME THAT'S HUMANE.
THESE ARISTO-BASTARDS, THEY'RE ALL, "HEY, THE FOXES GOTTA BE CULLED OR THEY'LL KILL OUR CHICKENS..." BUT THAT'S A TOTAL LAME-OUT.
TOTAL.
THERE'RE MORE EFFICIENT WAYS, Y'KNOW?
YOU MIND? TRYINNA SLEEP HERE.
I'M JUST SAYIN', MISTER. LIKE, 2004, BRITS MADE IT ILLEGAL. LOTSA HONKED-OFF SNOBS.
AND WHERE'S THE ONE PLACE LOVES TO SEE FOLK KILLING HARMLESS CRITTERS FOR KICKS?
'RAAAAAY FOR THE US OF A.
GOT A DILEMMA. SAY I SLICE-OFF MY EARS: WILL THEY GROW BACK BEFORE I GET SOME DAMN SHUTEYE?
DUDE, I DON'T THINK HE'S LISTENIN'.
NOT A PROBLEM, BENNY. TOMORROW HE'LL BE BEGGIN' TO HELP...
AND WHY'S THAT, PIXIEDUST?
'COS TOMORROW YOU GET TO MEET THE MORONS.

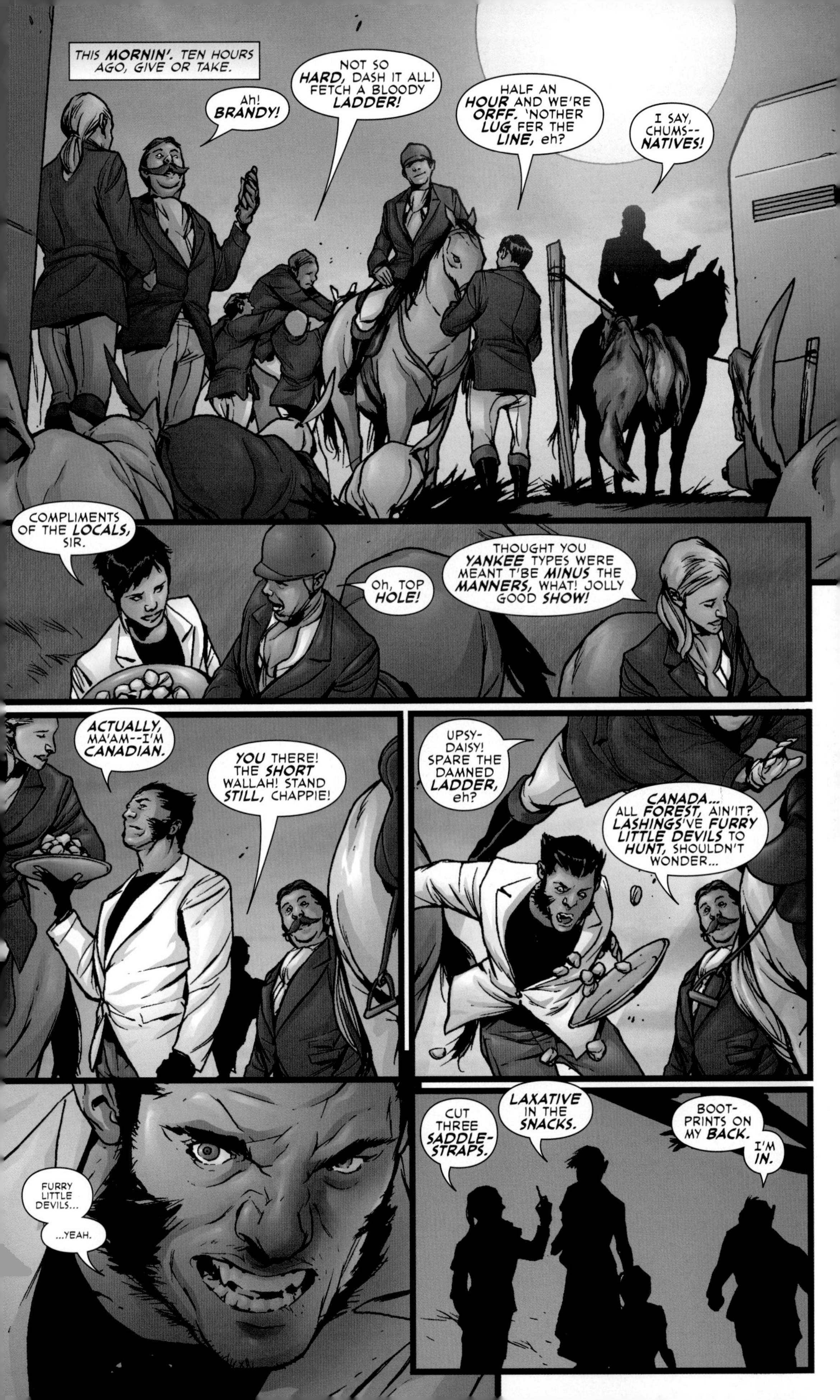
THIS MORNIN'. TEN HOURS AGO, GIVE OR TAKE.
Ah! BRANDY!
NOT SO HARD, DASH IT ALL! FETCH A BLOODY LADDER!
HALF AN HOUR AND WE'RE ORFF. 'NOTHER LUG FER THE LINE, eh?
I SAY, CHUMS-- NATIVES!
COMPLIMENTS OF THE LOCALS, SIR.
Oh, TOP HOLE!
THOUGHT YOU YANKEE TYPES WERE MEANT T'BE MINUS THE MANNERS, WHAT! JOLLY GOOD SHOW!
ACTUALLY, MA'AM--I'M CANADIAN.
YOU THERE! THE SHORT WALLAH! STAND STILL, CHAPPIE!
UPSY-DAISY! SPARE THE DAMNED LADDER, eh?
CANADA... ALL FOREST, AIN'T IT? LASHINGS'VE FURRY LITTLE DEVILS TO HUNT, SHOULDN'T WONDER...
FURRY LITTLE DEVILS...
...YEAH.
CUT THREE SADDLE-STRAPS.
LAXATIVE IN THE SNACKS.
BOOT-PRINTS ON MY BACK.
I'M IN.

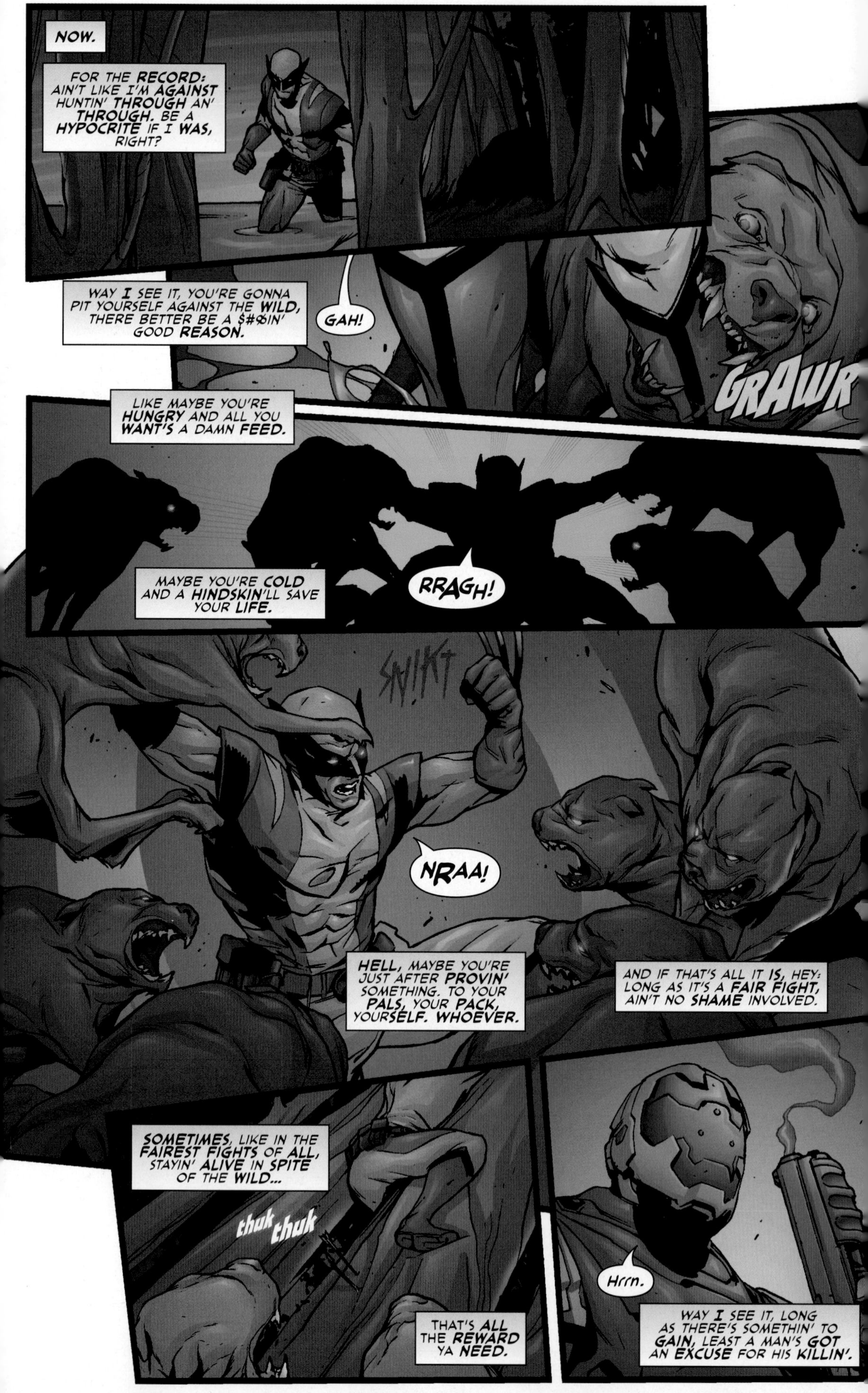

NOW.
FOR THE RECORD: AIN'T LIKE I'M AGAINST HUNTIN' THROUGH AN' THROUGH. BE A HYPOCRITE IF I WAS, RIGHT?
WAY I SEE IT, YOU'RE GONNA PIT YOURSELF AGAINST THE WILD, THERE BETTER BE A $#%IN' GOOD REASON.
GAH!
GRAWR
LIKE MAYBE YOU'RE HUNGRY AND ALL YOU WANT'S A DAMN FEED.
MAYBE YOU'RE COLD AND A HINDSKIN'LL SAVE YOUR LIFE.
RRAGH!
SNIKT
NRAA!
HELL, MAYBE YOU'RE JUST AFTER PROVIN' SOMETHING. TO YOUR PALS, YOUR PACK, YOURSELF. WHOEVER.
AND IF THAT'S ALL IT IS, HEY: LONG AS IT'S A FAIR FIGHT, AIN'T NO SHAME INVOLVED.
SOMETIMES, LIKE IN THE FAIREST FIGHTS OF ALL, STAYIN' ALIVE IN SPITE OF THE WILD...
thuk thuk
THAT'S ALL THE REWARD YA NEED.
Hrrn.
WAY I SEE IT, LONG AS THERE'S SOMETHIN' TO GAIN, LEAST A MAN'S GOT AN EXCUSE FOR HIS KILLIN'.

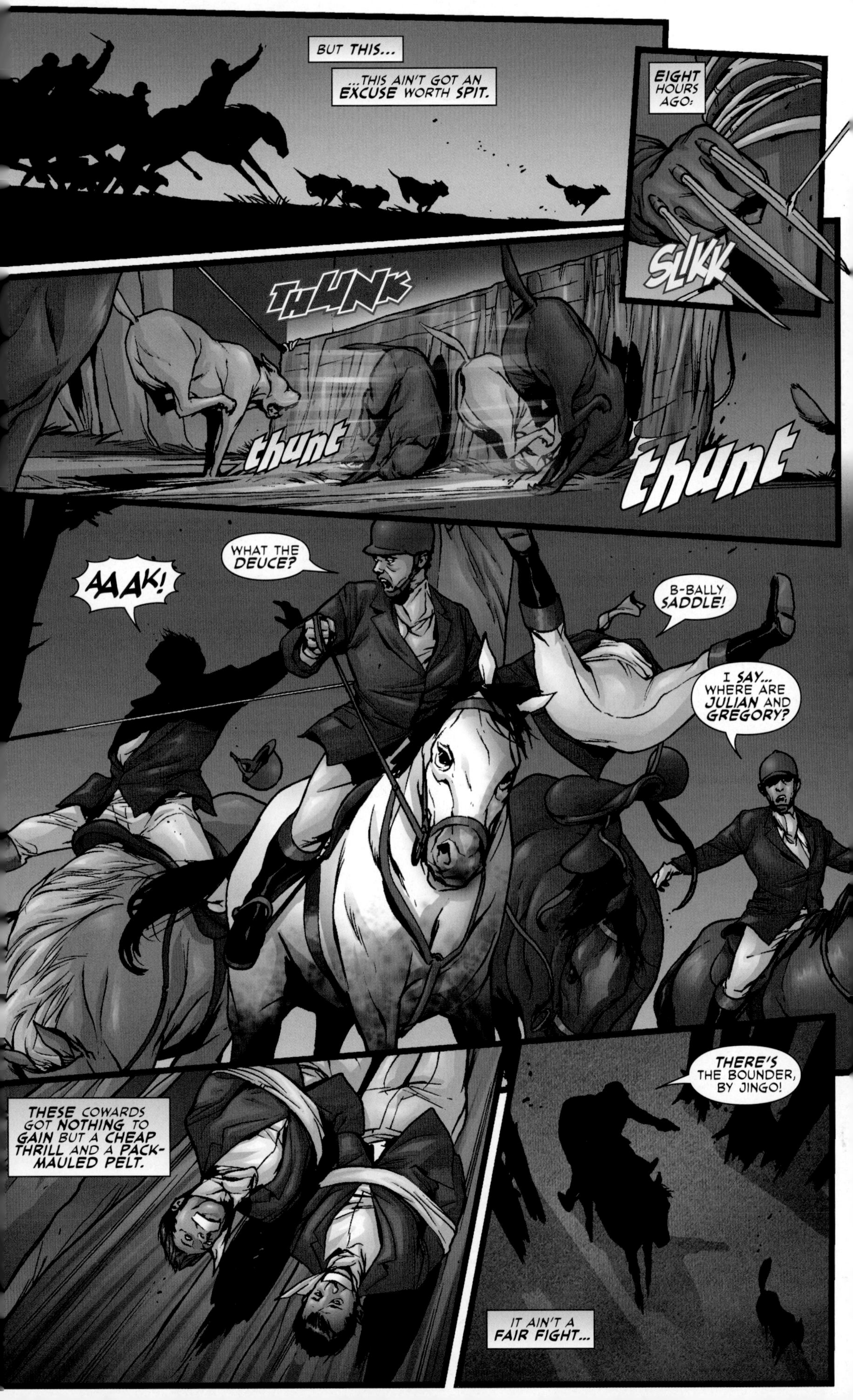
BUT THIS...
...THIS AIN'T GOT AN EXCUSE WORTH SPIT.
EIGHT HOURS AGO:
SLIKK
THUNK
thunt
thunt
WHAT THE DEUCE?
AAAK!
B-BALLY SADDLE!
I SAY... WHERE ARE JULIAN AND GREGORY?
THESE COWARDS GOT NOTHING TO GAIN BUT A CHEAP THRILL AND A PACK-MAULED PELT.
THERE'S THE BOUNDER, BY JINGO!
IT AIN'T A FAIR FIGHT...

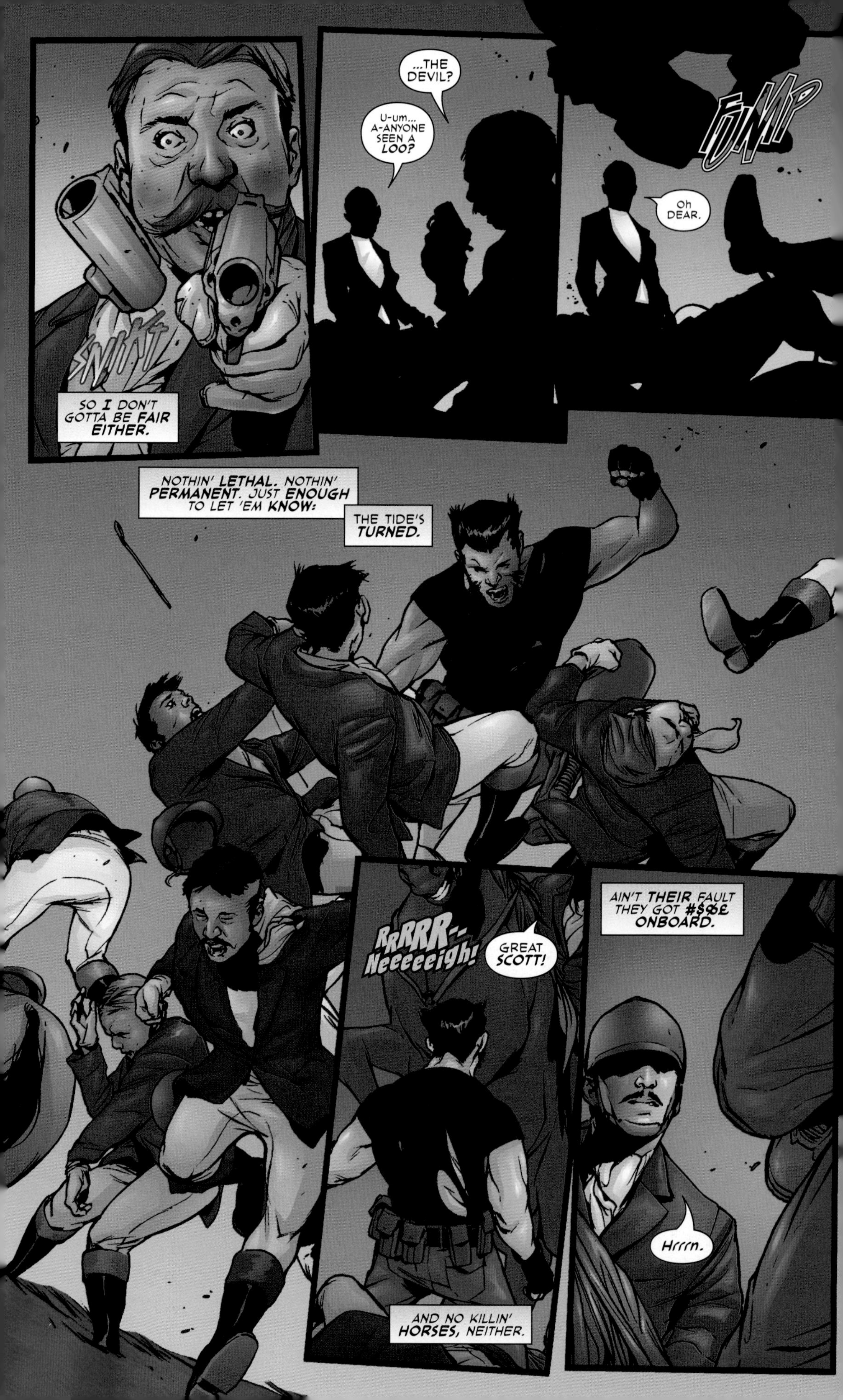
SNIKT
SO I DON'T GOTTA BE FAIR EITHER.
...THE DEVIL?
U-um... A-ANYONE SEEN A LOO?
FWMP
Oh DEAR.
NOTHIN' LETHAL. NOTHIN' PERMANENT. JUST ENOUGH TO LET 'EM KNOW:
THE TIDE'S TURNED.
RRRRR-- Neeeeeigh!
GREAT SCOTT!
AND NO KILLIN' HORSES, NEITHER.
AIN'T THEIR FAULT THEY GOT #$%£ ONBOARD.
Hrrrn.

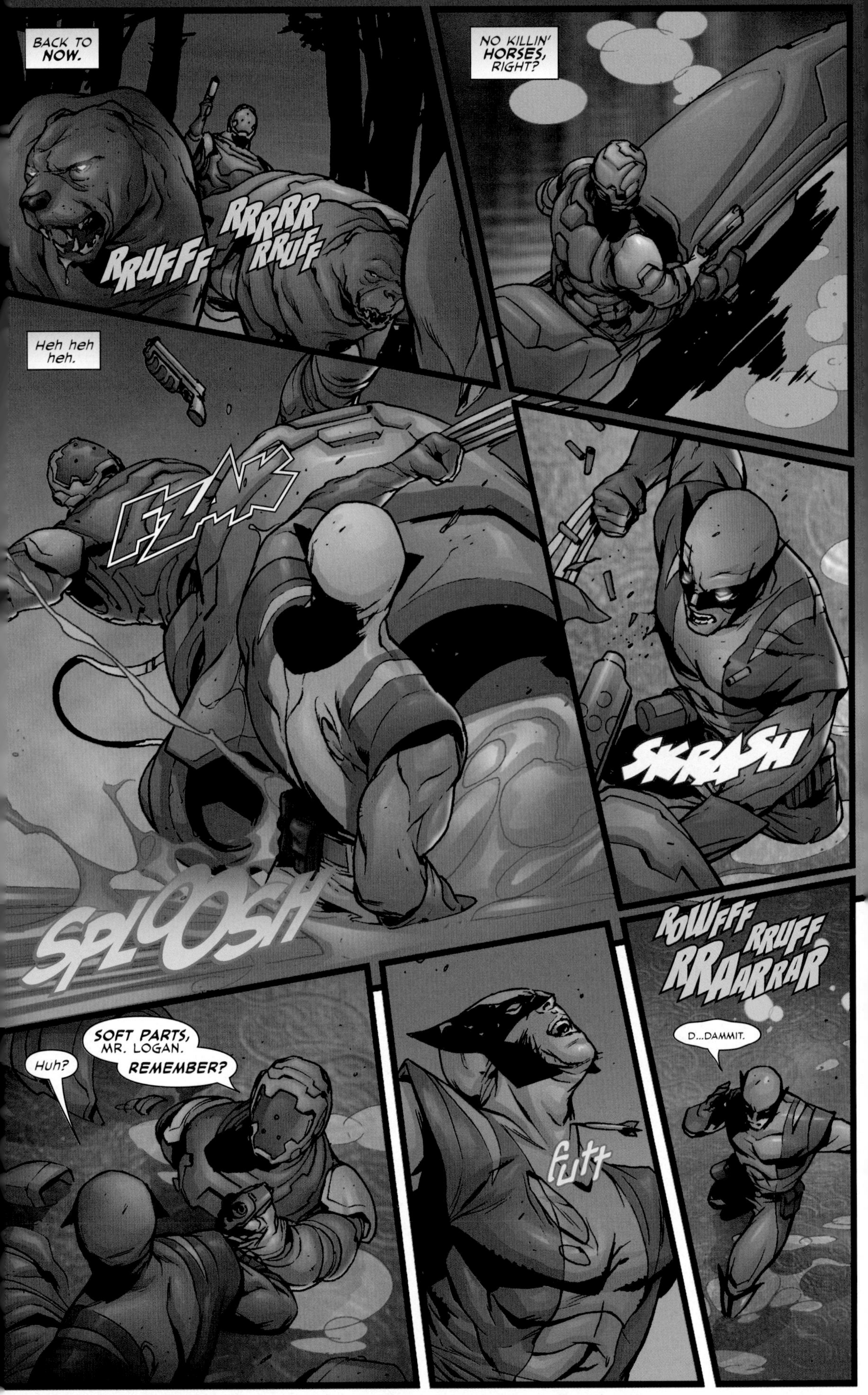
BACK TO NOW.
RRUFFF
RRRRR RRUFF
NO KILLIN' HORSES, RIGHT?
Heh heh heh.
FZAK
SKRASH
SPLOOSH
ROWFFF RRUFF RRAARRAR
Huh?
SOFT PARTS, MR. LOGAN. REMEMBER?
FUTT
D...DAMMIT.

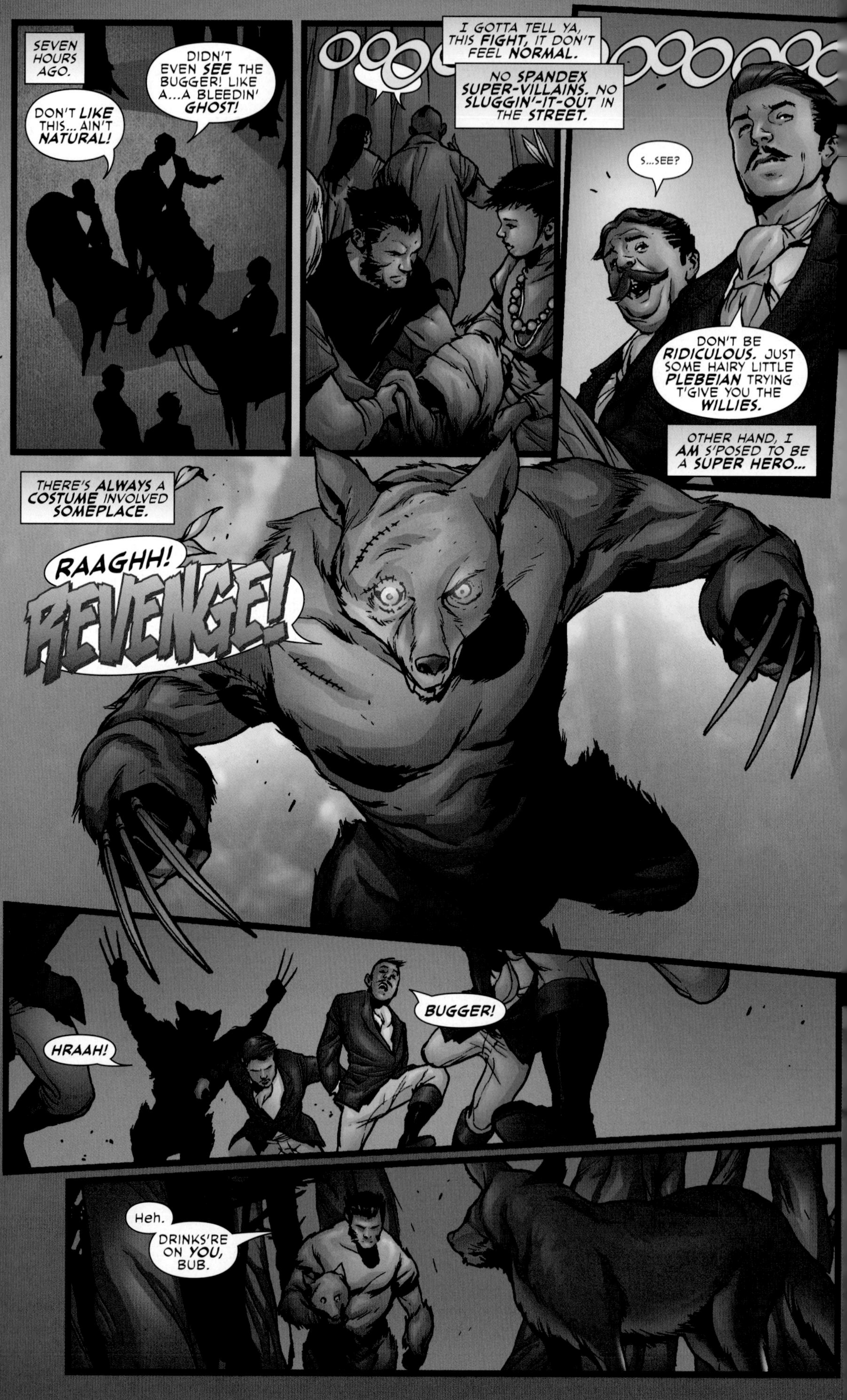

SEVEN HOURS AGO.
DON'T LIKE THIS... AIN'T NATURAL!
DIDN'T EVEN SEE THE BUGGER! LIKE A...A BLEEDIN' GHOST!
I GOTTA TELL YA, THIS FIGHT, IT DON'T FEEL NORMAL.
NO SPANDEX SUPER-VILLAINS. NO SLUGGIN'-IT-OUT IN THE STREET.
S...SEE?
DON'T BE RIDICULOUS. JUST SOME HAIRY LITTLE PLEBEIAN TRYING T'GIVE YOU THE WILLIES.
OTHER HAND, I AM S'POSED TO BE A SUPER HERO...
THERE'S ALWAYS A COSTUME INVOLVED SOMEPLACE.
RAAGHH! REVENGE!
HRAAH!
BUGGER!
Heh.
DRINKS'RE ON YOU, BUB.

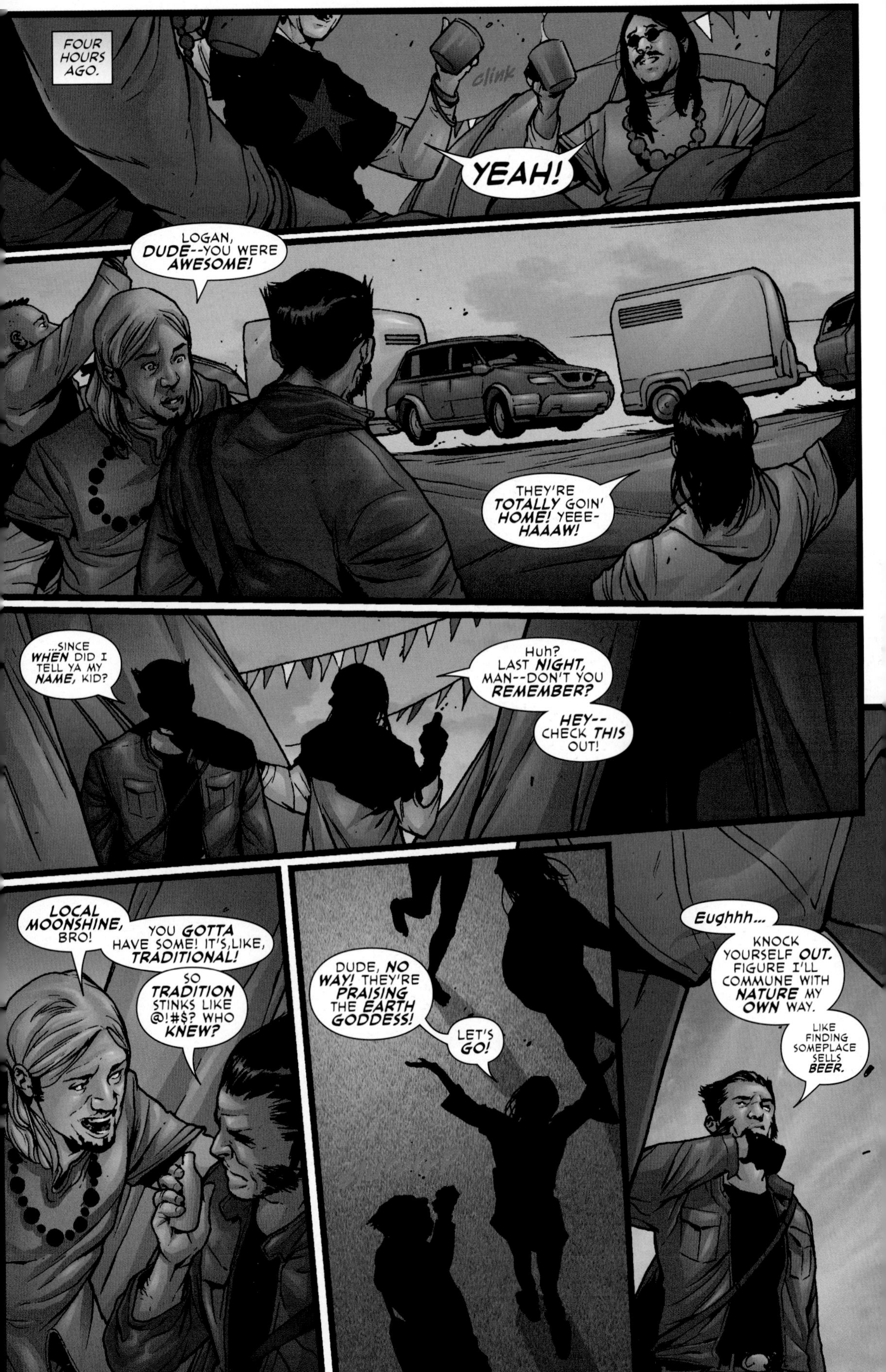

FOUR HOURS AGO.
clink
YEAH!
LOGAN, DUDE--YOU WERE AWESOME!
THEY'RE TOTALLY GOIN' HOME! YEEE-HAAAW!
...SINCE WHEN DID I TELL YA MY NAME, KID?
Huh? LAST NIGHT, MAN--DON'T YOU REMEMBER?
HEY--CHECK THIS OUT!
LOCAL MOONSHINE, BRO!
YOU GOTTA HAVE SOME! IT'S,LIKE, TRADITIONAL!
SO TRADITION STINKS LIKE @!#$? WHO KNEW?
DUDE, NO WAY! THEY'RE PRAISING THE EARTH GODDESS!
LET'S GO!
Eughhh...
KNOCK YOURSELF OUT. FIGURE I'LL COMMUNE WITH NATURE MY OWN WAY.
LIKE FINDING SOMEPLACE SELLS BEER.

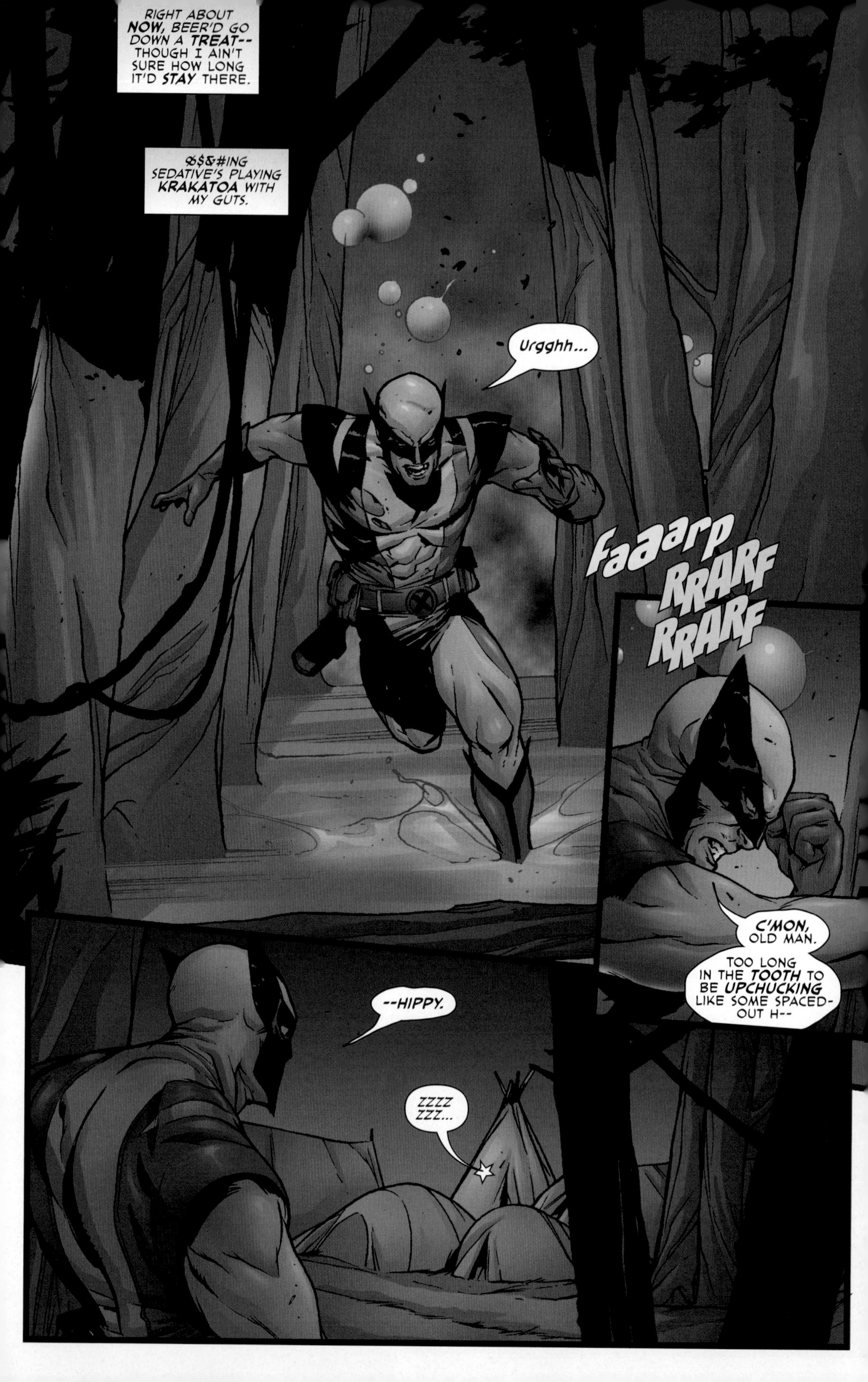
RIGHT ABOUT NOW, BEER'D GO DOWN A TREAT--THOUGH I AIN'T SURE HOW LONG IT'D STAY THERE.
%$&#ING SEDATIVE'S PLAYING KRAKATOA WITH MY GUTS.
Urgghh...
Faaaarp
RRARF
RRARF
C'MON, OLD MAN.
TOO LONG IN THE TOOTH TO BE UPCHUCKING LIKE SOME SPACED-OUT H--
--HIPPY.
ZZZZ ZZZ...

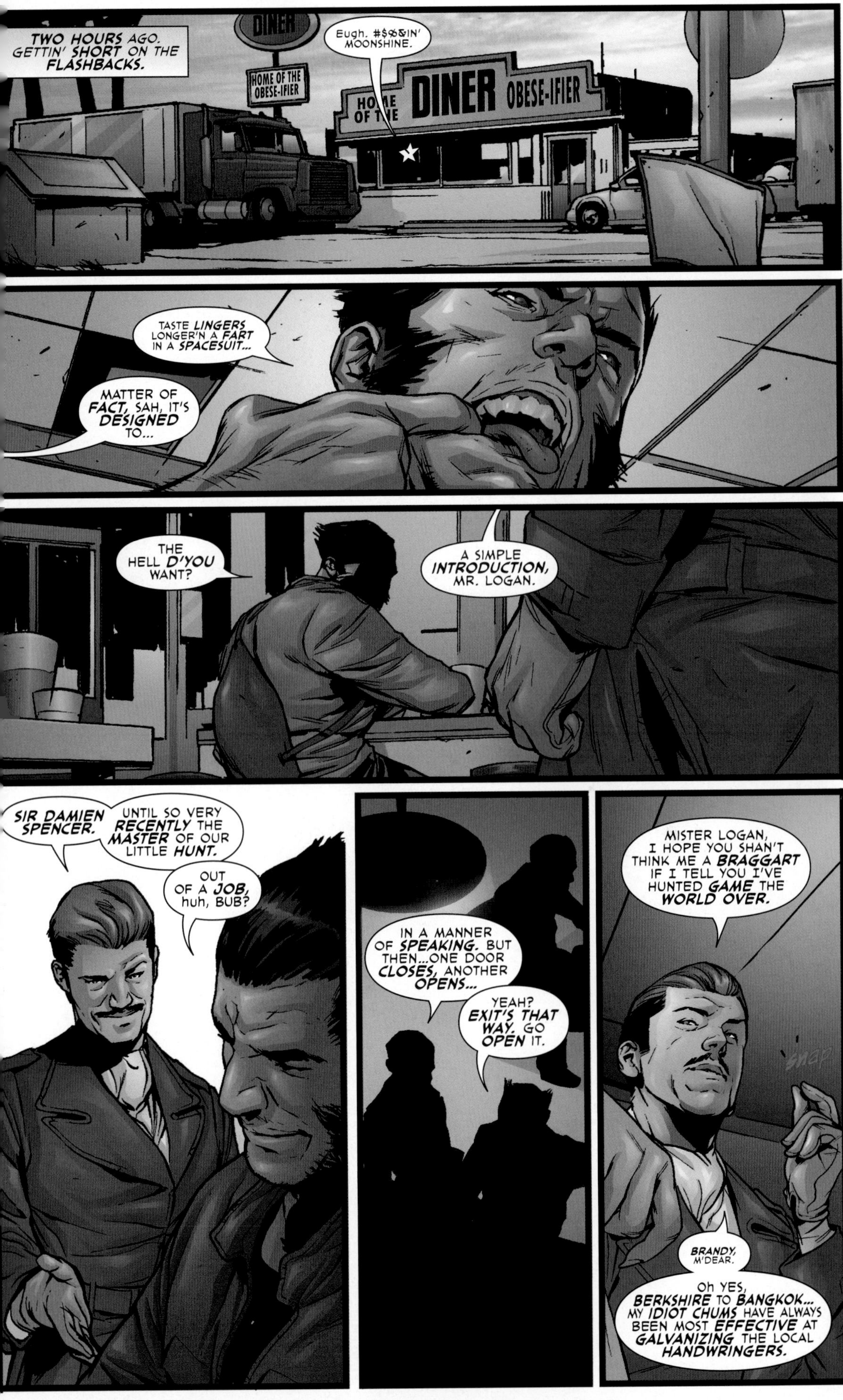
TWO HOURS AGO. GETTIN' SHORT ON THE FLASHBACKS.
DINER
HOME OF THE OBESE-IFIER
HOME OF THE DINER OBESE-IFIER
Eugh. #$%&IN' MOONSHINE.
TASTE LINGERS LONGER'N A FART IN A SPACESUIT...
MATTER OF FACT, SAH, IT'S DESIGNED TO...
THE HELL D'YOU WANT?
A SIMPLE INTRODUCTION, MR. LOGAN.
SIR DAMIEN SPENCER.
UNTIL SO VERY RECENTLY THE MASTER OF OUR LITTLE HUNT.
OUT OF A JOB, huh, BUB?
IN A MANNER OF SPEAKING. BUT THEN...ONE DOOR CLOSES, ANOTHER OPENS...
YEAH? EXIT'S THAT WAY. GO OPEN IT.
MISTER LOGAN, I HOPE YOU SHAN'T THINK ME A BRAGGART IF I TELL YOU I'VE HUNTED GAME THE WORLD OVER.
snap
BRANDY, M'DEAR.
Oh YES, BERKSHIRE TO BANGKOK... MY IDIOT CHUMS HAVE ALWAYS BEEN MOST EFFECTIVE AT GALVANIZING THE LOCAL HANDWRINGERS.

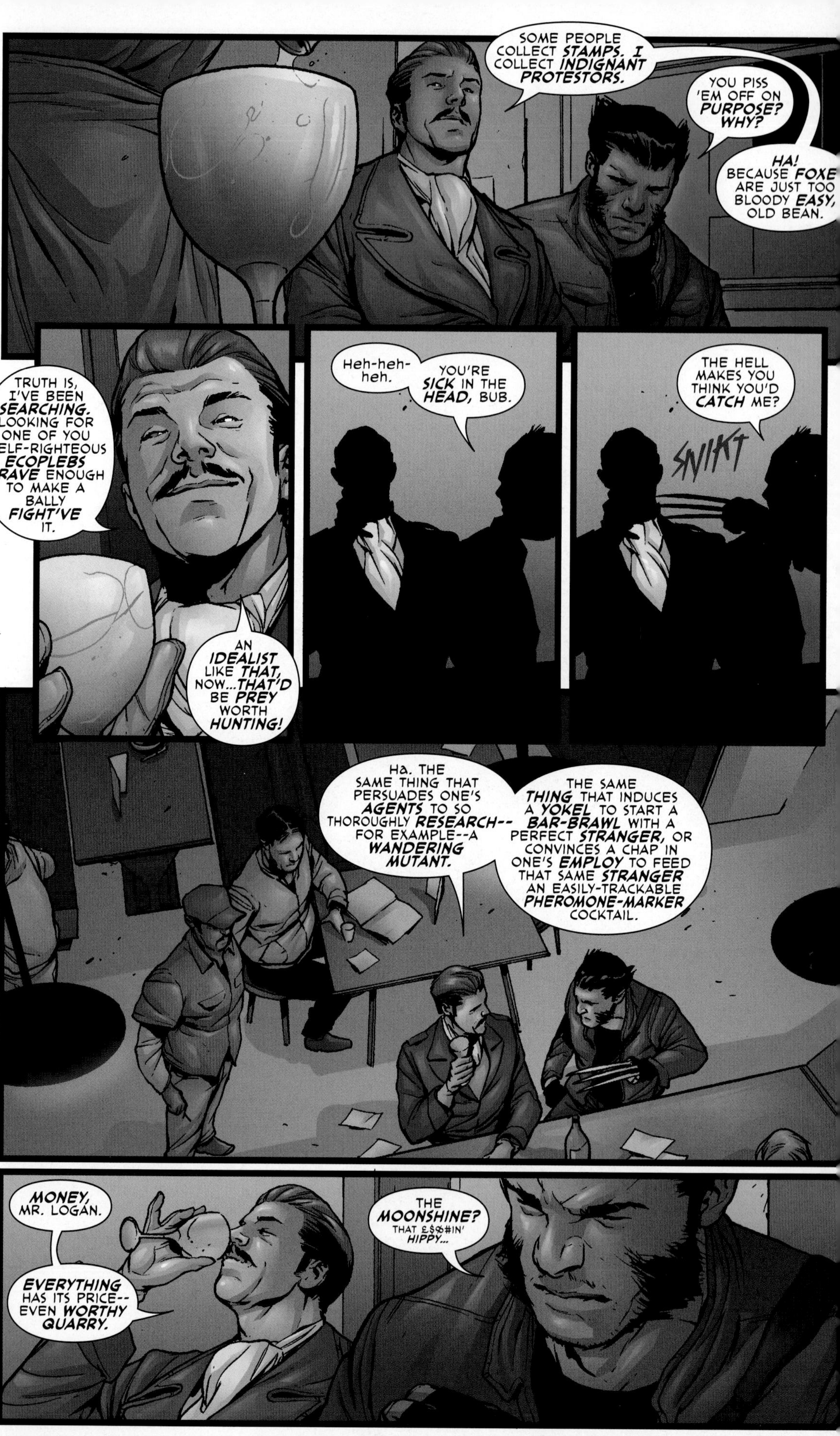

SOME PEOPLE COLLECT STAMPS. I COLLECT INDIGNANT PROTESTORS.
YOU PISS 'EM OFF ON PURPOSE? WHY?
HA! BECAUSE FOXES ARE JUST TOO BLOODY EASY, OLD BEAN.
TRUTH IS, I'VE BEEN SEARCHING. LOOKING FOR ONE OF YOU SELF-RIGHTEOUS ECOPLEBS BRAVE ENOUGH TO MAKE A BALLY FIGHT'VE IT.
AN IDEALIST LIKE THAT, NOW...THAT'D BE PREY WORTH HUNTING!
Heh-heh-heh.
YOU'RE SICK IN THE HEAD, BUB.
THE HELL MAKES YOU THINK YOU'D CATCH ME?
SNIKT
Ha. THE SAME THING THAT PERSUADES ONE'S AGENTS TO SO THOROUGHLY RESEARCH-- FOR EXAMPLE--A WANDERING MUTANT.
THE SAME THING THAT INDUCES A YOKEL TO START A BAR-BRAWL WITH A PERFECT STRANGER, OR CONVINCES A CHAP IN ONE'S EMPLOY TO FEED THAT SAME STRANGER AN EASILY-TRACKABLE PHEROMONE-MARKER COCKTAIL.
MONEY, MR. LOGAN.
EVERYTHING HAS ITS PRICE-- EVEN WORTHY QUARRY.
THE MOONSHINE? THAT £$%#IN' HIPPY...

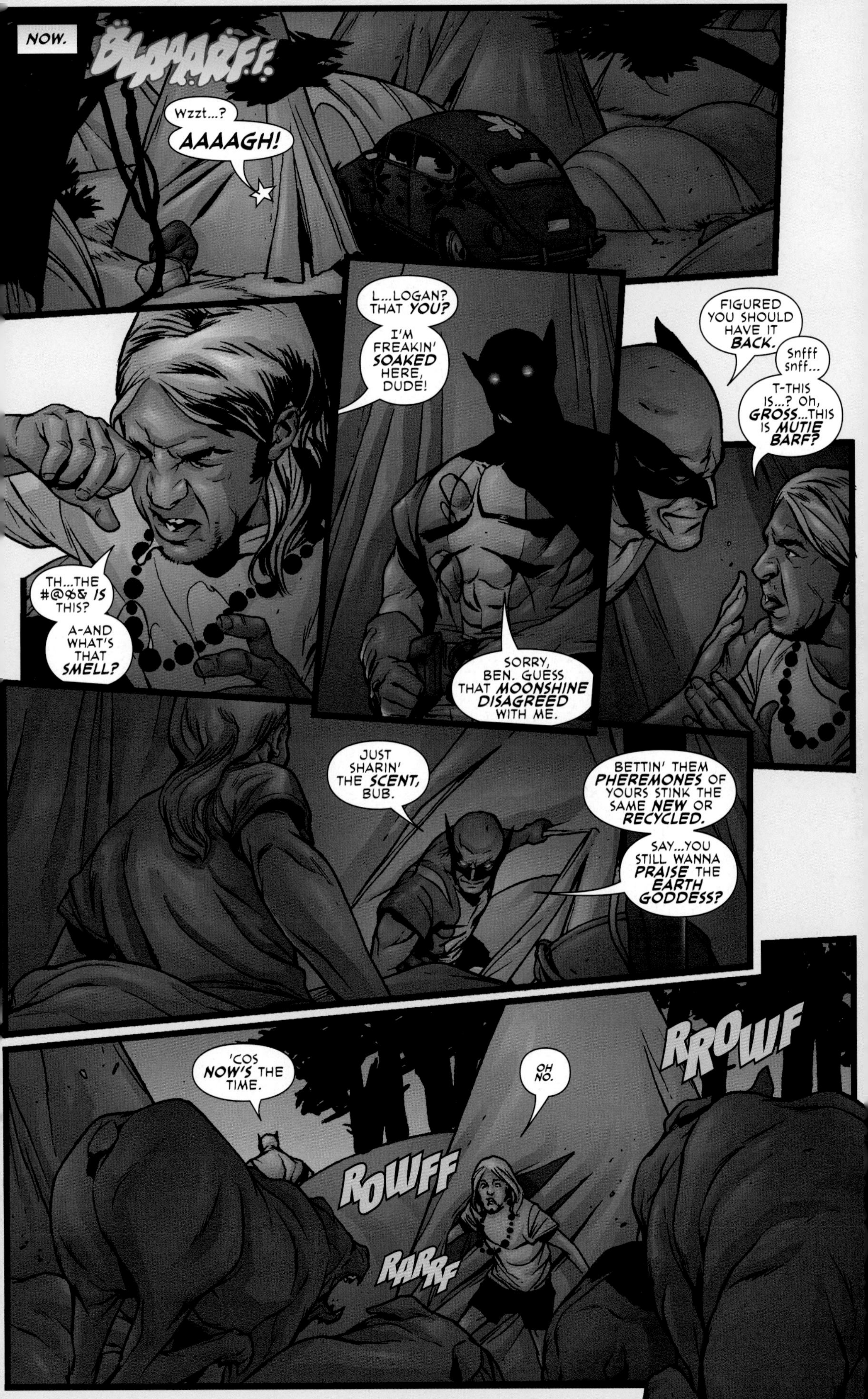

NOW.
BLAAARFF
Wzzt...?
AAAAGH!
TH...THE #@%& IS THIS?
A-AND WHAT'S THAT SMELL?
L...LOGAN? THAT YOU?
I'M FREAKIN' SOAKED HERE, DUDE!
SORRY, BEN. GUESS THAT MOONSHINE DISAGREED WITH ME.
FIGURED YOU SHOULD HAVE IT BACK.
Snfff snff...
T-THIS IS...? Oh, GROSS...THIS IS MUTIE BARF?
JUST SHARIN' THE SCENT, BUB.
BETTIN' THEM PHEREMONES OF YOURS STINK THE SAME NEW OR RECYCLED.
SAY...YOU STILL WANNA PRAISE THE EARTH GODDESS?
'COS NOW'S THE TIME.
OH NO.
RROWF
ROWFF
RARRF

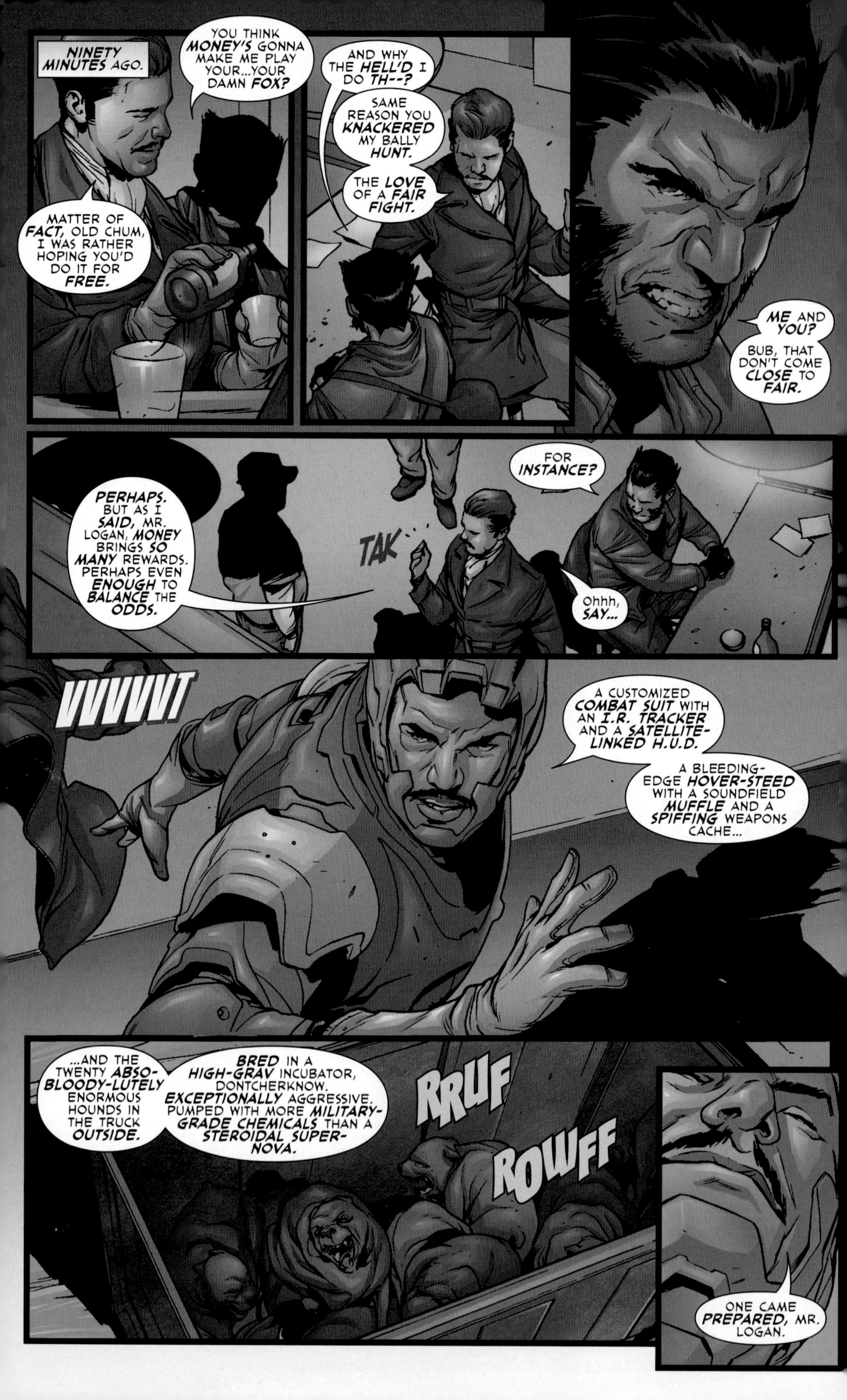
NINETY MINUTES AGO.
YOU THINK MONEY'S GONNA MAKE ME PLAY YOUR...YOUR DAMN FOX?
MATTER OF FACT, OLD CHUM, I WAS RATHER HOPING YOU'D DO IT FOR FREE.
AND WHY THE HELL'D I DO TH--?
SAME REASON YOU KNACKERED MY BALLY HUNT.
THE LOVE OF A FAIR FIGHT.
ME AND YOU?
BUB, THAT DON'T COME CLOSE TO FAIR.
PERHAPS. BUT AS I SAID, MR. LOGAN, MONEY BRINGS SO MANY REWARDS. PERHAPS EVEN ENOUGH TO BALANCE THE ODDS.
TAK
FOR INSTANCE?
Ohhh, SAY...
VVVVVVT
A CUSTOMIZED COMBAT SUIT WITH AN I.R. TRACKER AND A SATELLITE-LINKED H.U.D.
A BLEEDING-EDGE HOVER-STEED WITH A SOUNDFIELD MUFFLE AND A SPIFFING WEAPONS CACHE...
...AND THE TWENTY ABSO-BLOODY-LUTELY ENORMOUS HOUNDS IN THE TRUCK OUTSIDE.
BRED IN A HIGH-GRAV INCUBATOR, DONTCHERKNOW. EXCEPTIONALLY AGGRESSIVE. PUMPED WITH MORE MILITARY-GRADE CHEMICALS THAN A STEROIDAL SUPER-NOVA.
RRUF
ROWFF
ONE CAME PREPARED, MR. LOGAN.

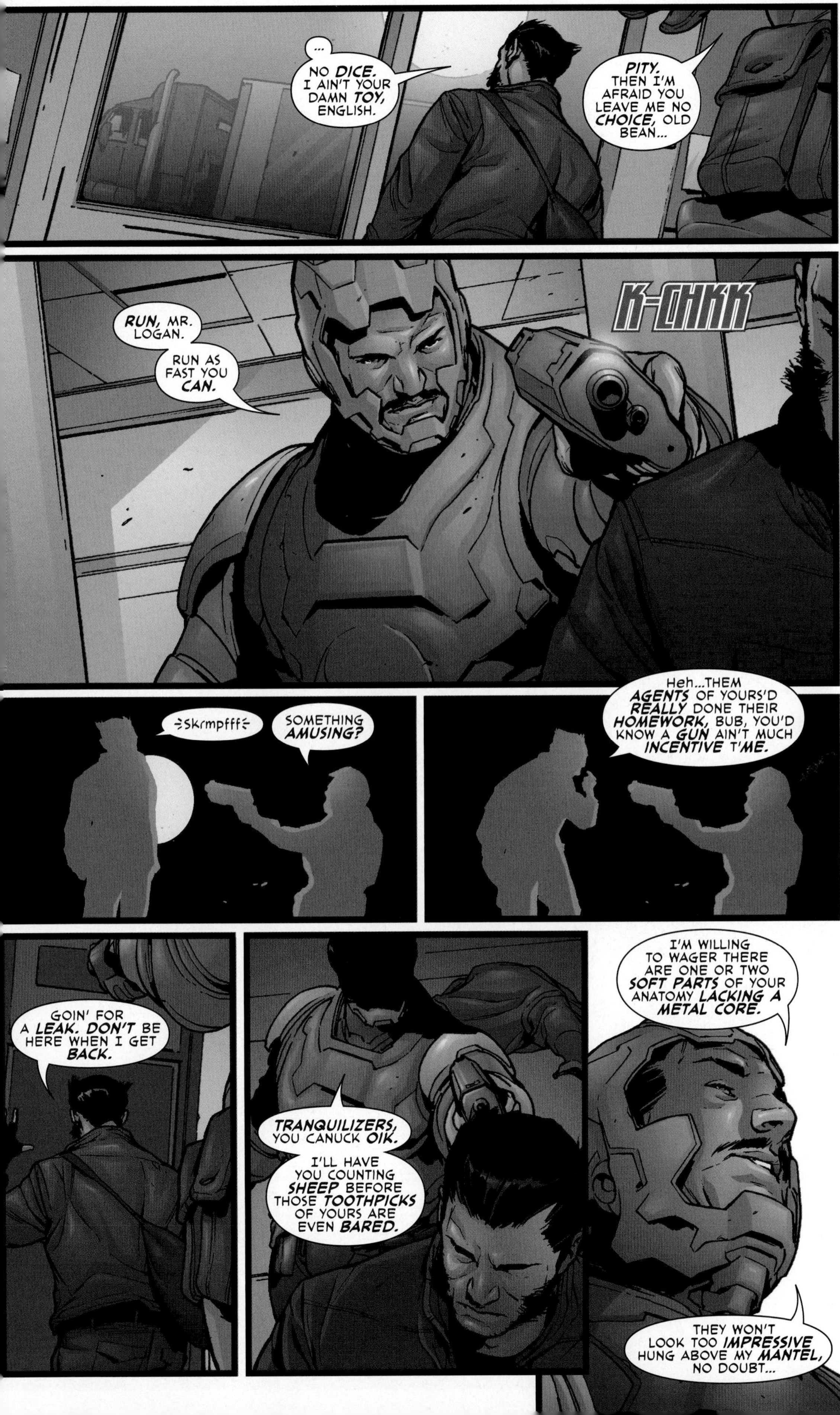

... NO DICE. I AIN'T YOUR DAMN TOY, ENGLISH.
PITY. THEN I'M AFRAID YOU LEAVE ME NO CHOICE, OLD BEAN...
RUN, MR. LOGAN.
RUN AS FAST YOU CAN.
K-CHKK
Skrmpfff
SOMETHING AMUSING?
Heh...THEM AGENTS OF YOURS'D REALLY DONE THEIR HOMEWORK, BUB, YOU'D KNOW A GUN AIN'T MUCH INCENTIVE T'ME.
GOIN' FOR A LEAK. DON'T BE HERE WHEN I GET BACK.
TRANQUILIZERS, YOU CANUCK OIK.
I'LL HAVE YOU COUNTING SHEEP BEFORE THOSE TOOTHPICKS OF YOURS ARE EVEN BARED.
I'M WILLING TO WAGER THERE ARE ONE OR TWO SOFT PARTS OF YOUR ANATOMY LACKING A METAL CORE.
THEY WON'T LOOK TOO IMPRESSIVE HUNG ABOVE MY MANTEL, NO DOUBT...

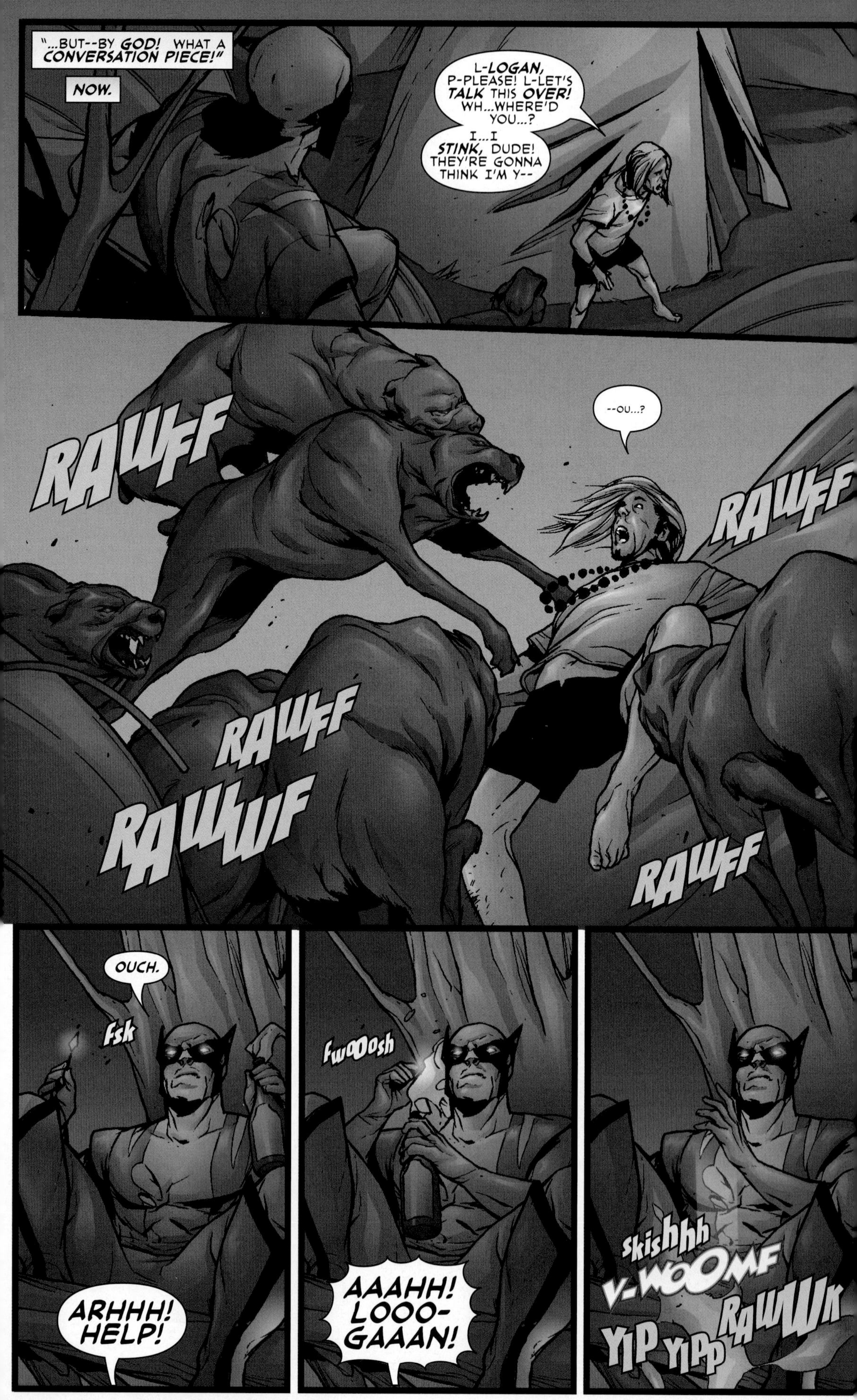
"...BUT--BY GOD! WHAT A CONVERSATION PIECE!"
NOW.
L-LOGAN, P-PLEASE! L-LET'S TALK THIS OVER! WH...WHERE'D YOU...?
I...I STINK, DUDE! THEY'RE GONNA THINK I'M Y--
--OU...?
RAWFF
RAWFF
RAWFF
RAWWF
RAWFF
OUCH.
Fsk
ARHHH! HELP!
Fwooosh
AAAHH! LOOO-GAAAN!
Skishhh
V-WOOMF
YIP
YIPP
RAWWK

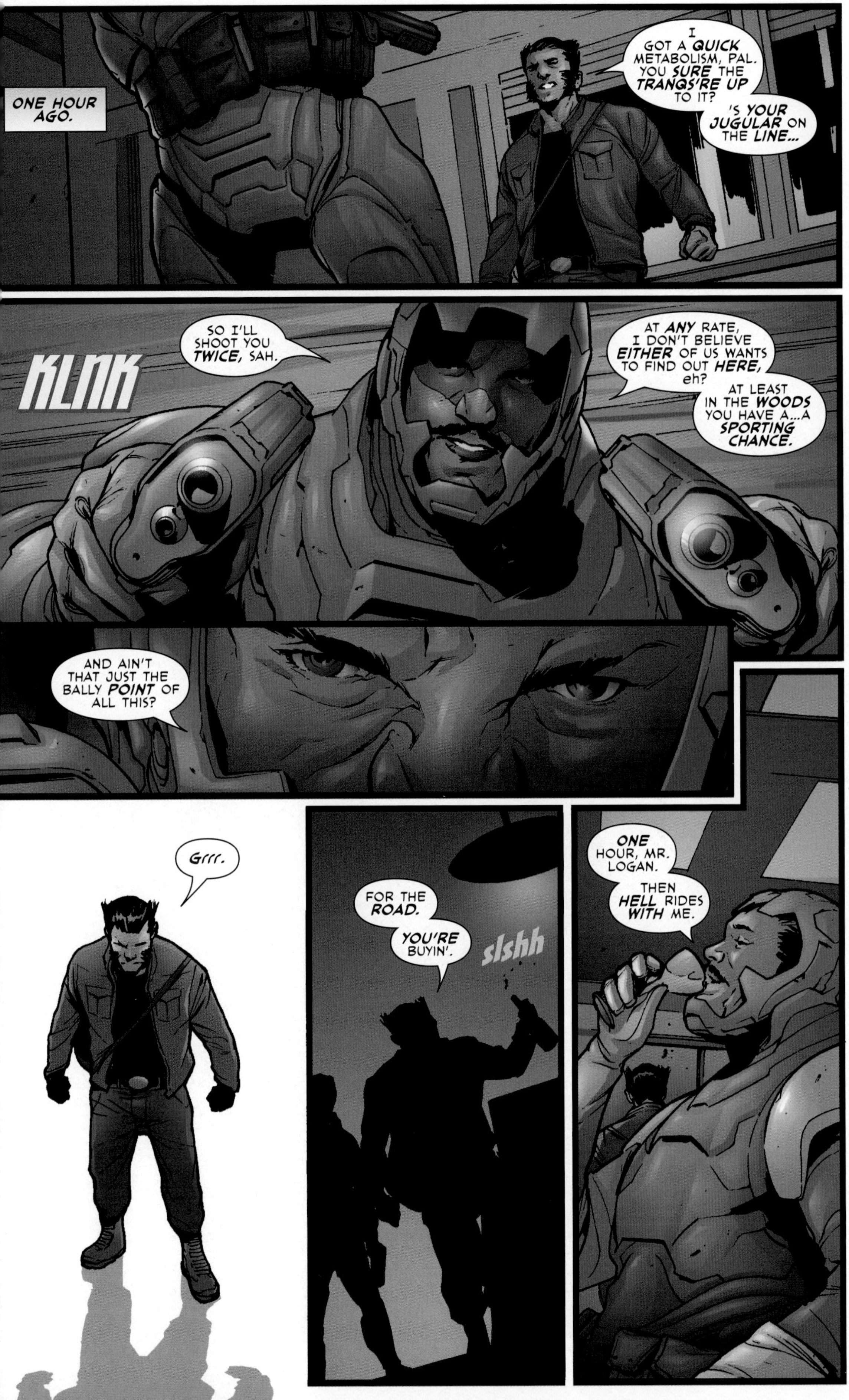

ONE HOUR AGO.
I GOT A QUICK METABOLISM, PAL. YOU SURE THE TRANQS'RE UP TO IT?
'S YOUR JUGULAR ON THE LINE...
KLNK
SO I'LL SHOOT YOU TWICE, SAH.
AT ANY RATE, I DON'T BELIEVE EITHER OF US WANTS TO FIND OUT HERE, eh?
AT LEAST IN THE WOODS YOU HAVE A...A SPORTING CHANCE.
AND AIN'T THAT JUST THE BALLY POINT OF ALL THIS?
Grrr.
FOR THE ROAD.
YOU'RE BUYIN'.
slshh
ONE HOUR, MR. LOGAN.
THEN HELL RIDES WITH ME.

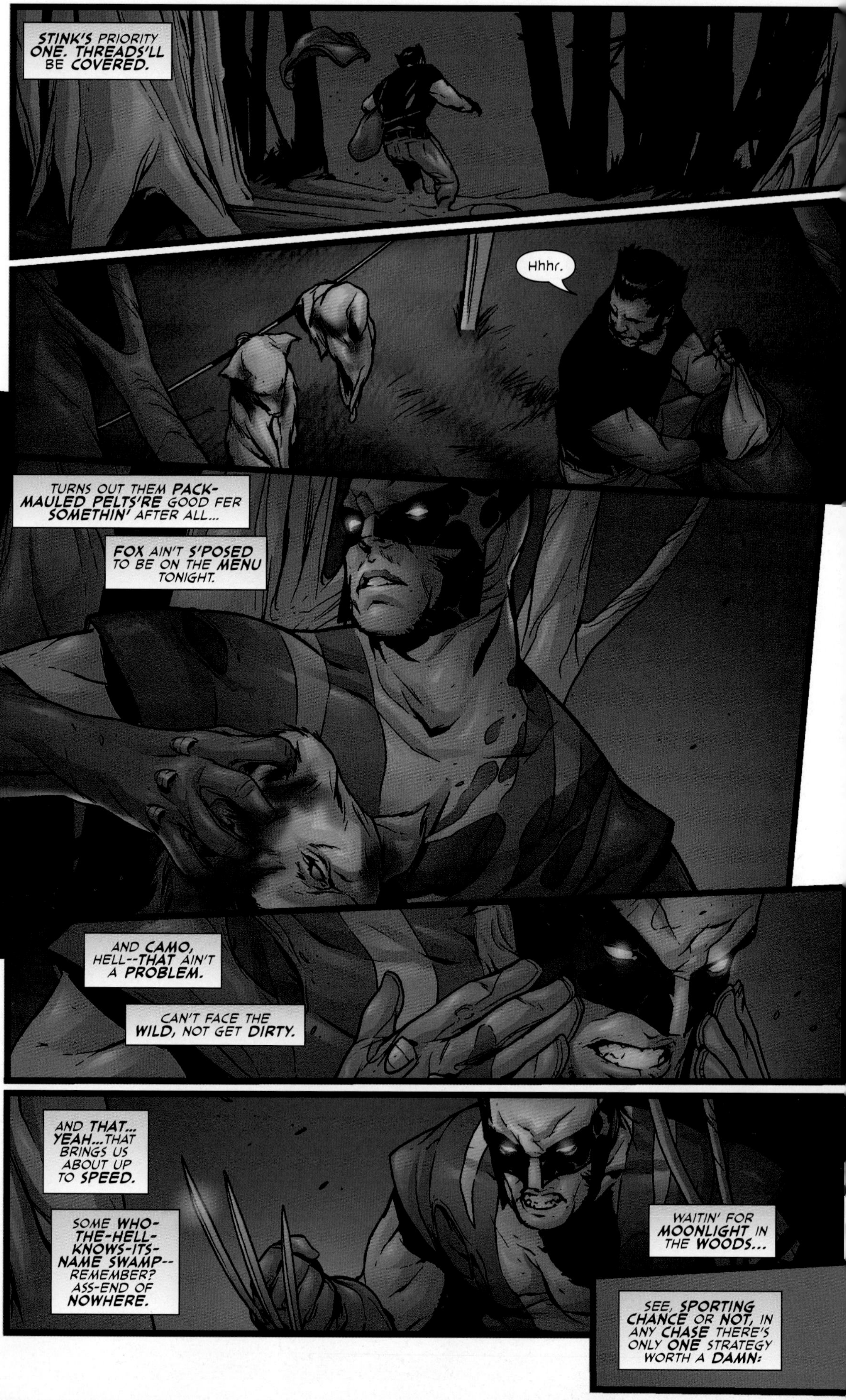
STINK'S PRIORITY ONE. THREADS'LL BE COVERED.
Hhhr.
TURNS OUT THEM PACK-MAULED PELTS'RE GOOD FER SOMETHIN' AFTER ALL...
FOX AIN'T S'POSED TO BE ON THE MENU TONIGHT.
AND CAMO, HELL--THAT AIN'T A PROBLEM.
CAN'T FACE THE WILD, NOT GET DIRTY.
AND THAT... YEAH...THAT BRINGS US ABOUT UP TO SPEED.
SOME WHO-THE-HELL-KNOWS-ITS-NAME SWAMP--REMEMBER? ASS-END OF NOWHERE.
WAITIN' FOR MOONLIGHT IN THE WOODS...
SEE, SPORTING CHANCE OR NOT, IN ANY CHASE THERE'S ONLY ONE STRATEGY WORTH A DAMN:

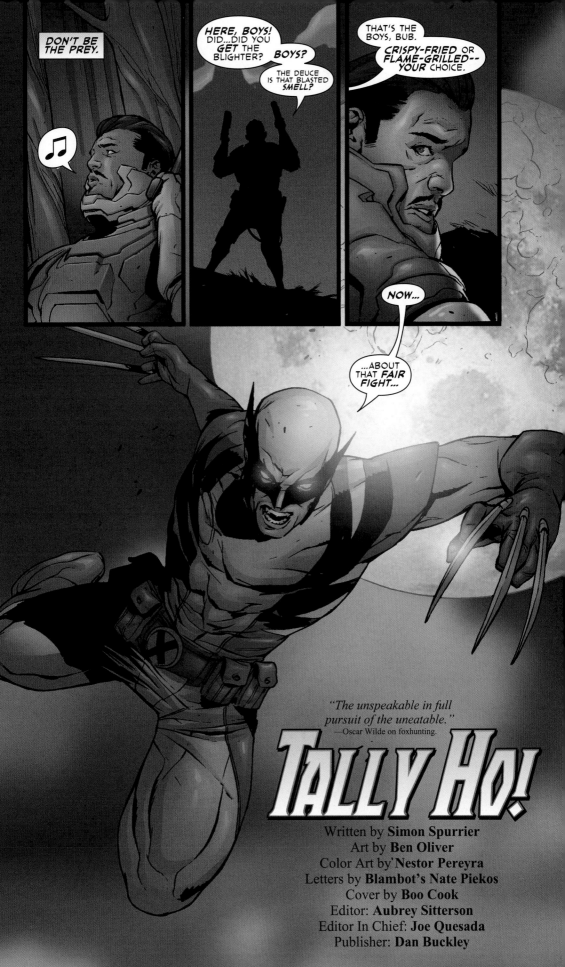

"The unspeakable in full pursuit of the uneatable."
—Oscar Wilde on foxhunting.

TALLY HO!

Written by **Simon Spurrier**
Art by **Ben Oliver**
Color Art by **Nestor Pereyra**
Letters by **Blambot's Nate Piekos**
Cover by **Boo Cook**
Editor: **Aubrey Sitterson**
Editor In Chief: **Joe Quesada**
Publisher: **Dan Buckley**

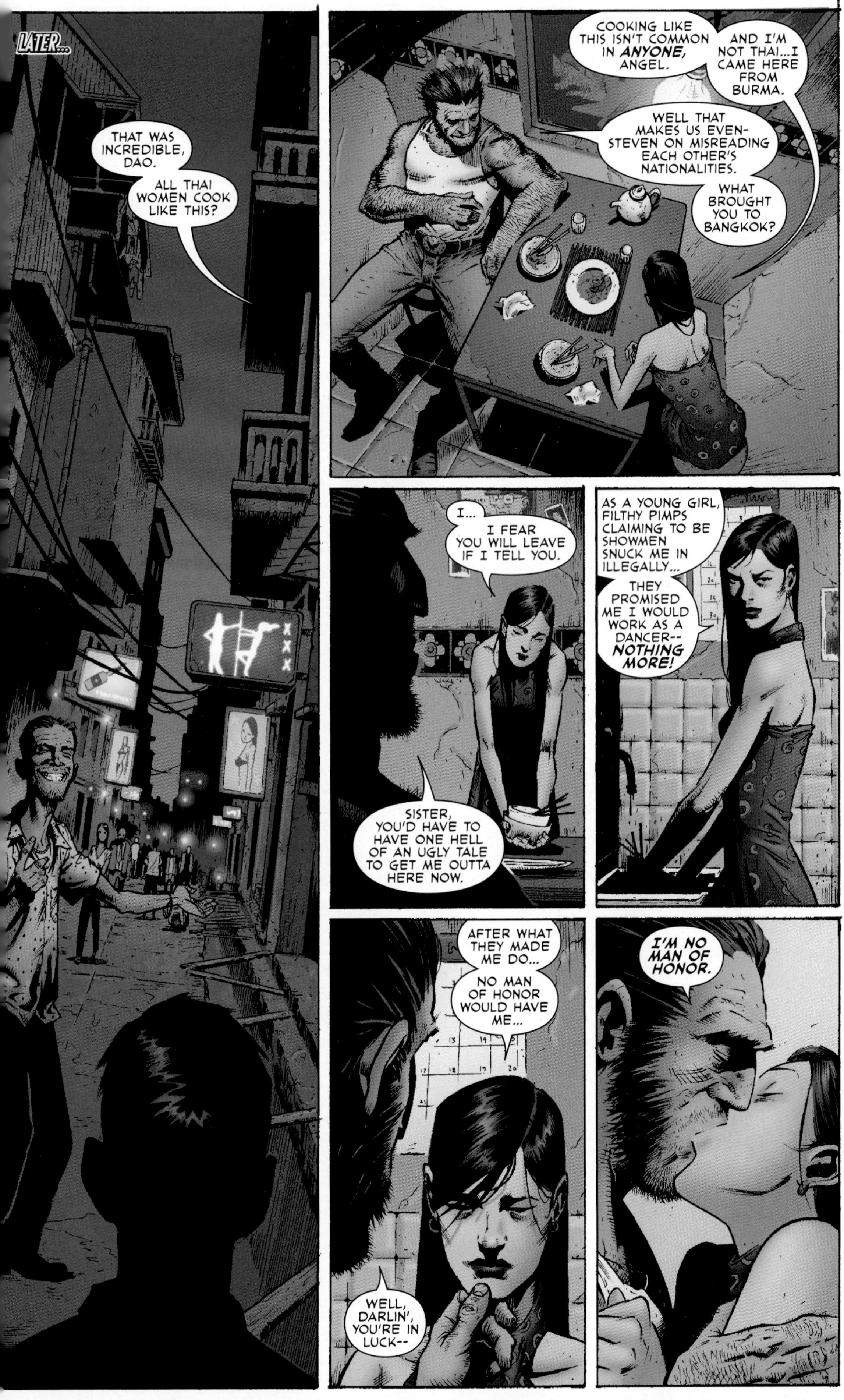
LATER...
THAT WAS INCREDIBLE, DAO.
ALL THAI WOMEN COOK LIKE THIS?
COOKING LIKE THIS ISN'T COMMON IN ANYONE, ANGEL.
AND I'M NOT THAI...I CAME HERE FROM BURMA.
WELL THAT MAKES US EVEN-STEVEN ON MISREADING EACH OTHER'S NATIONALITIES.
WHAT BROUGHT YOU TO BANGKOK?
I...
I FEAR YOU WILL LEAVE IF I TELL YOU.
SISTER, YOU'D HAVE TO HAVE ONE HELL OF AN UGLY TALE TO GET ME OUTTA HERE NOW.
AS A YOUNG GIRL, FILTHY PIMPS CLAIMING TO BE SHOWMEN SNUCK ME IN ILLEGALLY...
THEY PROMISED ME I WOULD WORK AS A DANCER-- NOTHING MORE!
AFTER WHAT THEY MADE ME DO...
NO MAN OF HONOR WOULD HAVE ME...
WELL, DARLIN', YOU'RE IN LUCK--
I'M NO MAN OF HONOR.

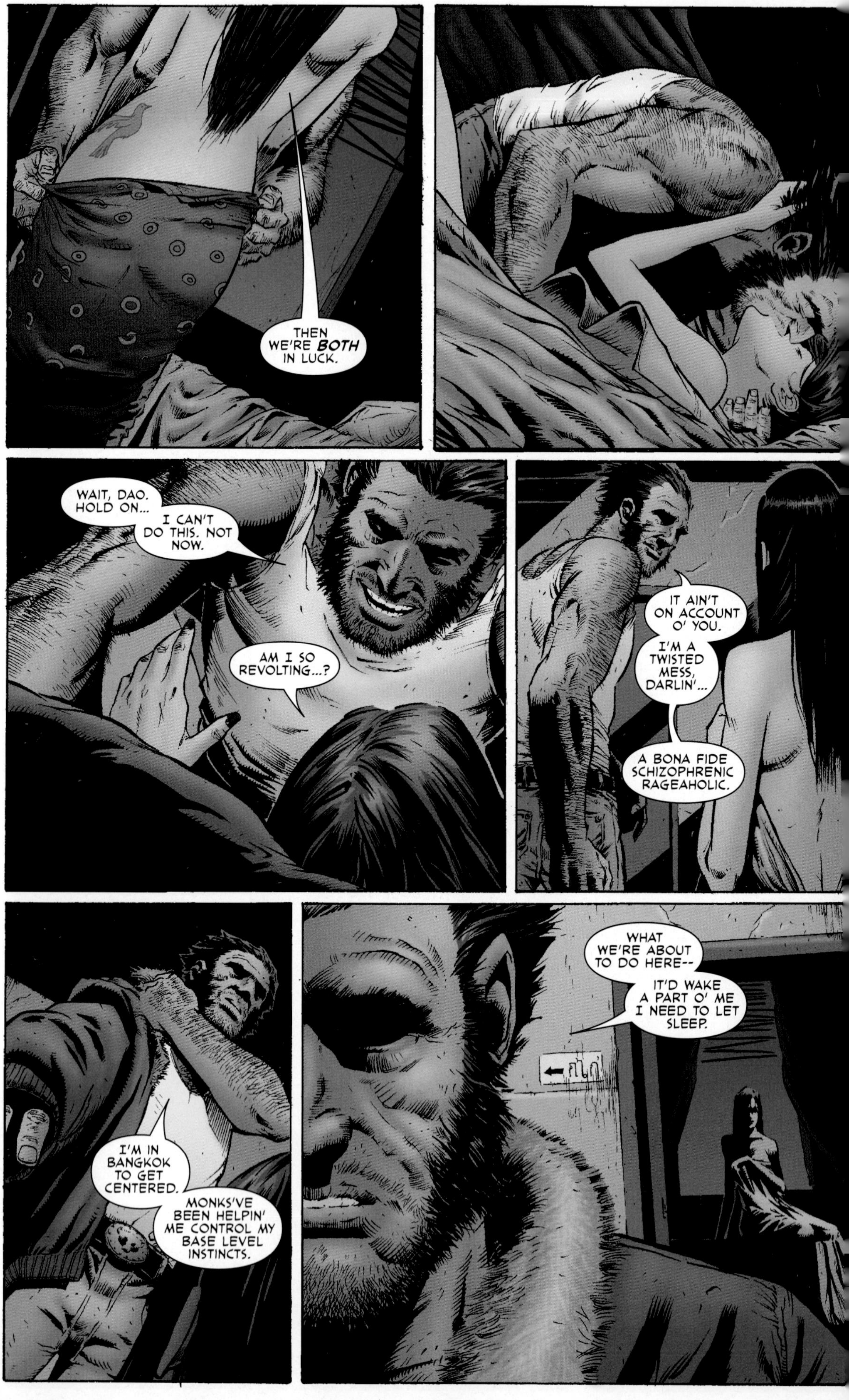
THEN WE'RE *BOTH* IN LUCK.
WAIT, DAO. HOLD ON...
I CAN'T DO THIS. NOT NOW.
AM I SO REVOLTING...?
IT AIN'T ON ACCOUNT O' YOU.
I'M A TWISTED MESS, DARLIN'...
A BONA FIDE SCHIZOPHRENIC RAGEAHOLIC.
I'M IN BANGKOK TO GET CENTERED.
MONKS'VE BEEN HELPIN' ME CONTROL MY BASE LEVEL INSTINCTS.
WHAT WE'RE ABOUT TO DO HERE--
IT'D WAKE A PART O' ME I NEED TO LET SLEEP.

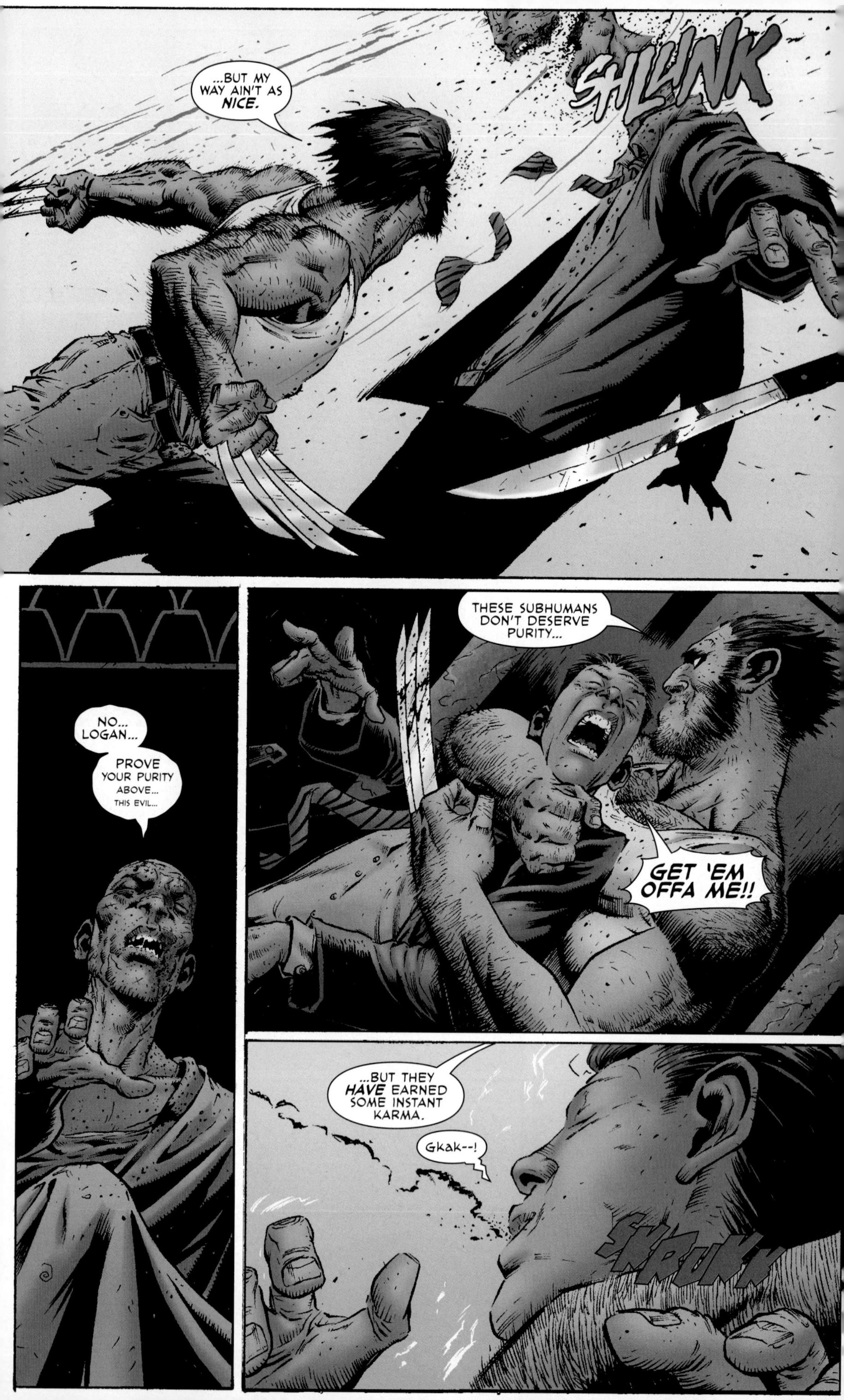
...BUT MY WAY AIN'T AS NICE.
SHLUNK
NO... LOGAN...
PROVE YOUR PURITY ABOVE... THIS EVIL...
THESE SUBHUMANS DON'T DESERVE PURITY...
GET 'EM OFFA ME!!
...BUT THEY HAVE EARNED SOME INSTANT KARMA.
Gkak--!

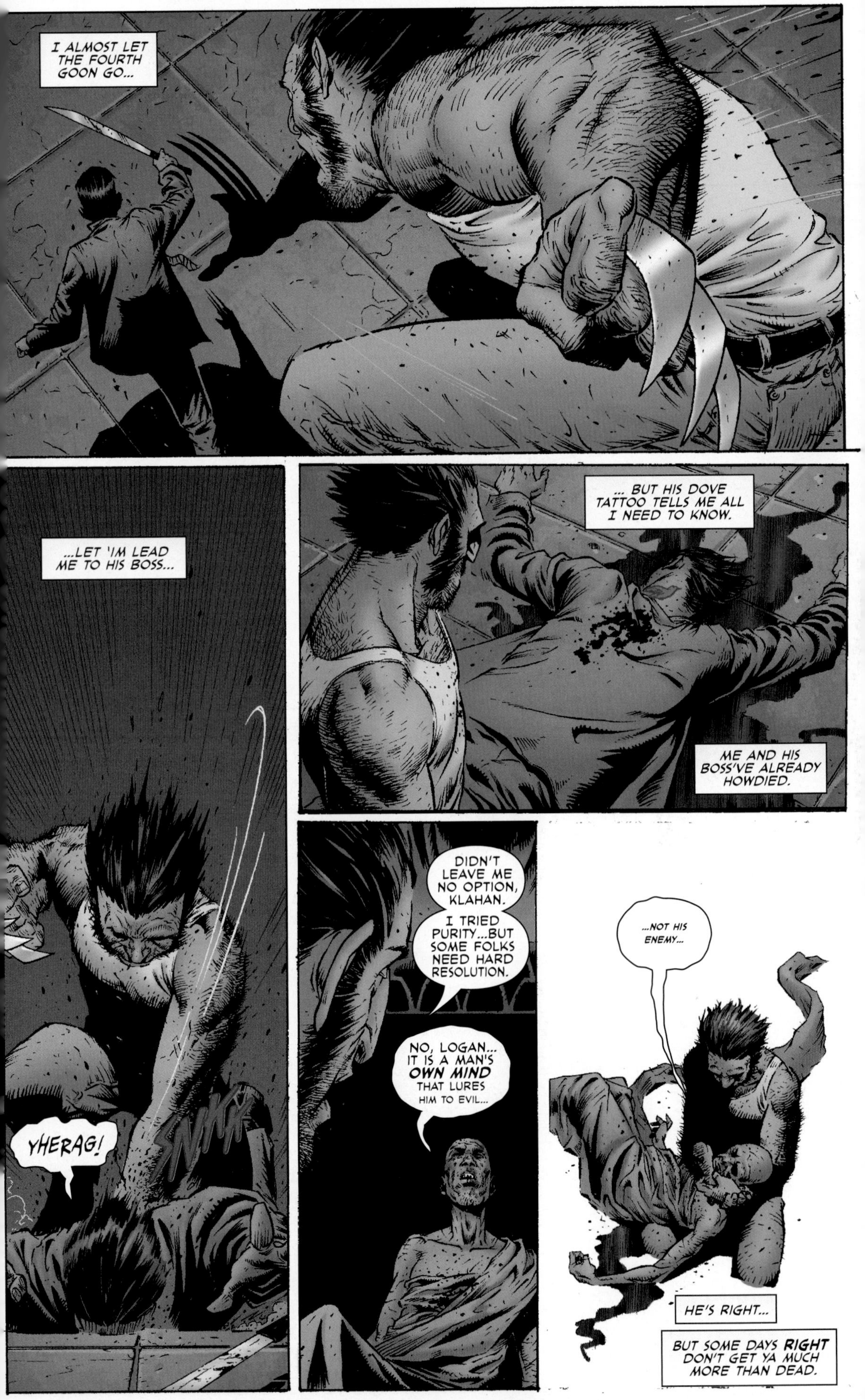
I ALMOST LET THE FOURTH GOON GO...
...LET 'IM LEAD ME TO HIS BOSS...
YHERAG!
... BUT HIS DOVE TATTOO TELLS ME ALL I NEED TO KNOW.
ME AND HIS BOSS'VE ALREADY HOWDIED.
DIDN'T LEAVE ME NO OPTION, KLAHAN.
I TRIED PURITY...BUT SOME FOLKS NEED HARD RESOLUTION.
NO, LOGAN... IT IS A MAN'S OWN MIND THAT LURES HIM TO EVIL...
...NOT HIS ENEMY...
HE'S RIGHT...
BUT SOME DAYS RIGHT DON'T GET YA MUCH MORE THAN DEAD.

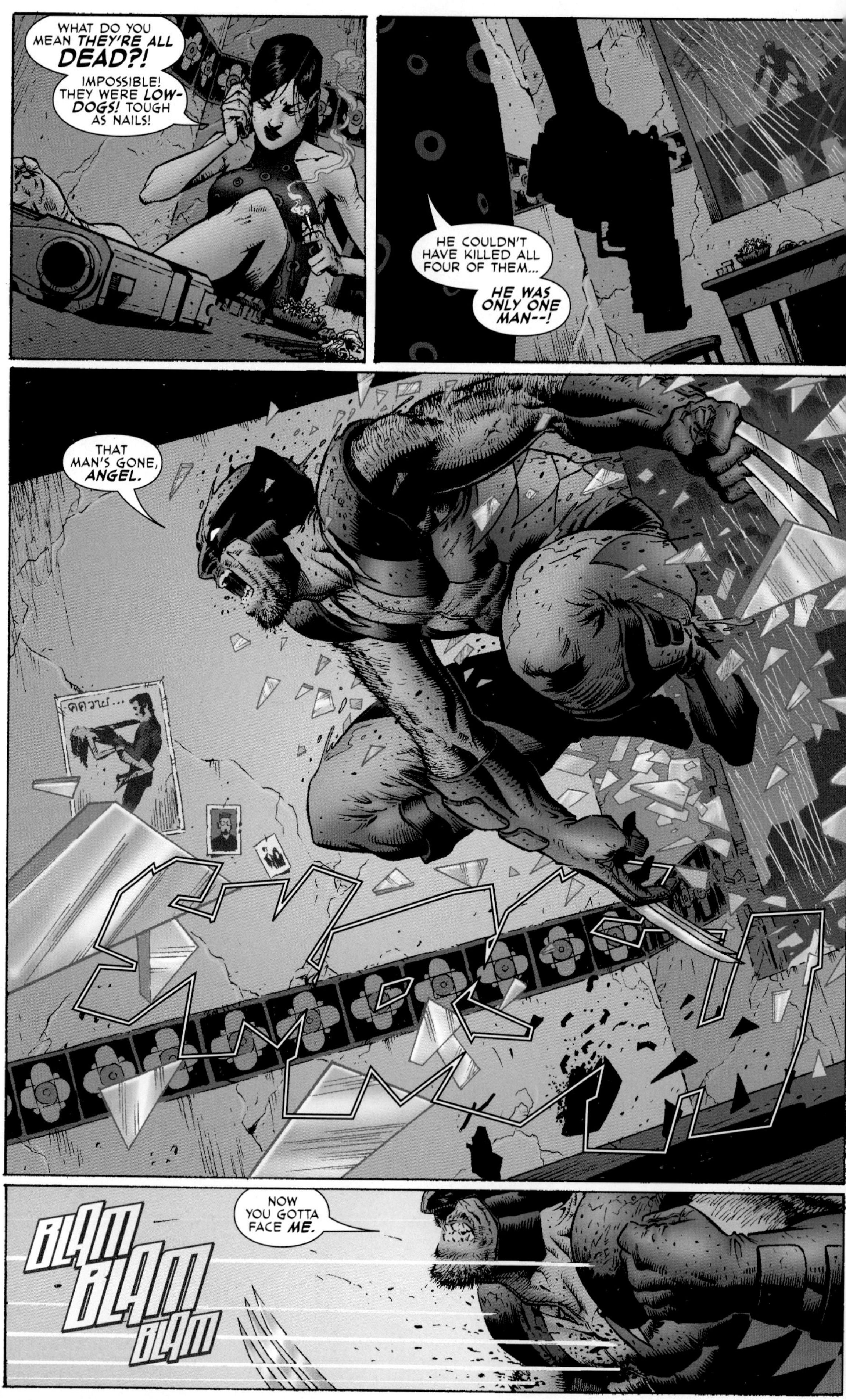

WHAT DO YOU MEAN THEY'RE ALL DEAD?!
IMPOSSIBLE! THEY WERE LOW-DOGS! TOUGH AS NAILS!
HE COULDN'T HAVE KILLED ALL FOUR OF THEM...
HE WAS ONLY ONE MAN--!
THAT MAN'S GONE, ANGEL.
BLAM BLAM BLAM
NOW YOU GOTTA FACE ME.

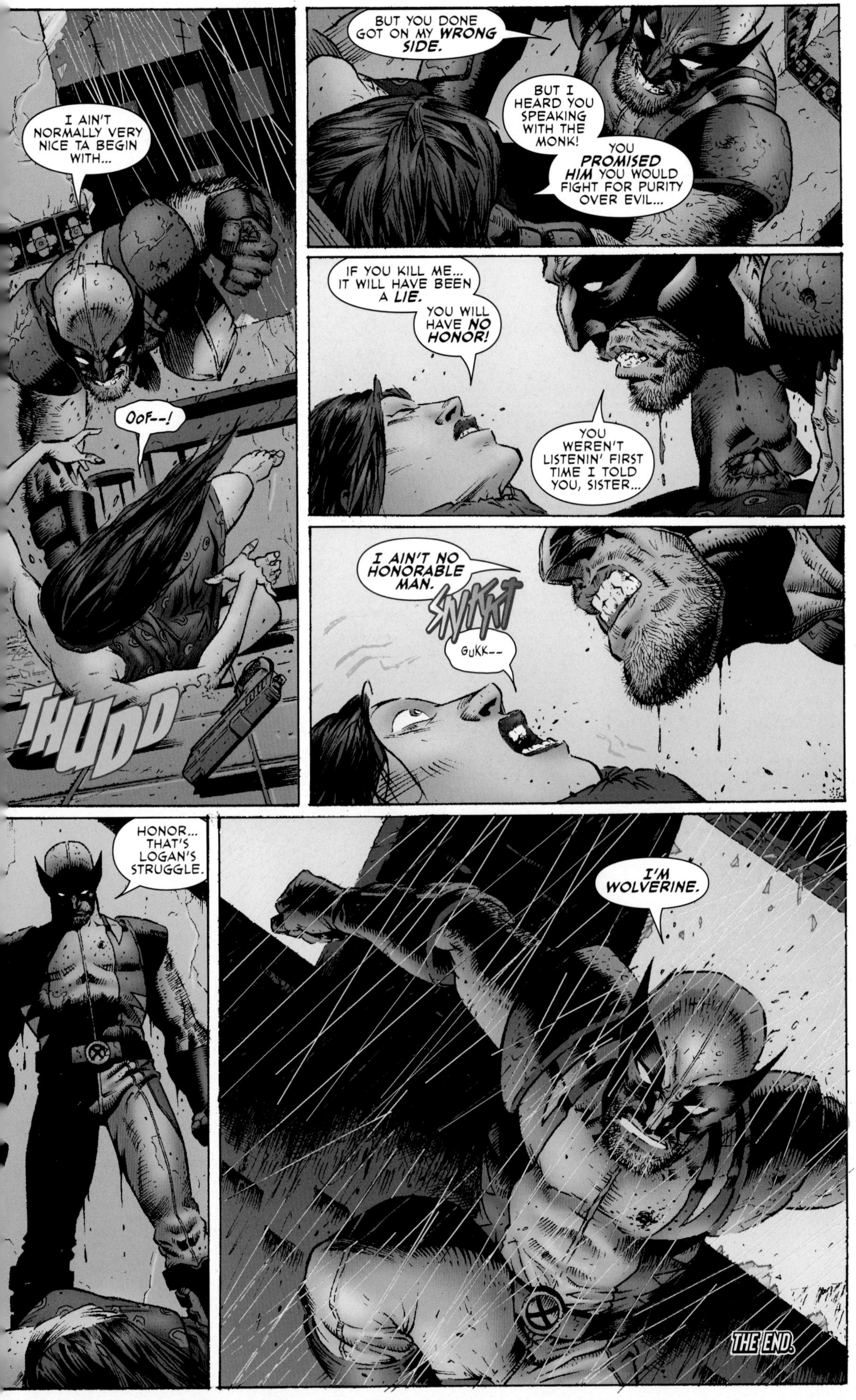
I AIN'T NORMALLY VERY NICE TA BEGIN WITH...
OOF--!
THUDD
BUT YOU DONE GOT ON MY WRONG SIDE.
BUT I HEARD YOU SPEAKING WITH THE MONK!
YOU PROMISED HIM YOU WOULD FIGHT FOR PURITY OVER EVIL...
IF YOU KILL ME... IT WILL HAVE BEEN A LIE.
YOU WILL HAVE NO HONOR!
YOU WEREN'T LISTENIN' FIRST TIME I TOLD YOU, SISTER...
I AIN'T NO HONORABLE MAN.
SNIKT
GUKK--
HONOR... THAT'S LOGAN'S STRUGGLE.
I'M WOLVERINE.
THE END.

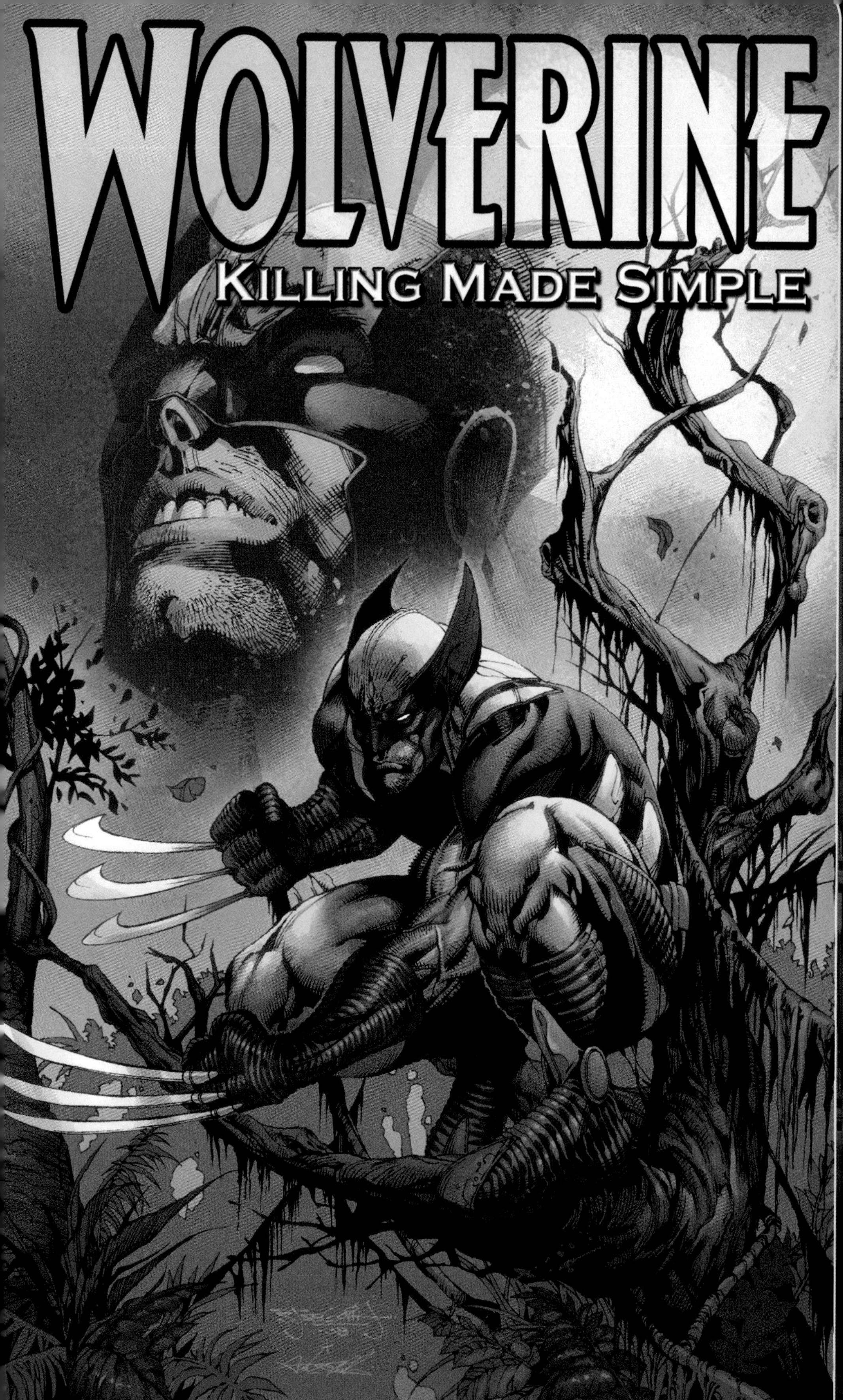
WOLVERINE
KILLING MADE SIMPLE

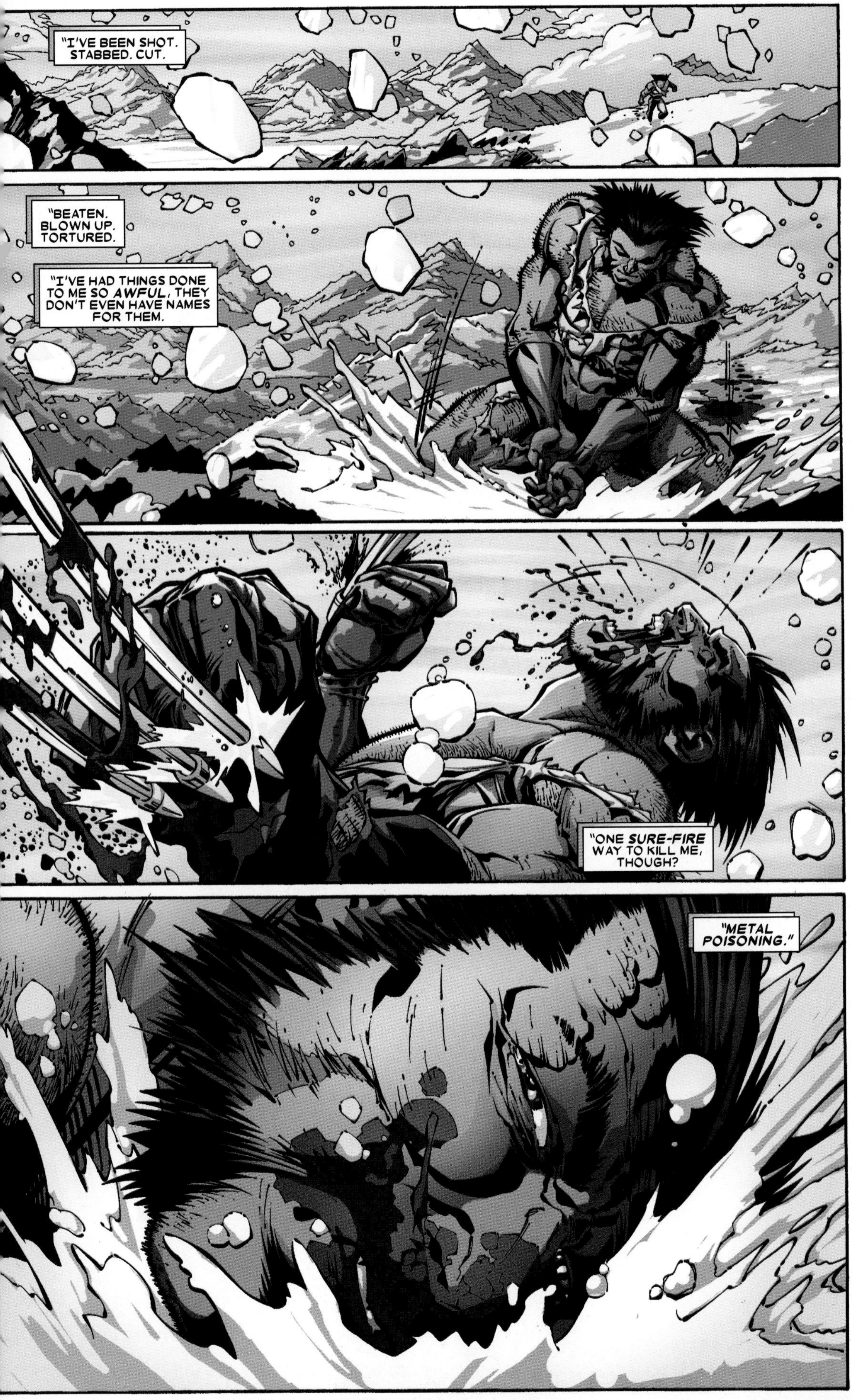
"I'VE BEEN SHOT. STABBED. CUT.
"BEATEN. BLOWN UP. TORTURED.
"I'VE HAD THINGS DONE TO ME SO AWFUL, THEY DON'T EVEN HAVE NAMES FOR THEM.
"ONE SURE-FIRE WAY TO KILL ME, THOUGH?
"METAL POISONING."

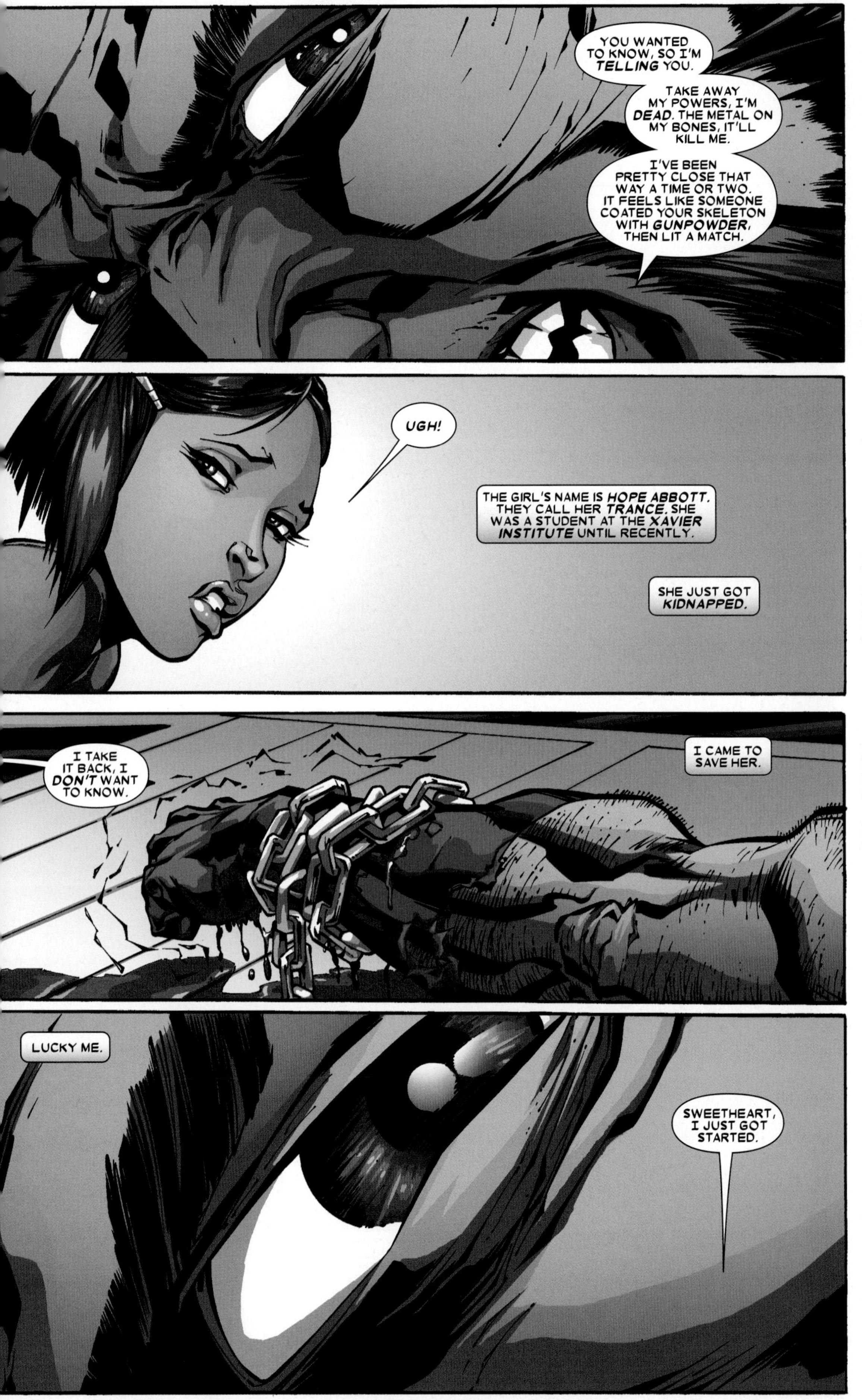
YOU WANTED TO KNOW, SO I'M TELLING YOU.
TAKE AWAY MY POWERS, I'M DEAD. THE METAL ON MY BONES, IT'LL KILL ME.
I'VE BEEN PRETTY CLOSE THAT WAY A TIME OR TWO. IT FEELS LIKE SOMEONE COATED YOUR SKELETON WITH GUNPOWDER, THEN LIT A MATCH.
UGH!
THE GIRL'S NAME IS HOPE ABBOTT. THEY CALL HER TRANCE. SHE WAS A STUDENT AT THE XAVIER INSTITUTE UNTIL RECENTLY.
SHE JUST GOT KIDNAPPED.
I TAKE IT BACK, I DON'T WANT TO KNOW.
I CAME TO SAVE HER.
LUCKY ME.
SWEETHEART, I JUST GOT STARTED.

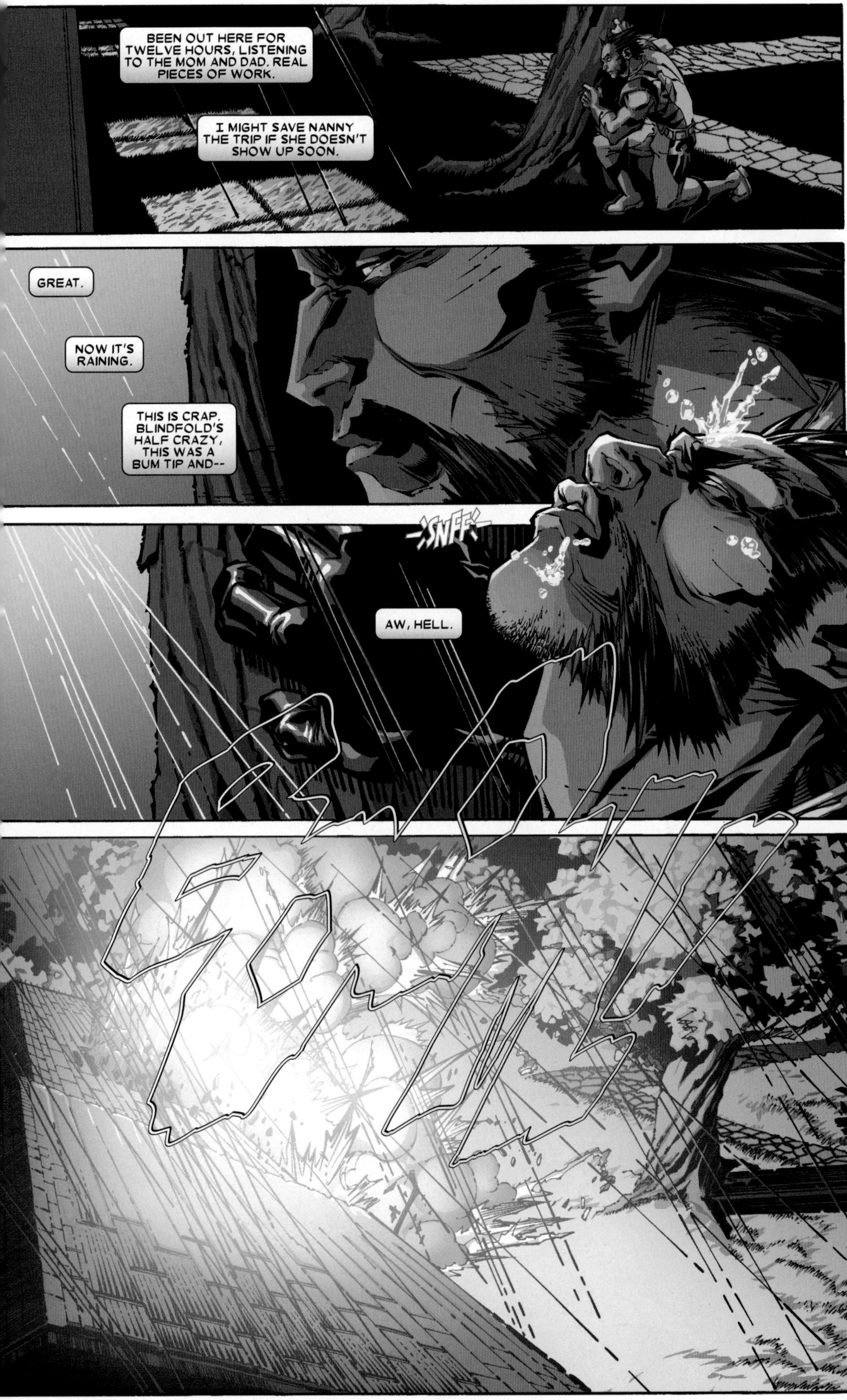

BEEN OUT HERE FOR TWELVE HOURS, LISTENING TO THE MOM AND DAD. REAL PIECES OF WORK.
I MIGHT SAVE NANNY THE TRIP IF SHE DOESN'T SHOW UP SOON.
GREAT.
NOW IT'S RAINING.
THIS IS CRAP. BLINDFOLD'S HALF CRAZY, THIS WAS A BUM TIP AND--
SNFF
AW, HELL.

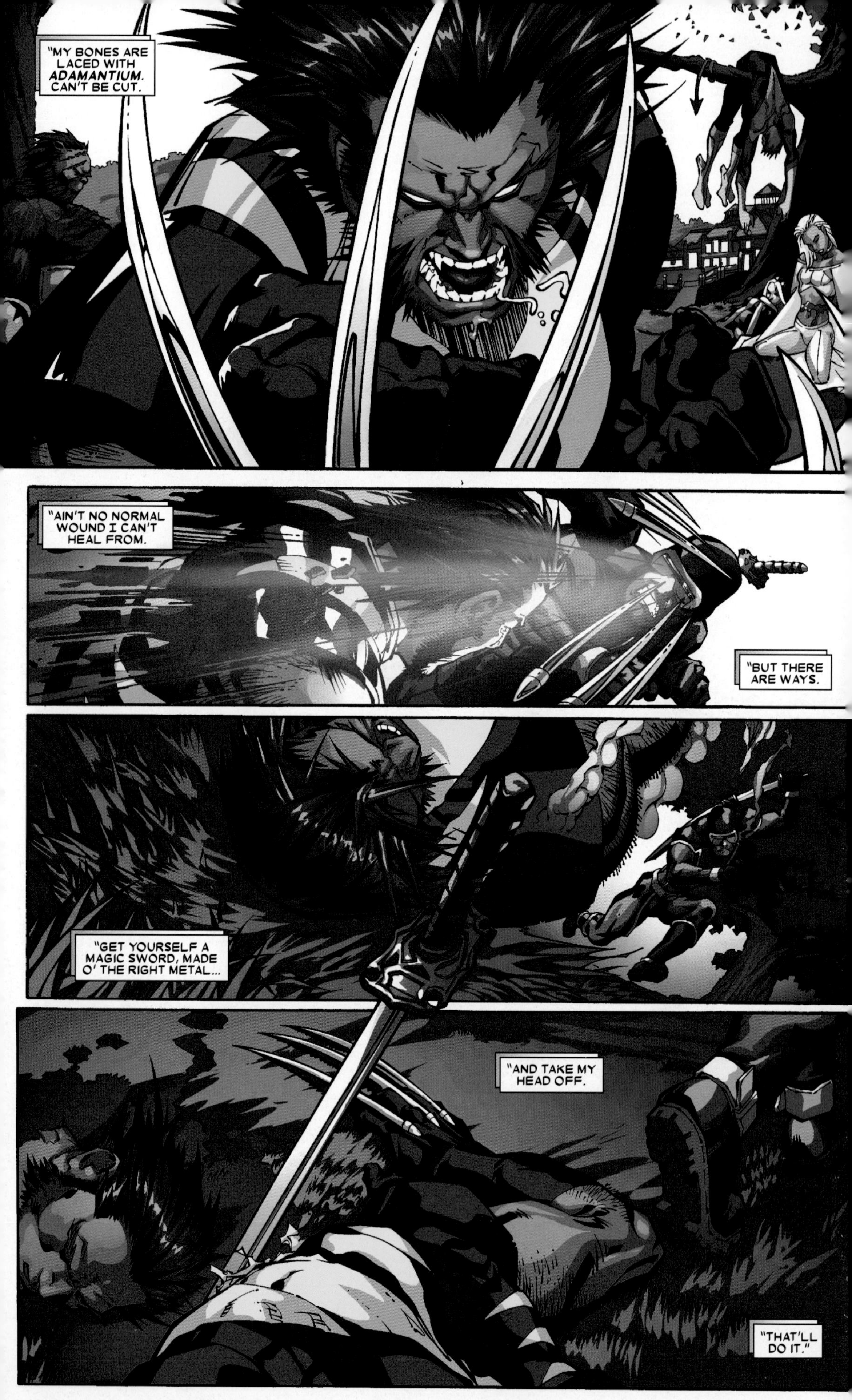
"MY BONES ARE LACED WITH *ADAMANTIUM*. CAN'T BE CUT.
"AIN'T NO NORMAL WOUND I CAN'T HEAL FROM.
"BUT THERE ARE WAYS.
"GET YOURSELF A MAGIC SWORD, MADE O' THE RIGHT METAL...
"AND TAKE MY HEAD OFF.
"THAT'LL DO IT."

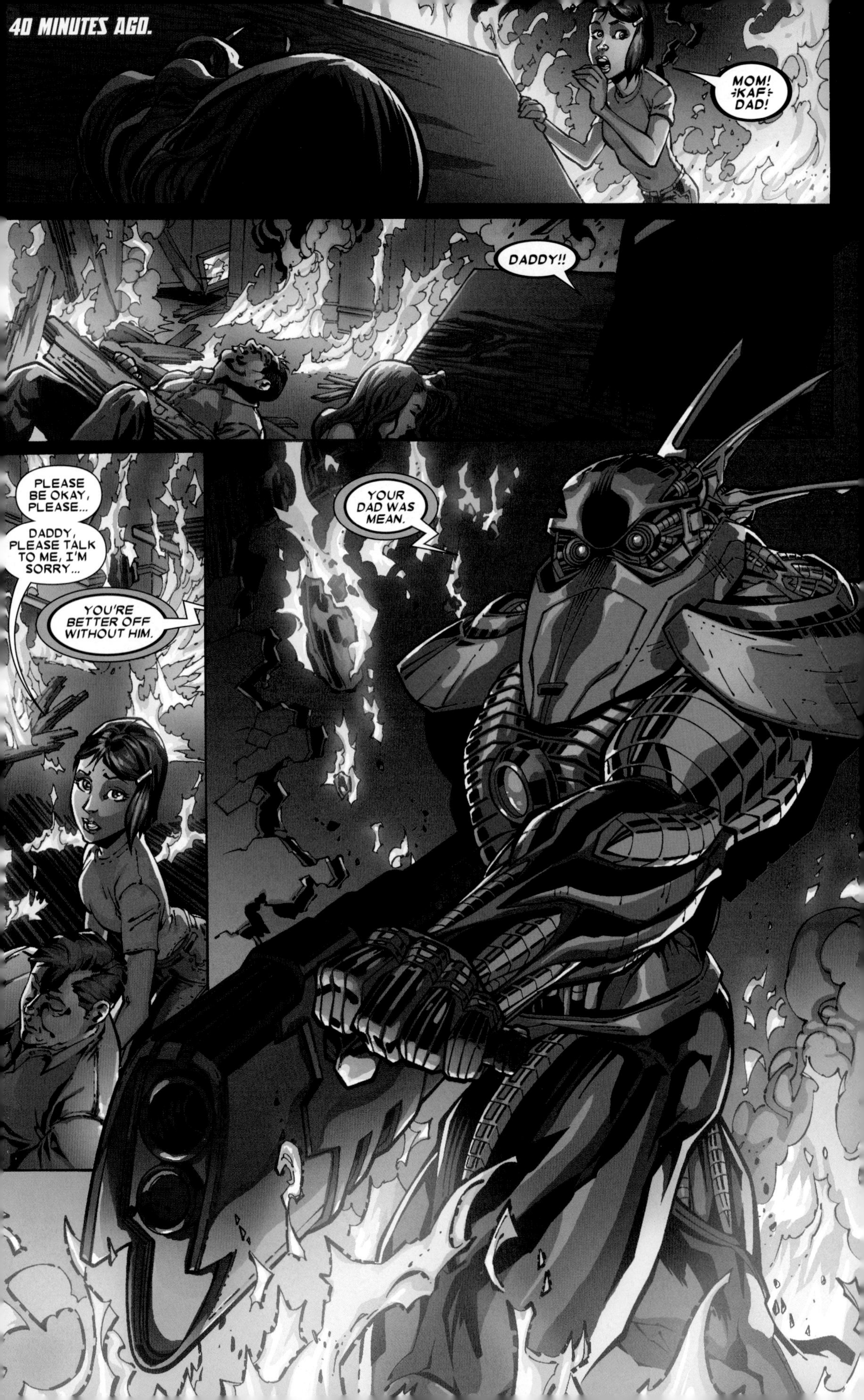
40 MINUTES AGO.
MOM! ÷KAF÷ DAD!
DADDY!!
PLEASE BE OKAY, PLEASE...
DADDY, PLEASE TALK TO ME, I'M SORRY...
YOUR DAD WAS MEAN.
YOU'RE BETTER OFF WITHOUT HIM.

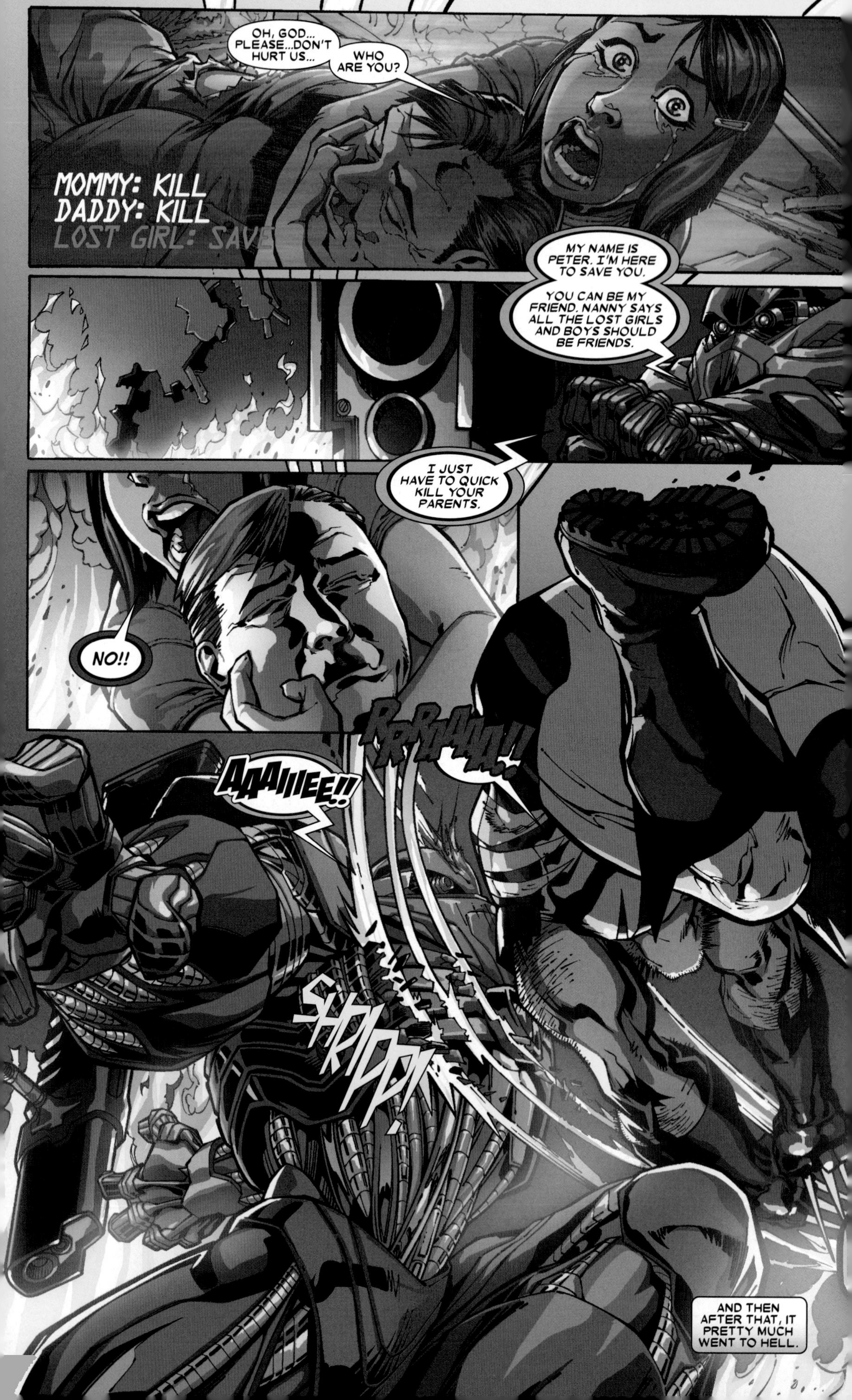

OH, GOD... PLEASE...DON'T HURT US...
WHO ARE YOU?
MOMMY: KILL
DADDY: KILL
LOST GIRL: SAVE
MY NAME IS PETER. I'M HERE TO SAVE YOU.
YOU CAN BE MY FRIEND. NANNY SAYS ALL THE LOST GIRLS AND BOYS SHOULD BE FRIENDS.
I JUST HAVE TO QUICK KILL YOUR PARENTS.
NO!!
RRRAAAA!!
AAAIIIEE!!
SHRIPP!
AND THEN AFTER THAT, IT PRETTY MUCH WENT TO HELL.

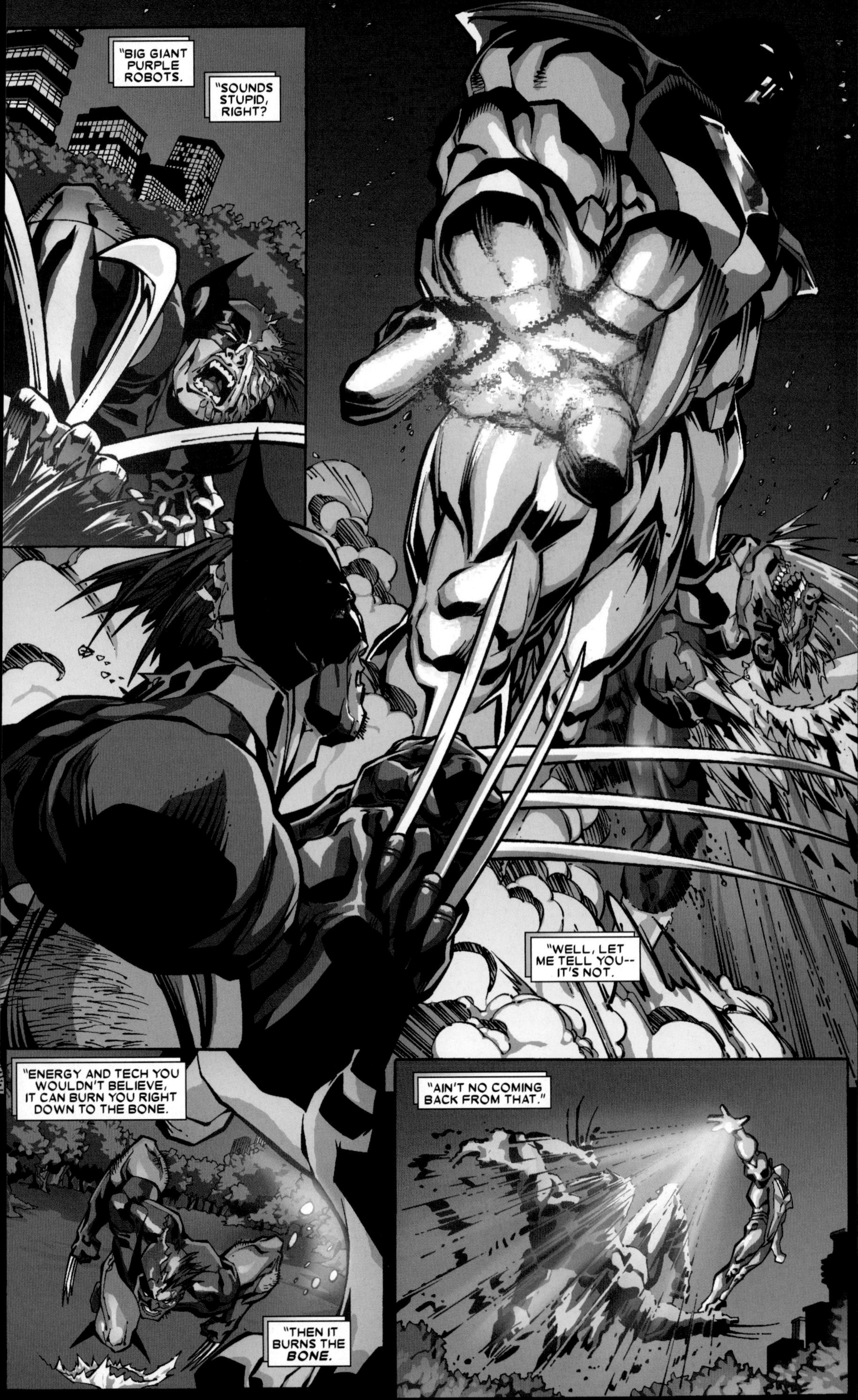
"BIG GIANT PURPLE ROBOTS.
"SOUNDS STUPID, RIGHT?
"WELL, LET ME TELL YOU-- IT'S NOT.
"ENERGY AND TECH YOU WOULDN'T BELIEVE, IT CAN BURN YOU RIGHT DOWN TO THE BONE.
"THEN IT BURNS THE *BONE*.
"AIN'T NO COMING BACK FROM THAT."

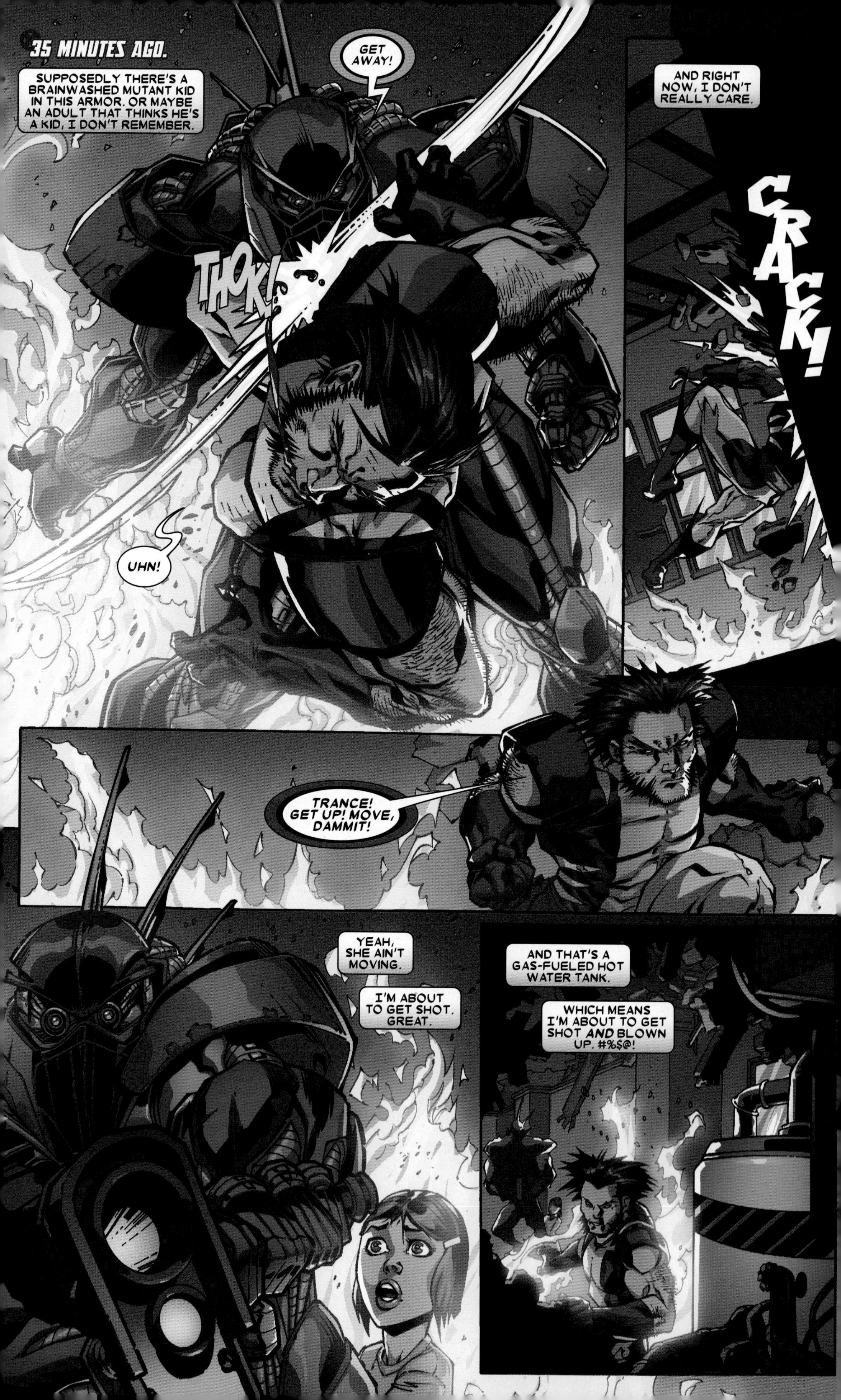
35 MINUTES AGO.
SUPPOSEDLY THERE'S A BRAINWASHED MUTANT KID IN THIS ARMOR. OR MAYBE AN ADULT THAT THINKS HE'S A KID, I DON'T REMEMBER.
GET AWAY!
THOK!
UHN!
AND RIGHT NOW, I DON'T REALLY CARE.
CRACK!
TRANCE! GET UP! MOVE, DAMMIT!
YEAH, SHE AIN'T MOVING.
I'M ABOUT TO GET SHOT. GREAT.
AND THAT'S A GAS-FUELED HOT WATER TANK.
WHICH MEANS I'M ABOUT TO GET SHOT AND BLOWN UP. #%$@!

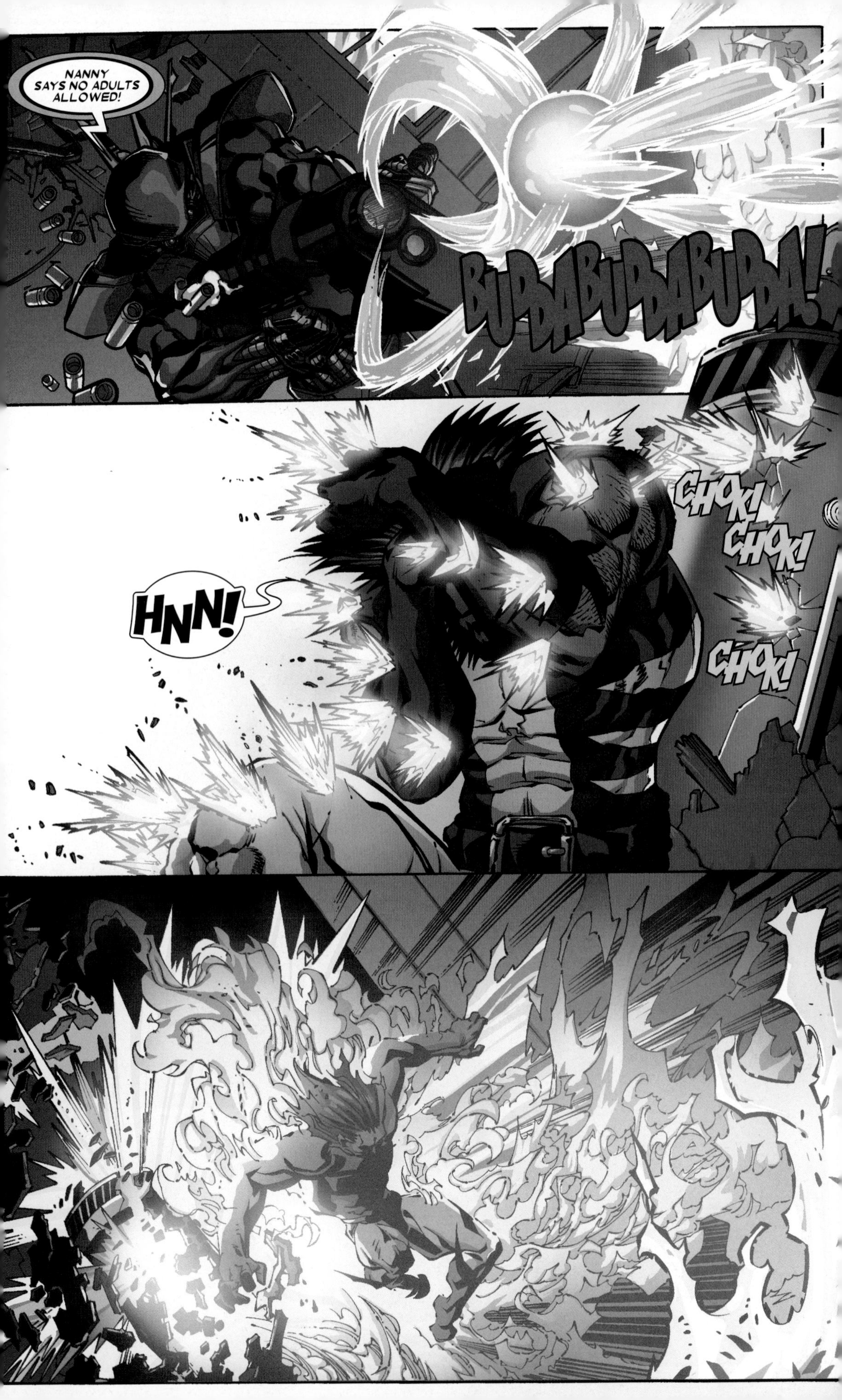
NANNY SAYS NO ADULTS ALLOWED!
BUDDABUDDABUDDA!
CHOK!
CHOK!
HNN!
CHOK!

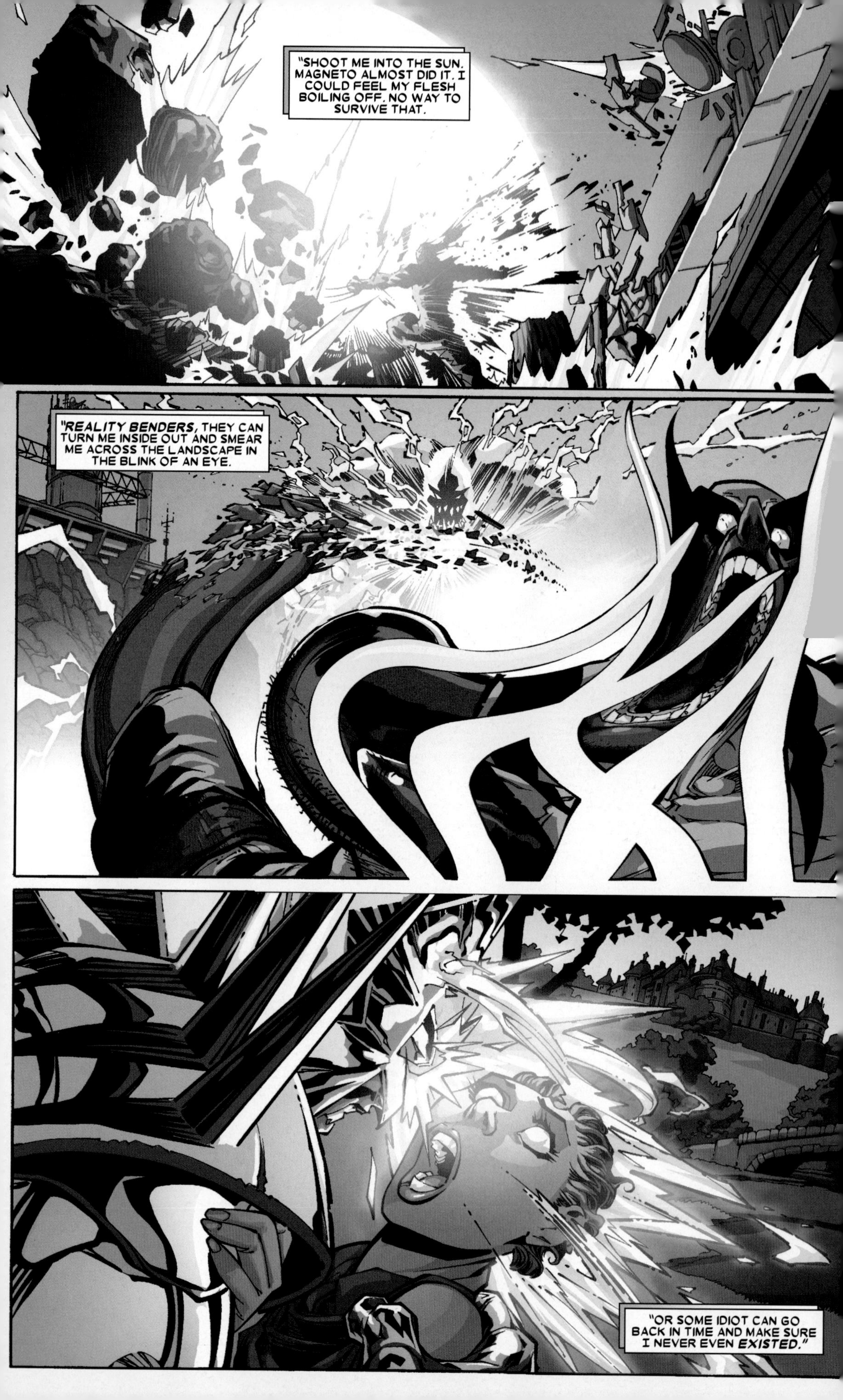
"SHOOT ME INTO THE SUN. MAGNETO ALMOST DID IT. I COULD FEEL MY FLESH BOILING OFF. NO WAY TO SURVIVE THAT.
"REALITY BENDERS, THEY CAN TURN ME INSIDE OUT AND SMEAR ME ACROSS THE LANDSCAPE IN THE BLINK OF AN EYE.
"OR SOME IDIOT CAN GO BACK IN TIME AND MAKE SURE I NEVER EVEN EXISTED."

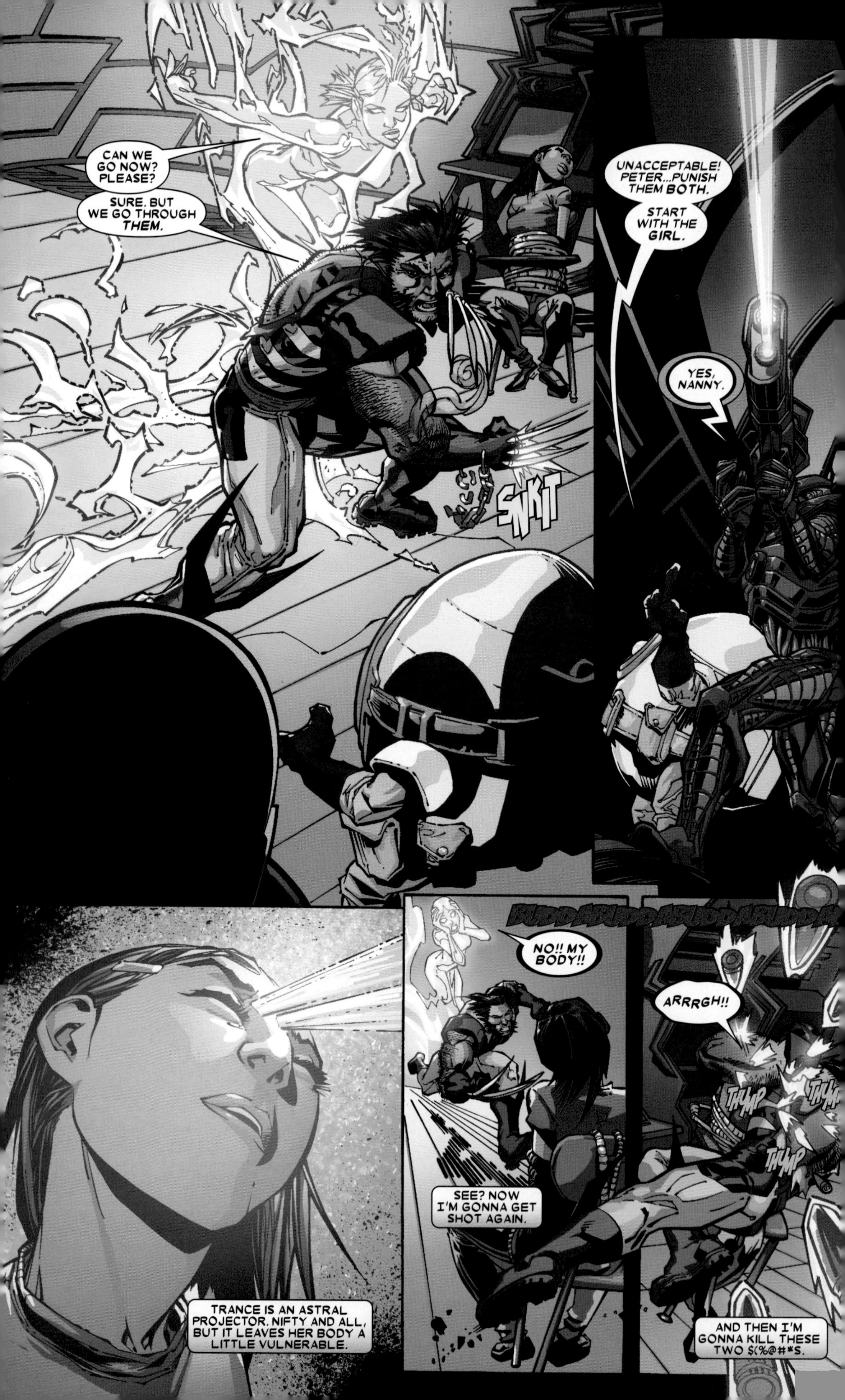
CAN WE GO NOW? PLEASE?
SURE. BUT WE GO THROUGH *THEM.*
SNKT
UNACCEPTABLE! PETER...PUNISH THEM BOTH.
START WITH THE GIRL.
YES, NANNY.
TRANCE IS AN ASTRAL PROJECTOR. NIFTY AND ALL, BUT IT LEAVES HER BODY A LITTLE VULNERABLE.
NO!! MY BODY!!
SEE? NOW I'M GONNA GET SHOT AGAIN.
ARRRGH!!
THUMP
THUMP
THUMP
AND THEN I'M GONNA KILL THESE TWO $(%@#*S.

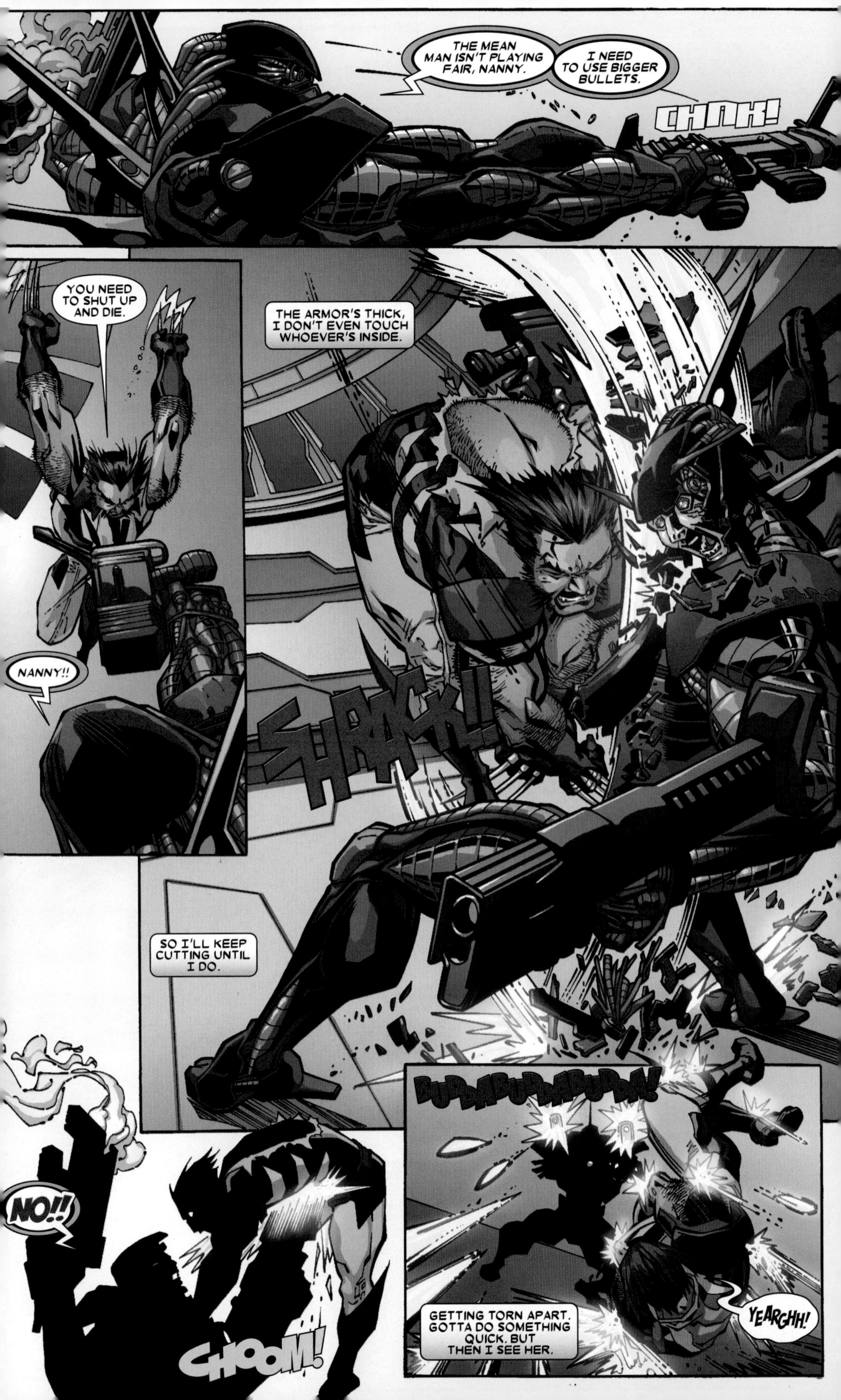
THE MEAN MAN ISN'T PLAYING FAIR, NANNY.
I NEED TO USE BIGGER BULLETS.
CHNK!
YOU NEED TO SHUT UP AND DIE.
THE ARMOR'S THICK, I DON'T EVEN TOUCH WHOEVER'S INSIDE.
NANNY!!
SHRACK!!
SO I'LL KEEP CUTTING UNTIL I DO.
BUDDABUDDABUDDA!
NO!!
CHOOM!
GETTING TORN APART. GOTTA DO SOMETHING QUICK. BUT THEN I SEE HER.
YEARGHH!

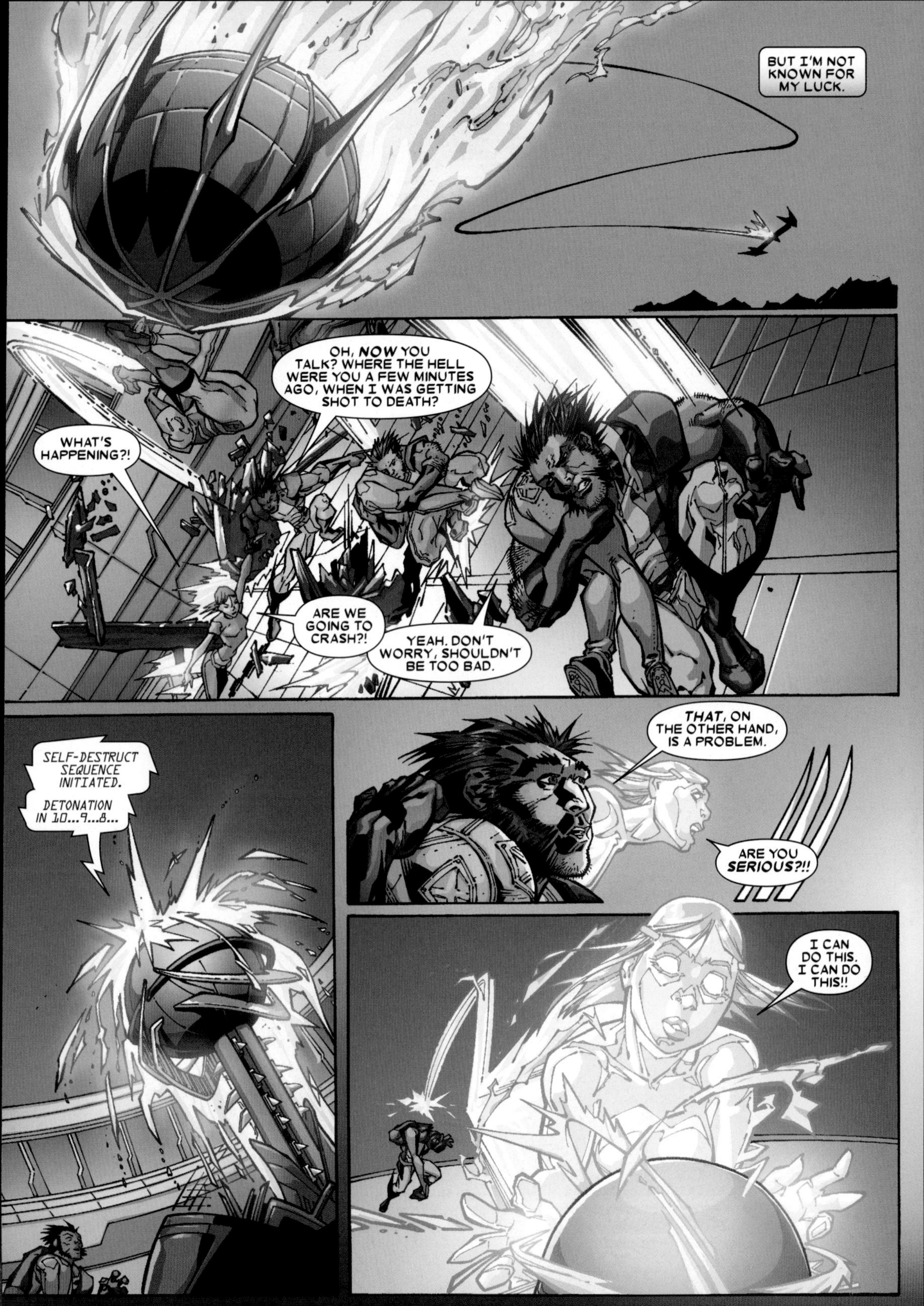
BUT I'M NOT KNOWN FOR MY LUCK.
OH, NOW YOU TALK? WHERE THE HELL WERE YOU A FEW MINUTES AGO, WHEN I WAS GETTING SHOT TO DEATH?
WHAT'S HAPPENING?!
ARE WE GOING TO CRASH?!
YEAH. DON'T WORRY, SHOULDN'T BE TOO BAD.
SELF-DESTRUCT SEQUENCE INITIATED.
DETONATION IN 10...9...8...
THAT, ON THE OTHER HAND, IS A PROBLEM.
ARE YOU SERIOUS?!!
I CAN DO THIS. I CAN DO THIS!!

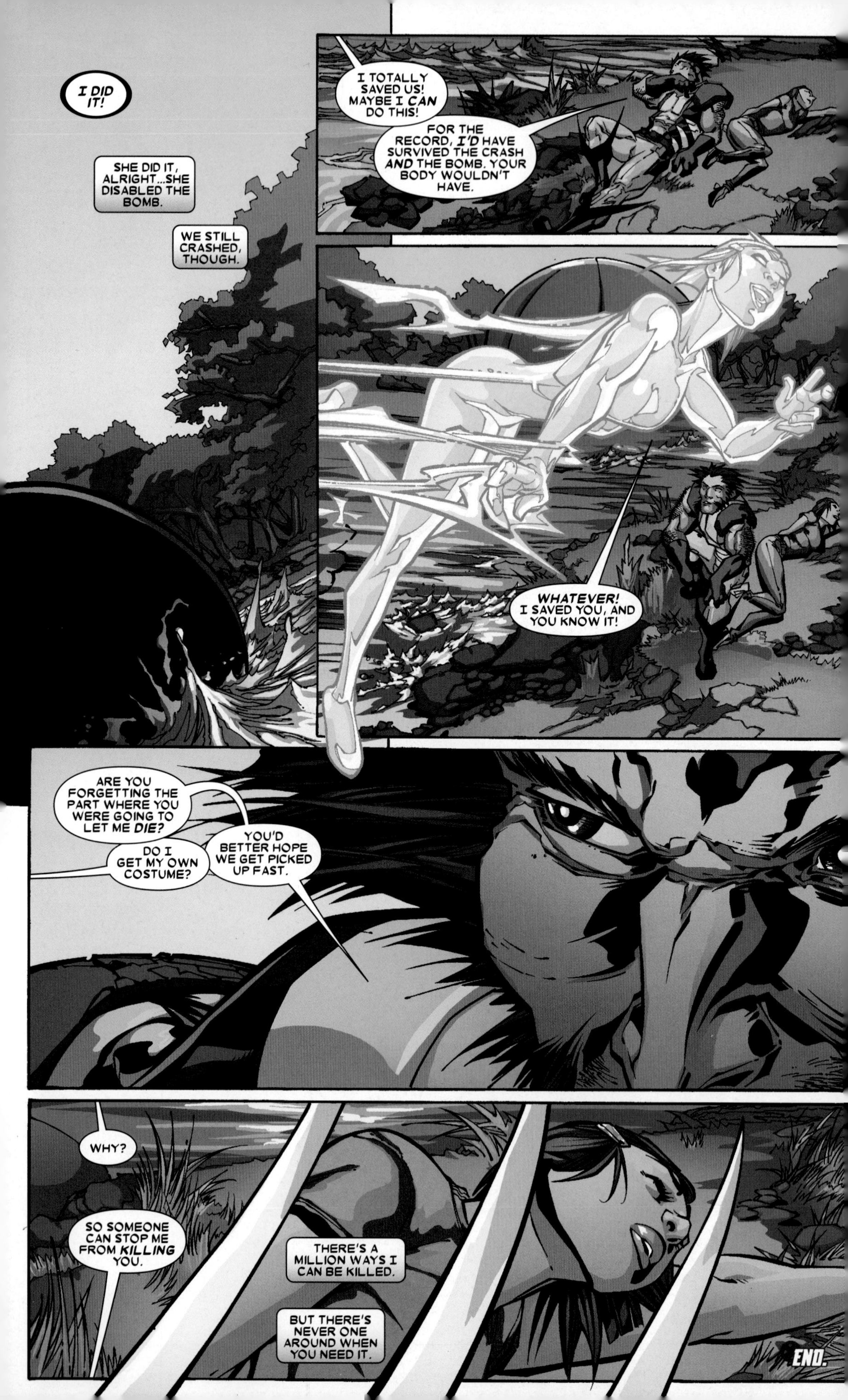
I DID IT!
SHE DID IT, ALRIGHT...SHE DISABLED THE BOMB.
WE STILL CRASHED, THOUGH.
I TOTALLY SAVED US! MAYBE I CAN DO THIS!
FOR THE RECORD, I'D HAVE SURVIVED THE CRASH AND THE BOMB. YOUR BODY WOULDN'T HAVE.
WHATEVER! I SAVED YOU, AND YOU KNOW IT!
ARE YOU FORGETTING THE PART WHERE YOU WERE GOING TO LET ME DIE?
DO I GET MY OWN COSTUME?
YOU'D BETTER HOPE WE GET PICKED UP FAST.
WHY?
SO SOMEONE CAN STOP ME FROM KILLING YOU.
THERE'S A MILLION WAYS I CAN BE KILLED.
BUT THERE'S NEVER ONE AROUND WHEN YOU NEED IT.
END.

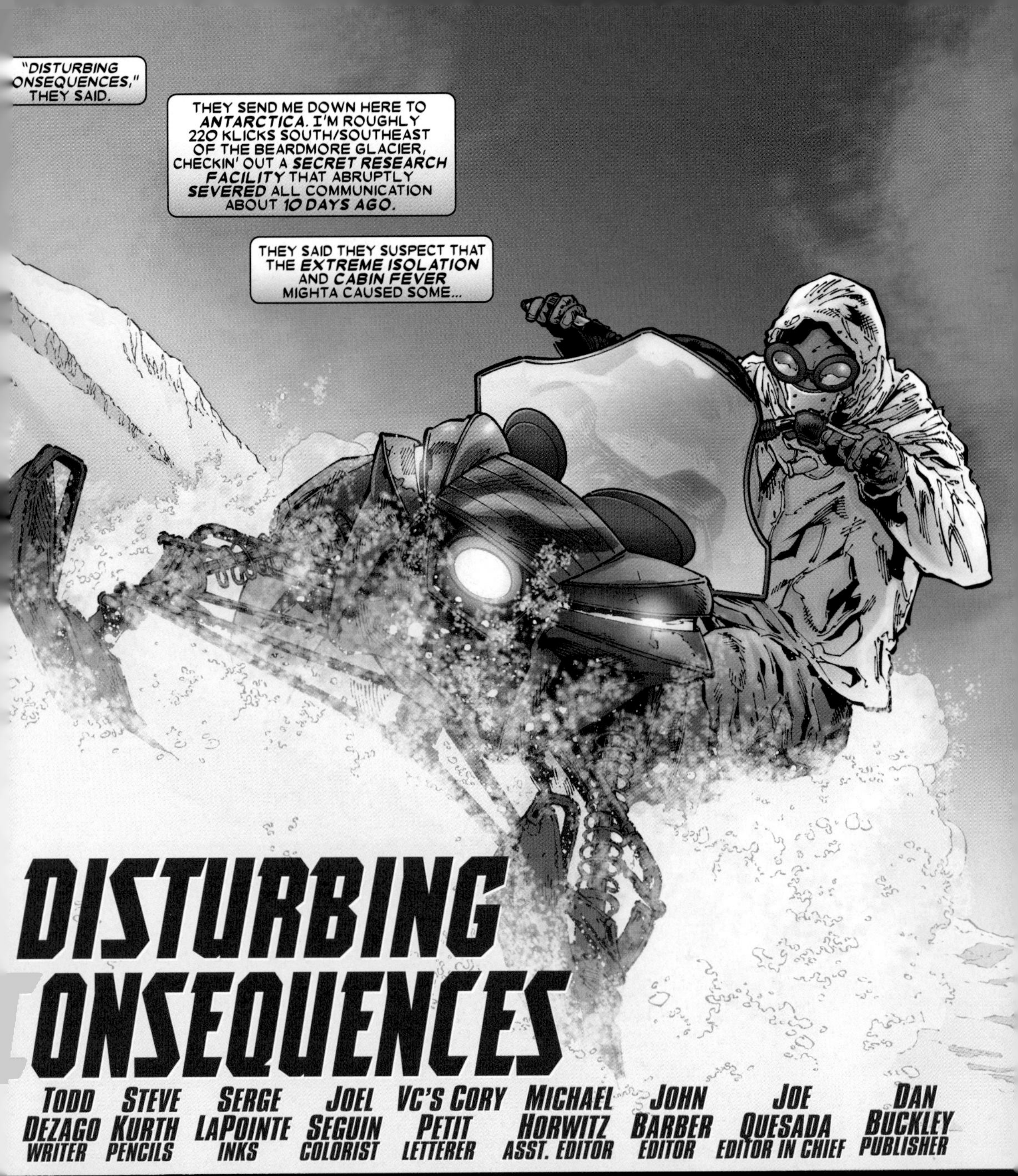
"DISTURBING
ONSEQUENCES,"
THEY SAID.
THEY SEND ME DOWN HERE TO ANTARCTICA. I'M ROUGHLY 220 KLICKS SOUTH/SOUTHEAST OF THE BEARDMORE GLACIER, CHECKIN' OUT A SECRET RESEARCH FACILITY THAT ABRUPTLY SEVERED ALL COMMUNICATION ABOUT 10 DAYS AGO.
THEY SAID THEY SUSPECT THAT THE EXTREME ISOLATION AND CABIN FEVER MIGHTA CAUSED SOME...
DISTURBING
ONSEQUENCES
TODD DEZAGO WRITER
STEVE KURTH PENCILS
SERGE LAPOINTE INKS
JOEL SEGUIN COLORIST
VC'S CORY PETIT LETTERER
MICHAEL HORWITZ ASST. EDITOR
JOHN BARBER EDITOR
JOE QUESADA EDITOR IN CHIEF
DAN BUCKLEY PUBLISHER

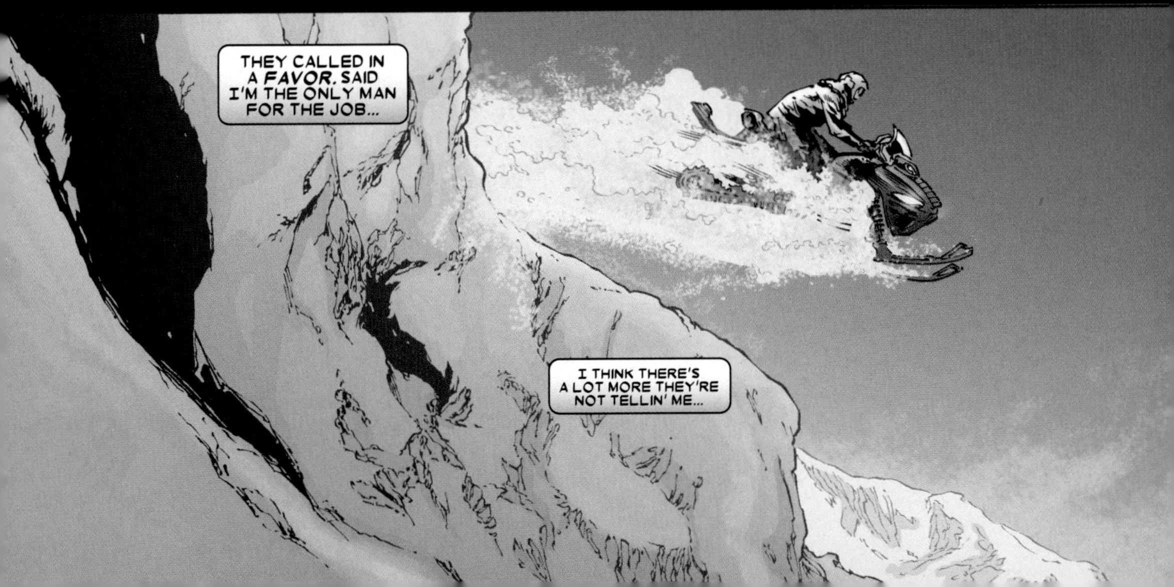
THEY CALLED IN A FAVOR. SAID I'M THE ONLY MAN FOR THE JOB...
I THINK THERE'S A LOT MORE THEY'RE NOT TELLIN' ME...

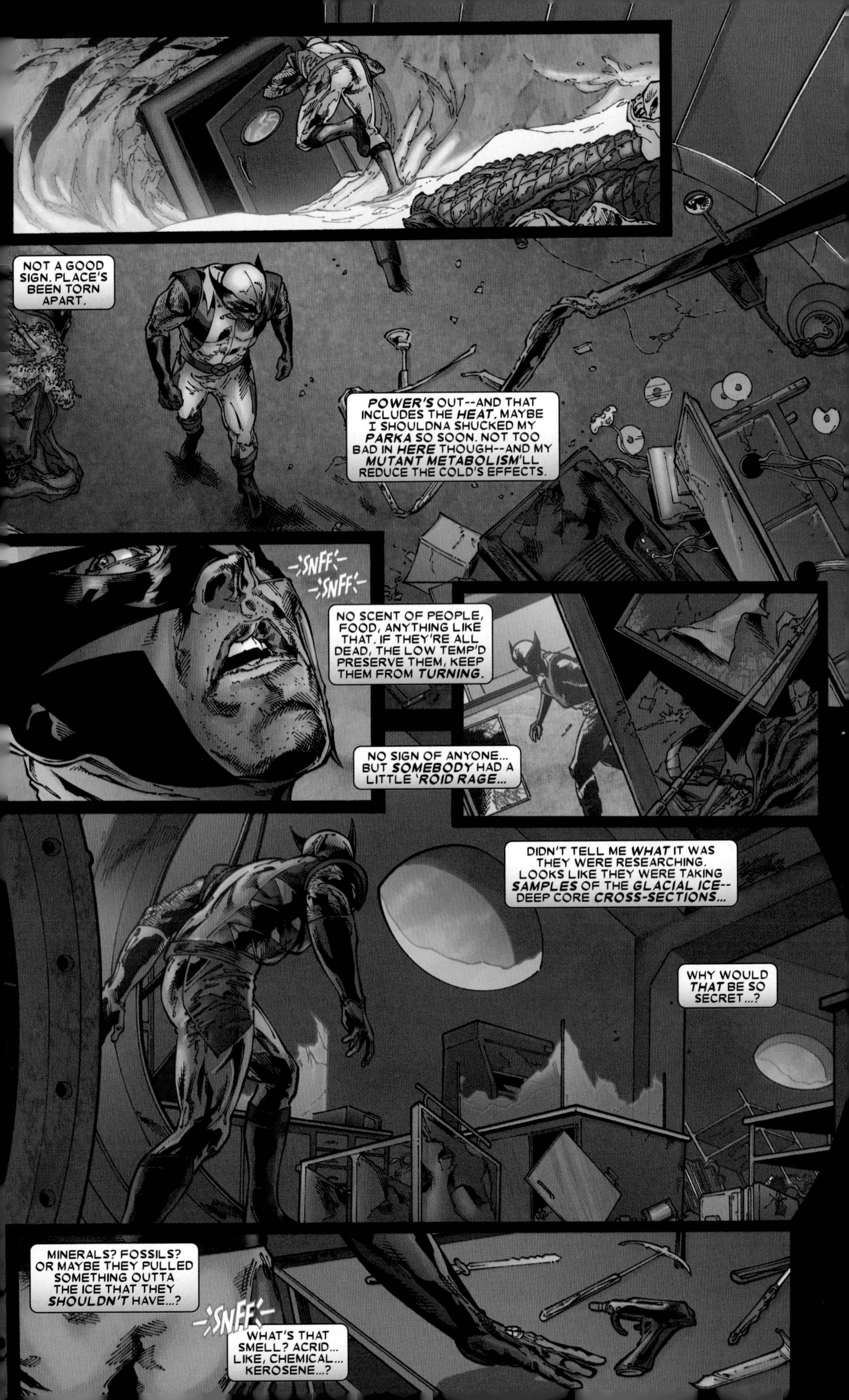
NOT A GOOD SIGN. PLACE'S BEEN TORN APART.
POWER'S OUT--AND THAT INCLUDES THE HEAT. MAYBE I SHOULDNA SHUCKED MY PARKA SO SOON. NOT TOO BAD IN HERE THOUGH--AND MY MUTANT METABOLISM'LL REDUCE THE COLD'S EFFECTS.
SNFF
SNFF
NO SCENT OF PEOPLE, FOOD, ANYTHING LIKE THAT. IF THEY'RE ALL DEAD, THE LOW TEMP'D PRESERVE THEM, KEEP THEM FROM TURNING.
NO SIGN OF ANYONE... BUT SOMEBODY HAD A LITTLE 'ROID RAGE...
DIDN'T TELL ME WHAT IT WAS THEY WERE RESEARCHING. LOOKS LIKE THEY WERE TAKING SAMPLES OF THE GLACIAL ICE--DEEP CORE CROSS-SECTIONS...
WHY WOULD THAT BE SO SECRET...?
MINERALS? FOSSILS? OR MAYBE THEY PULLED SOMETHING OUTTA THE ICE THAT THEY SHOULDN'T HAVE...?
SNFF
WHAT'S THAT SMELL? ACRID... LIKE, CHEMICAL... KEROSENE...?

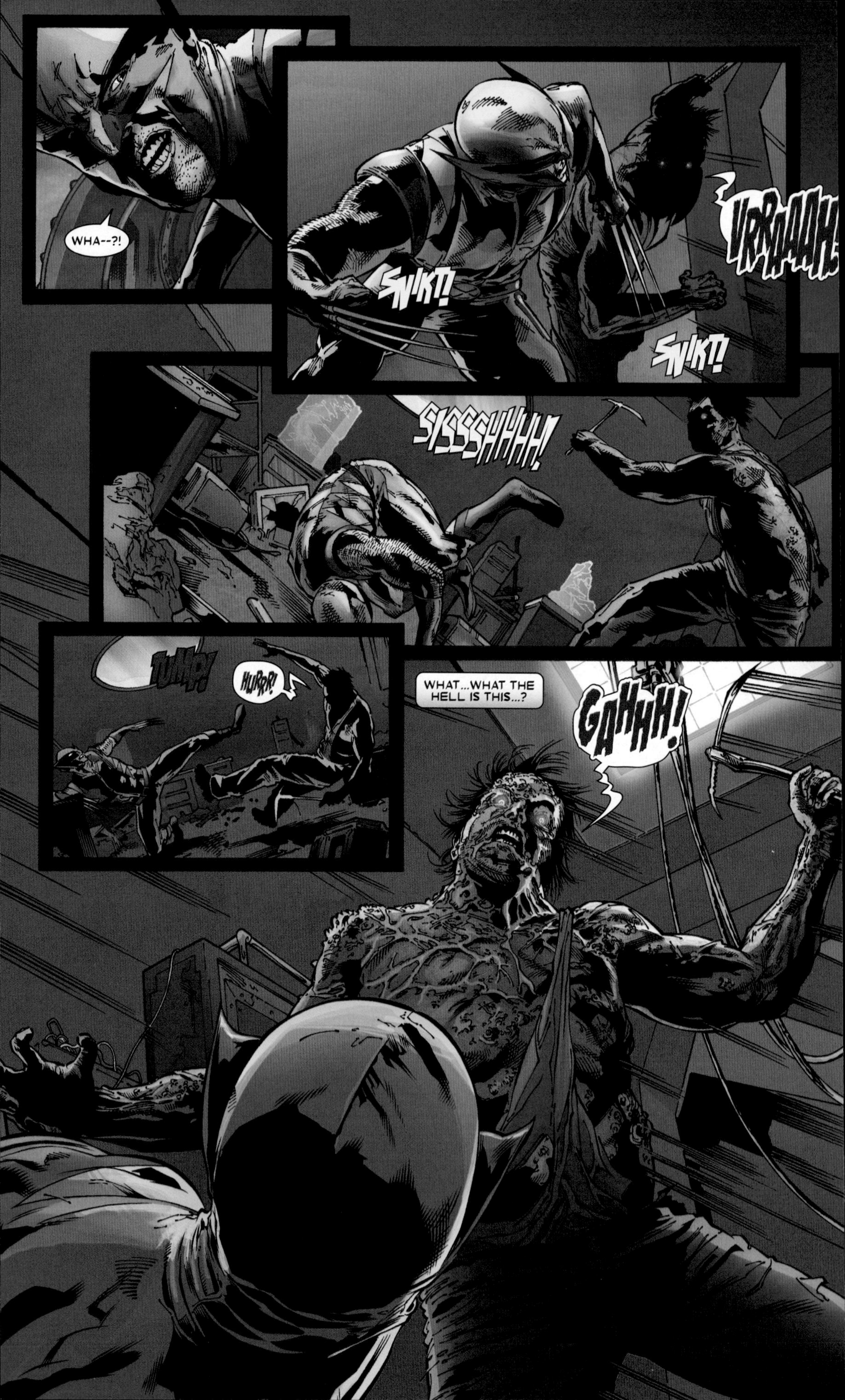
WHA--?!
SNIKT!
VRRAAAH!
SNIKT!
SISSSHHHH!
THMP!
HURRR!
WHAT...WHAT THE HELL IS THIS...?
GAHHH!

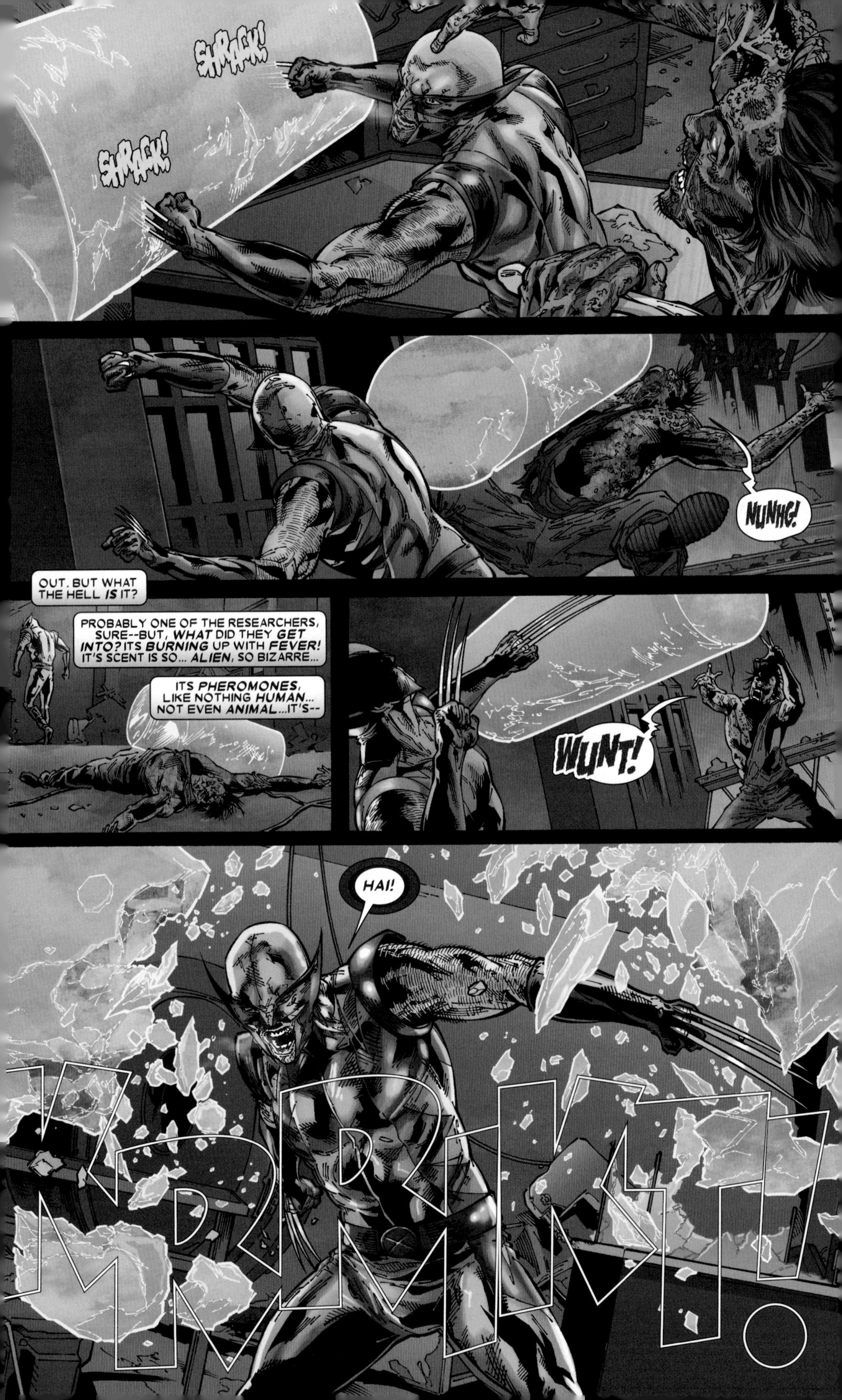
SHRACK!
SHRACK!
NUNHG!
OUT. BUT WHAT THE HELL *IS* IT?
PROBABLY ONE OF THE RESEARCHERS, SURE--BUT, *WHAT* DID THEY *GET INTO?* ITS *BURNING* UP WITH *FEVER!* IT'S SCENT IS SO... *ALIEN*, SO BIZARRE...
ITS *PHEROMONES*, LIKE NOTHING *HUMAN*... NOT EVEN *ANIMAL*...IT'S--
WUNT!
HAI!

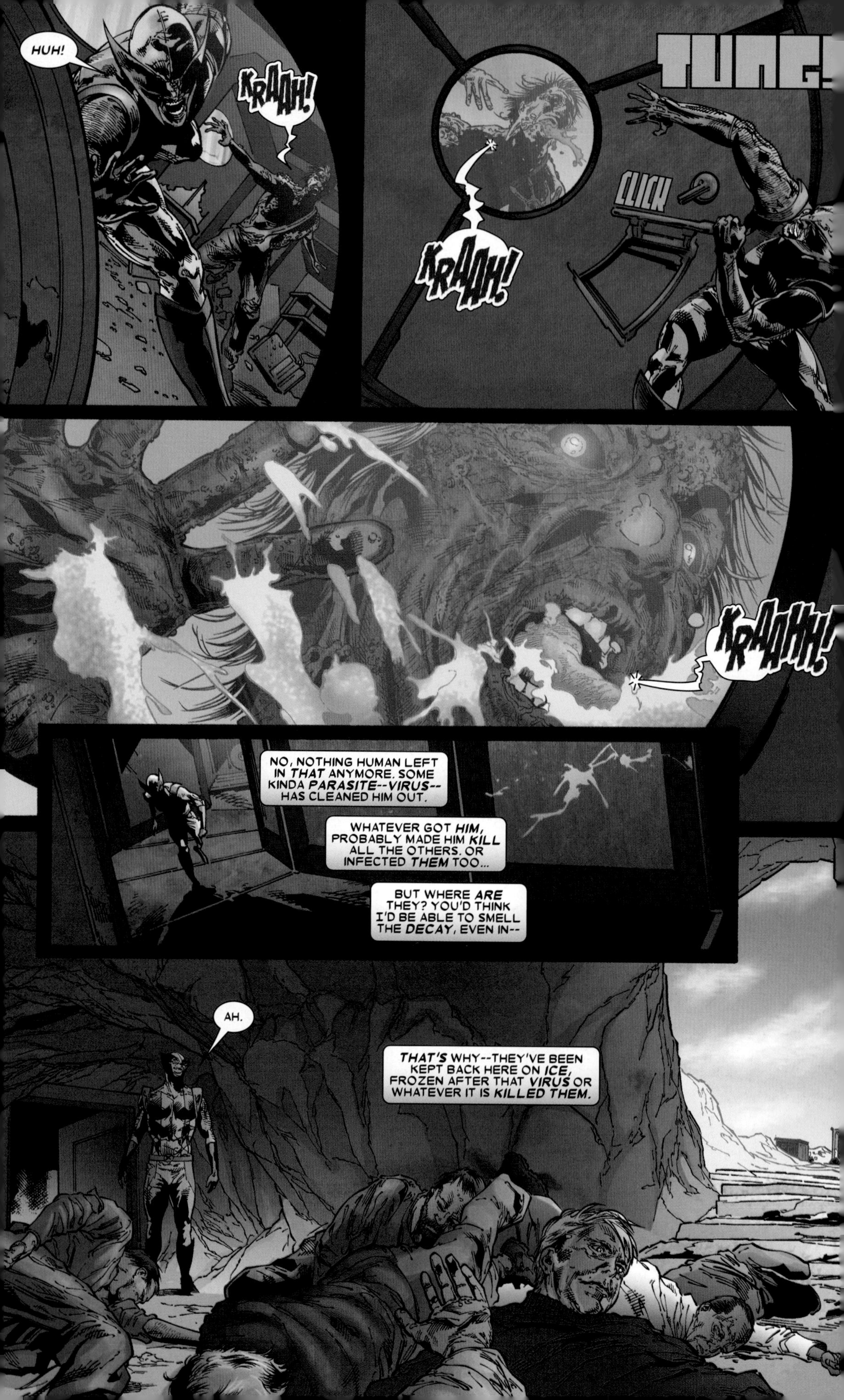
HUH!
KRAAH!
TUNG!
KRAAH!
CLICK
KRAAHH!
NO, NOTHING HUMAN LEFT IN *THAT* ANYMORE. SOME KINDA *PARASITE--VIRUS--* HAS CLEANED HIM OUT.
WHATEVER GOT *HIM*, PROBABLY MADE HIM *KILL* ALL THE OTHERS. OR INFECTED *THEM* TOO...
BUT WHERE *ARE* THEY? YOU'D THINK I'D BE ABLE TO SMELL THE *DECAY*, EVEN IN--
AH.
THAT'S WHY--THEY'VE BEEN KEPT BACK HERE ON *ICE*, FROZEN AFTER THAT *VIRUS* OR WHATEVER IT IS *KILLED THEM*.

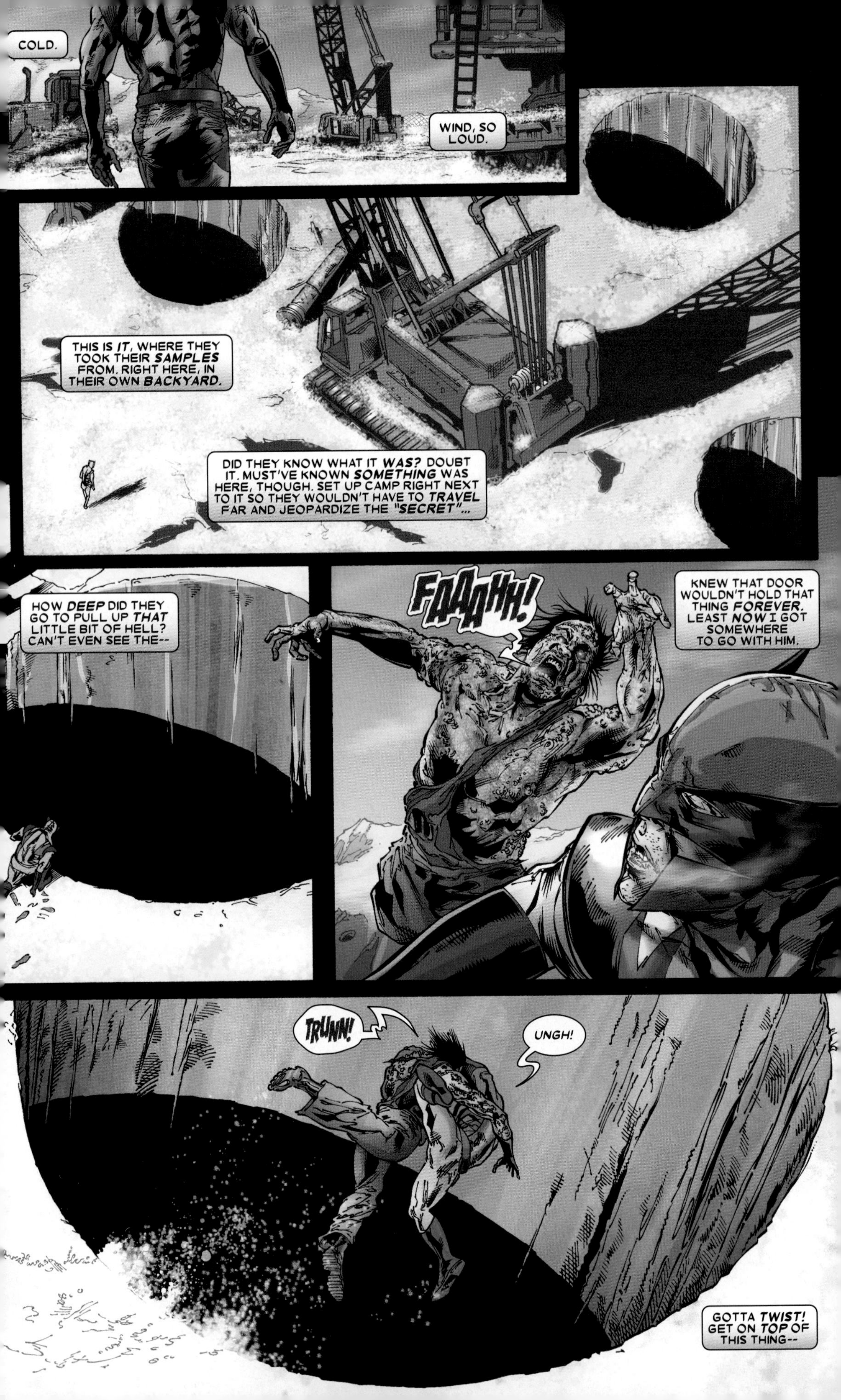
COLD.
WIND, SO LOUD.
THIS IS *IT*, WHERE THEY TOOK THEIR *SAMPLES* FROM. RIGHT HERE, IN THEIR OWN *BACKYARD.*
DID THEY KNOW WHAT IT *WAS?* DOUBT IT. MUST'VE KNOWN *SOMETHING* WAS HERE, THOUGH. SET UP CAMP RIGHT NEXT TO IT SO THEY WOULDN'T HAVE TO *TRAVEL* FAR AND JEOPARDIZE THE *"SECRET"*...
HOW *DEEP* DID THEY GO TO PULL UP *THAT* LITTLE BIT OF HELL? CAN'T EVEN SEE THE--
FAAAHH!
KNEW THAT DOOR WOULDN'T HOLD THAT THING *FOREVER.* LEAST *NOW* I GOT SOMEWHERE TO GO WITH HIM.
TRUNN!
UNGH!
GOTTA *TWIST!* GET ON *TOP* OF THIS THING--

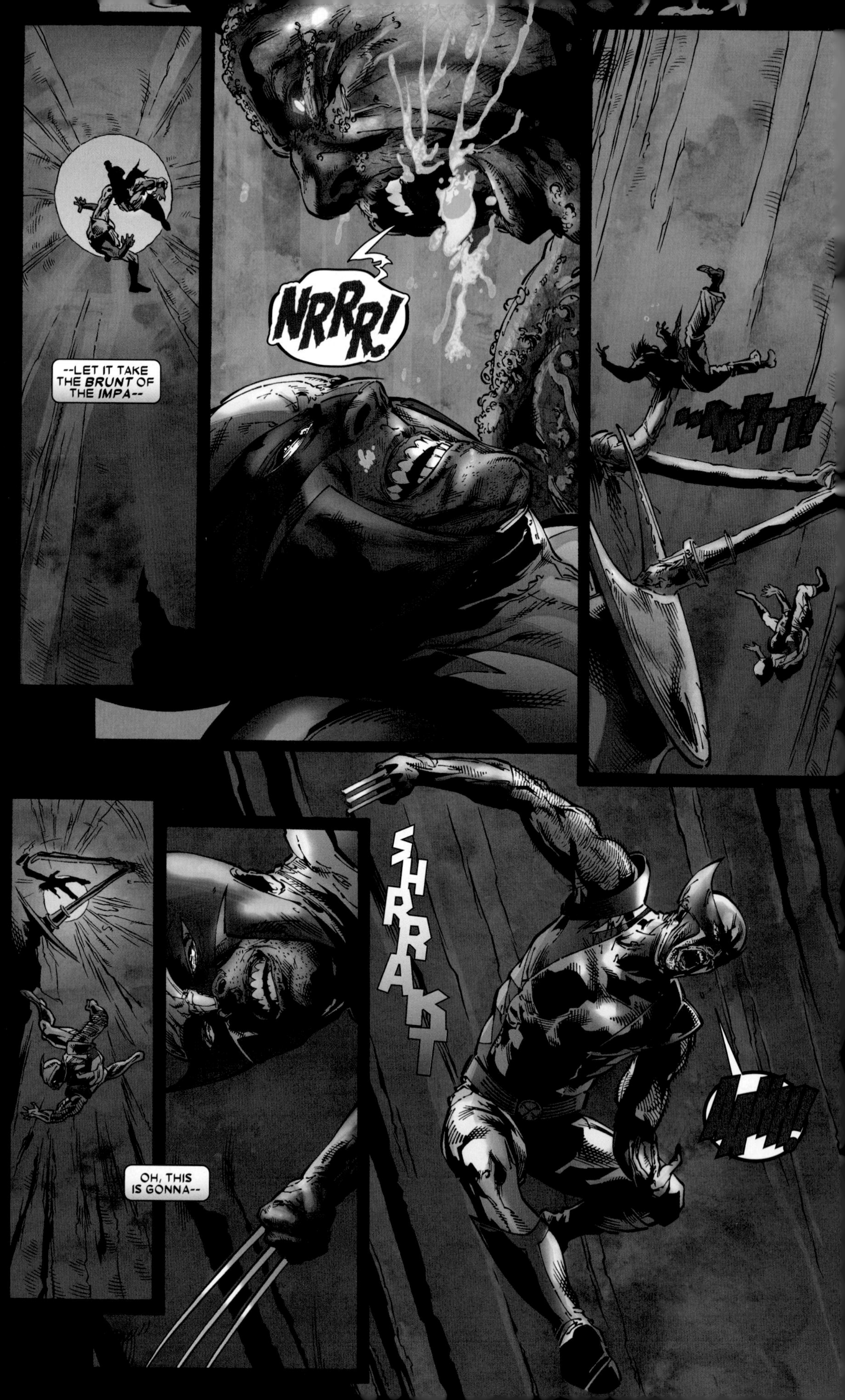

--LET IT TAKE THE *BRUNT* OF THE *IMPA*--
NRRR!
--KTTT!
OH, THIS IS GONNA--
SHRRAKT

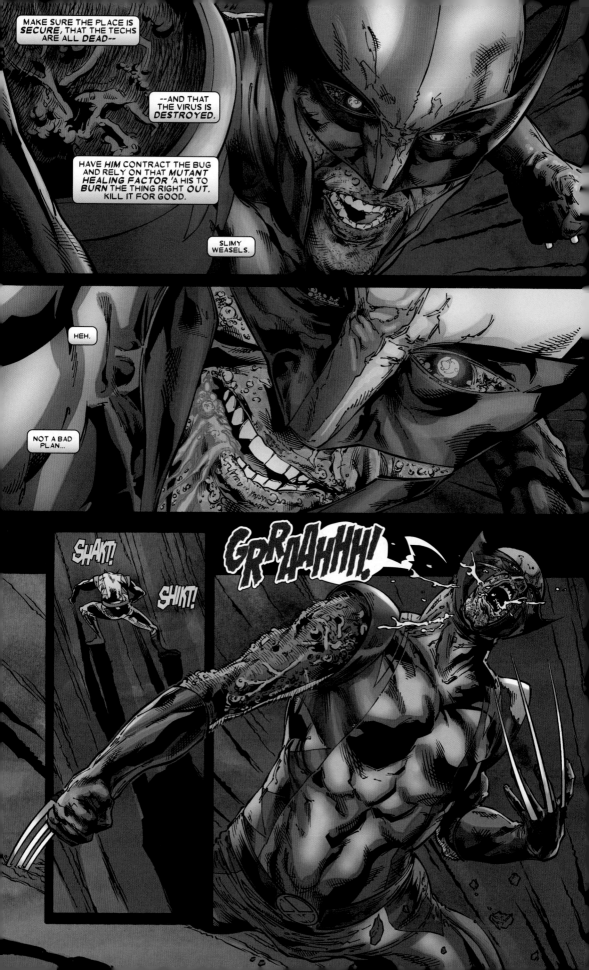

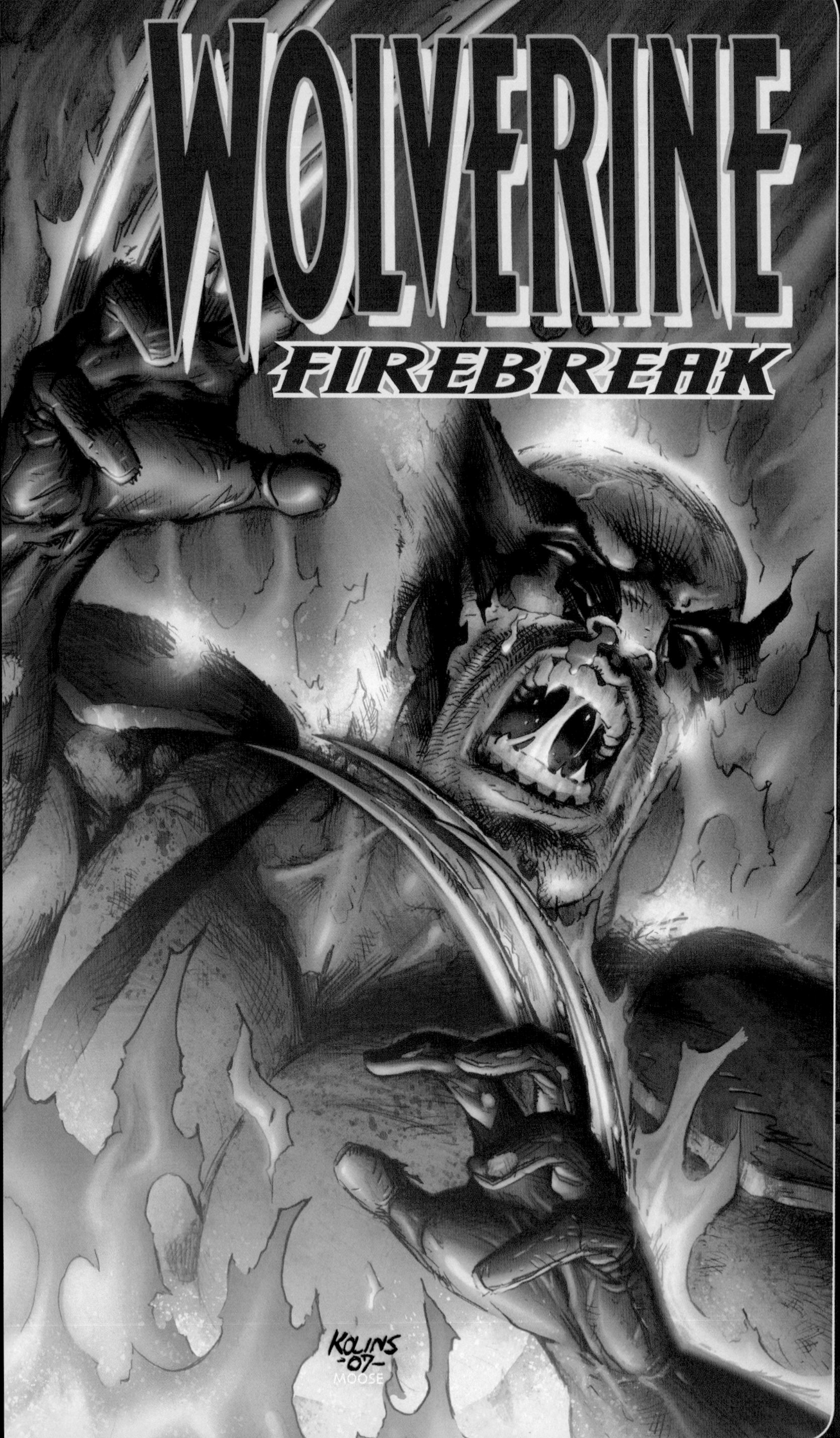
WOLVERINE
FIREBREAK
KOLINS
-07-
MOOSE

Then there was a sound like  **SNIKT!**

And something _else_ came out of the fire. Something that smelled of burned _meat_.

And sulphur.

And _blood._

FIREBREAK

MIKE CAREY WRITER
SCOTT KOLINS PENCILER
MOOSE BAUMANN COLORIST
TROY PETERI LETTERER
AUBREY SITTERSON EDITOR
JOE QUESADA EDITOR IN CHIEF
DAN BUCKLEY PUBLISHER

 _GRAAAH!_

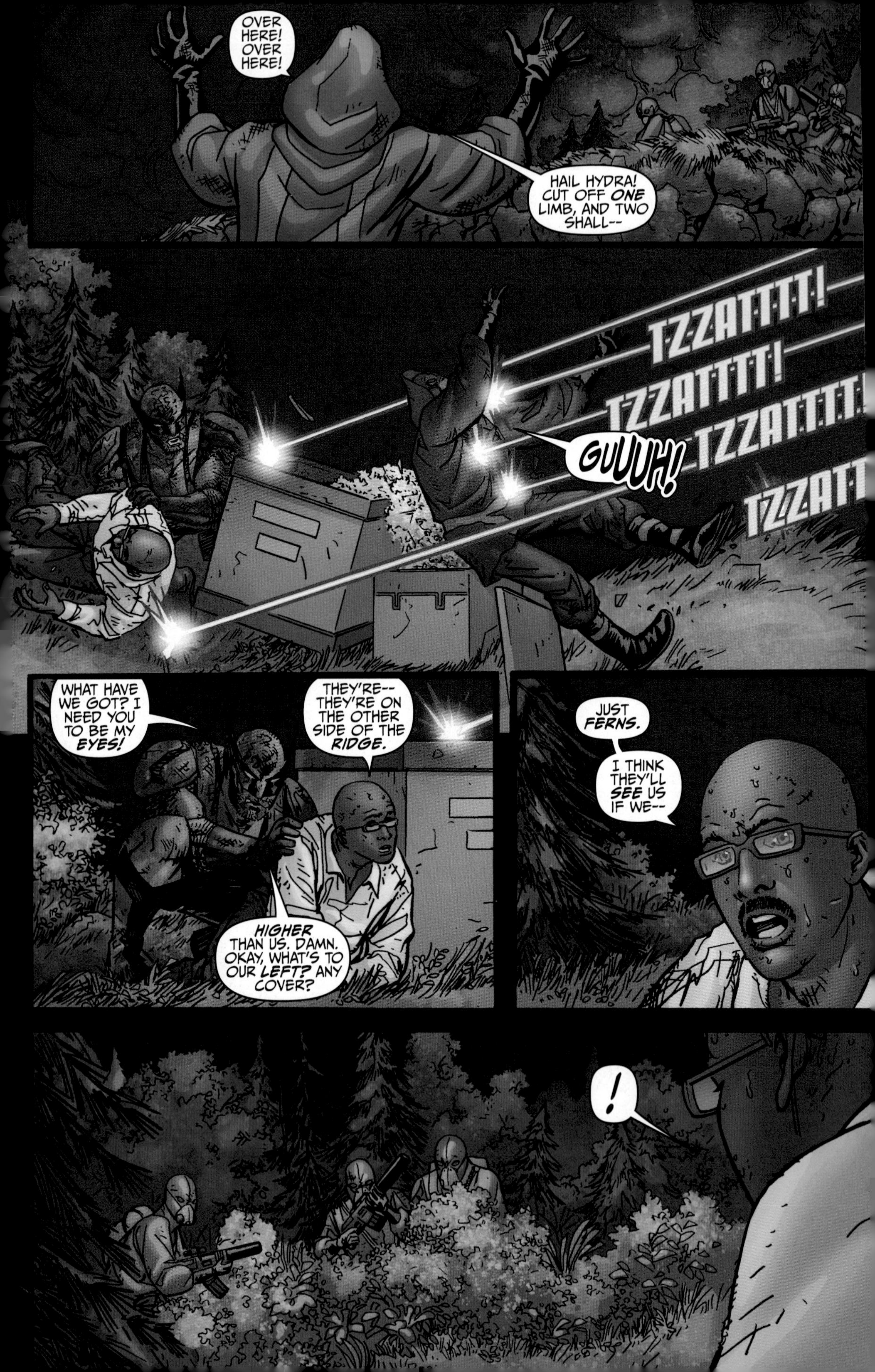
OVER HERE! OVER HERE!
HAIL HYDRA! CUT OFF ONE LIMB, AND TWO SHALL--
T-Z-ZAT-T-T-T!
TZZATTTT!
TZZAT-T-T-T!
TZZAT-T-T-T!
GUUUH!
TZZAT-
WHAT HAVE WE GOT? I NEED YOU TO BE MY EYES!
THEY'RE-- THEY'RE ON THE OTHER SIDE OF THE RIDGE.
HIGHER THAN US. DAMN. OKAY, WHAT'S TO OUR LEFT? ANY COVER?
JUST FERNS.
I THINK THEY'LL SEE US IF WE--
!

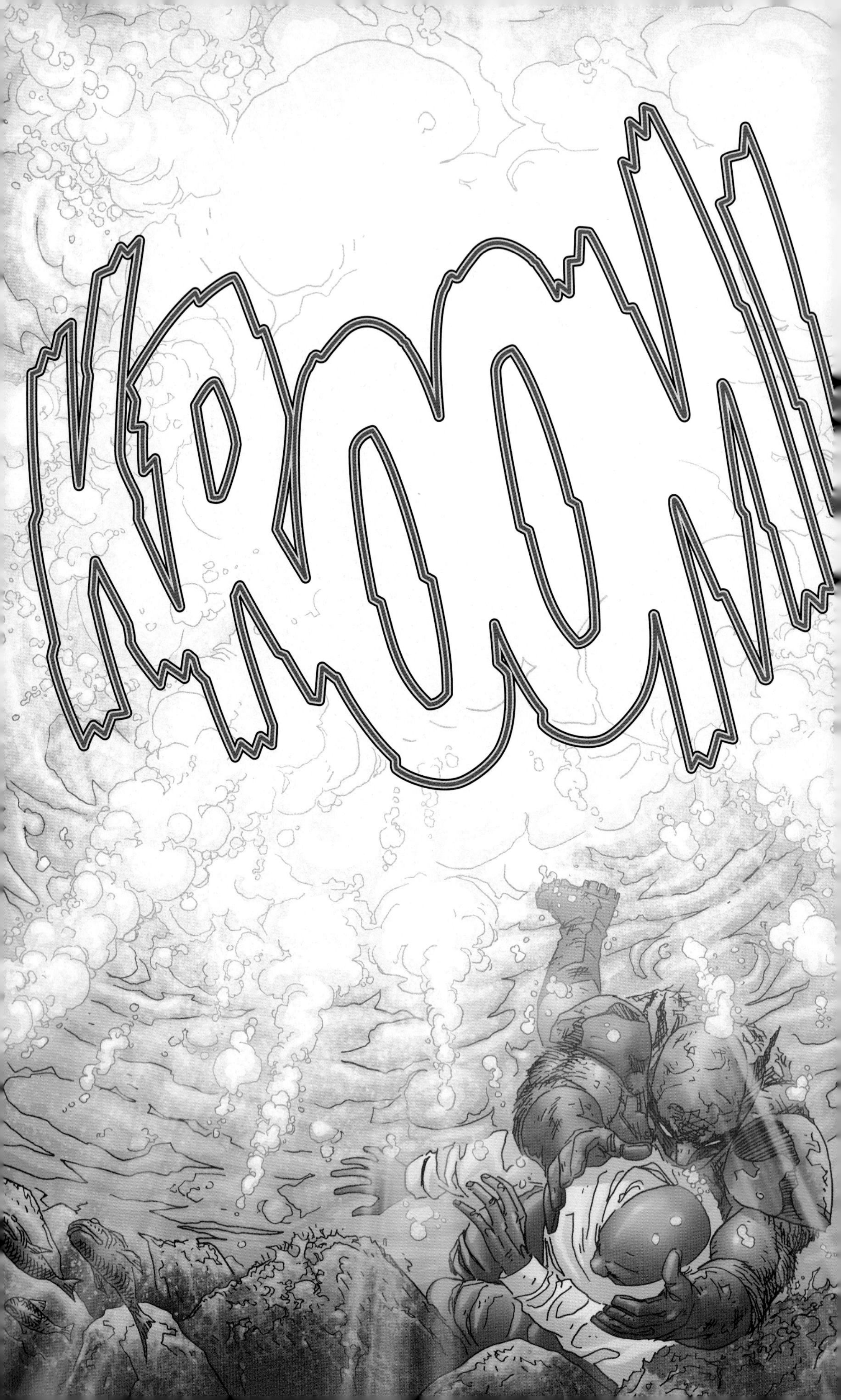
KRRROOM!!

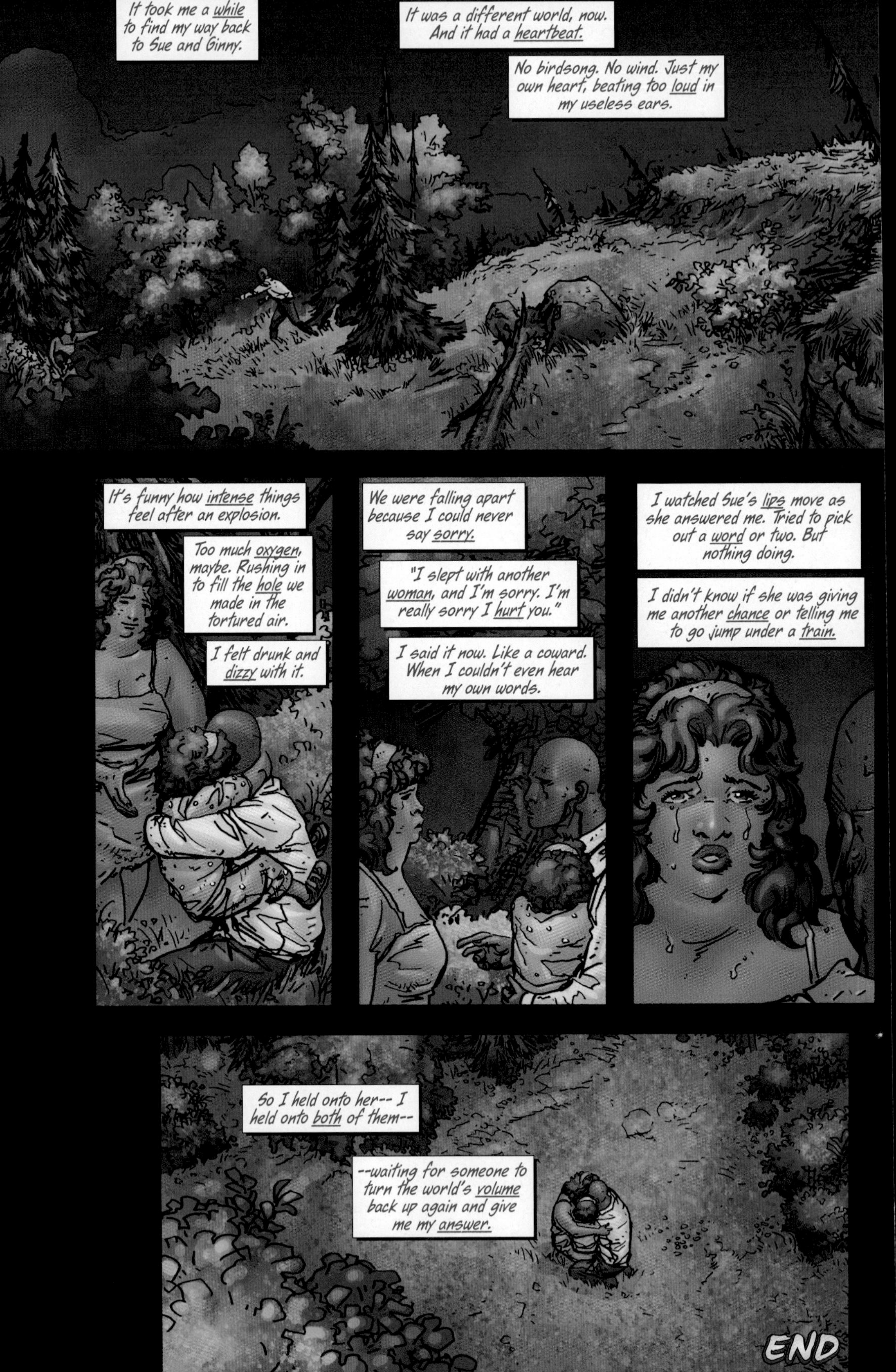
It took me a while to find my way back to Sue and Ginny.
It was a different world, now. And it had a heartbeat.
No birdsong. No wind. Just my own heart, beating too loud in my useless ears.
It's funny how intense things feel after an explosion.
Too much oxygen, maybe. Rushing in to fill the hole we made in the tortured air.
I felt drunk and dizzy with it.
We were falling apart because I could never say sorry.
"I slept with another woman, and I'm sorry. I'm really sorry I hurt you."
I said it now. Like a coward. When I couldn't even hear my own words.
I watched Sue's lips move as she answered me. Tried to pick out a word or two. But nothing doing.
I didn't know if she was giving me another chance or telling me to go jump under a train.
So I held onto her-- I held onto both of them--
--waiting for someone to turn the world's volume back up again and give me my answer.
END

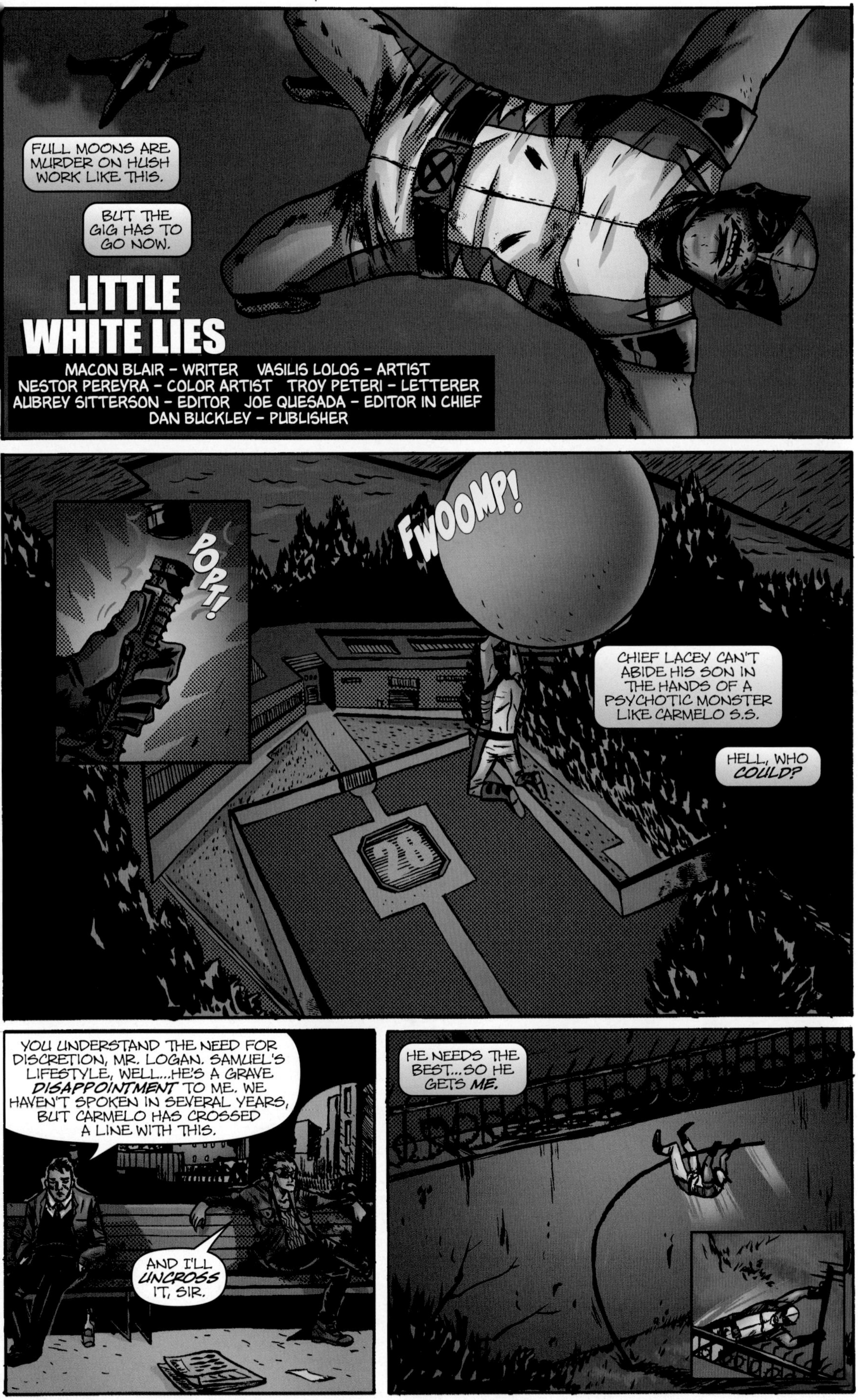

FULL MOONS ARE MURDER ON HUSH WORK LIKE THIS.
BUT THE GIG HAS TO GO NOW.
LITTLE WHITE LIES
MACON BLAIR – WRITER VASILIS LOLOS – ARTIST
NESTOR PEREYRA – COLOR ARTIST TROY PETERI – LETTERER
AUBREY SITTERSON – EDITOR JOE QUESADA – EDITOR IN CHIEF
DAN BUCKLEY – PUBLISHER
POPT!
FWOOMP!
CHIEF LACEY CAN'T ABIDE HIS SON IN THE HANDS OF A PSYCHOTIC MONSTER LIKE CARMELO S.S.
HELL, WHO *COULD?*
28
YOU UNDERSTAND THE NEED FOR DISCRETION, MR. LOGAN. SAMUEL'S LIFESTYLE, WELL...HE'S A GRAVE *DISAPPOINTMENT* TO ME. WE HAVEN'T SPOKEN IN SEVERAL YEARS, BUT CARMELO HAS CROSSED A LINE WITH THIS.
AND I'LL *UNCROSS* IT, SIR.
HE NEEDS THE BEST...SO HE GETS *ME.*

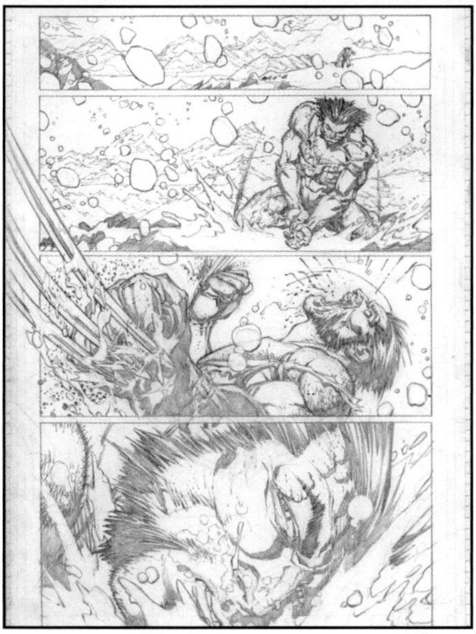
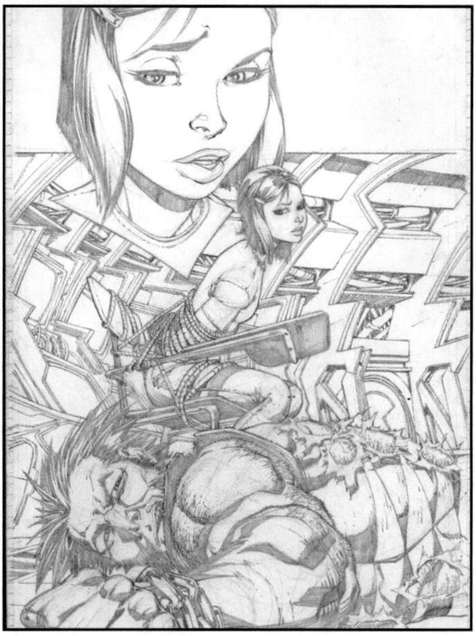
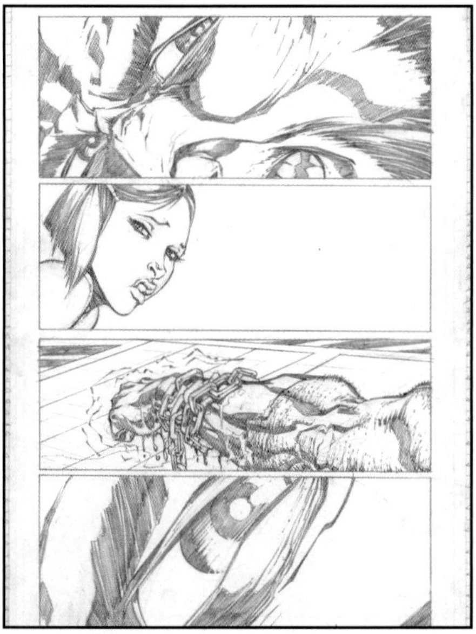
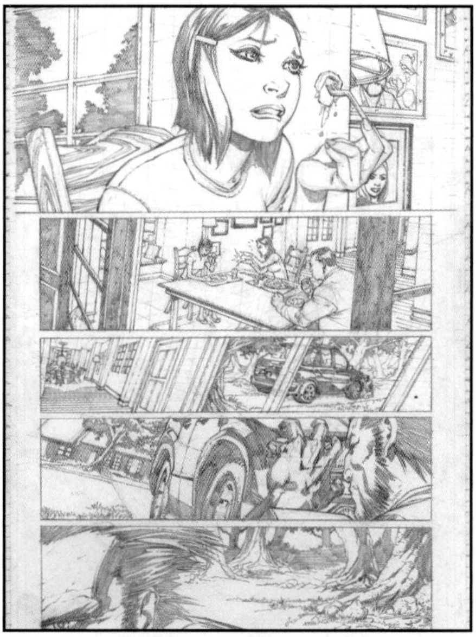
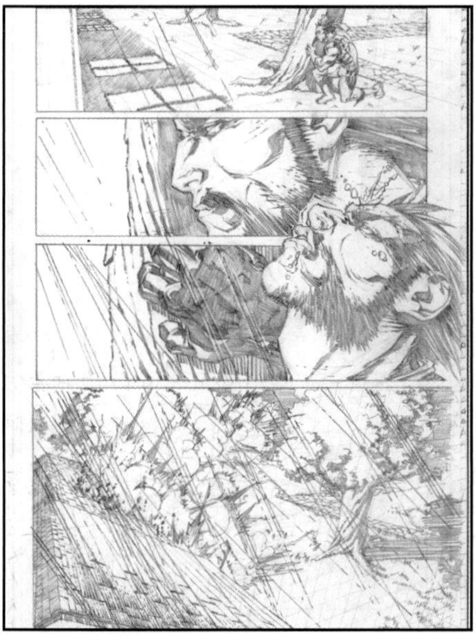
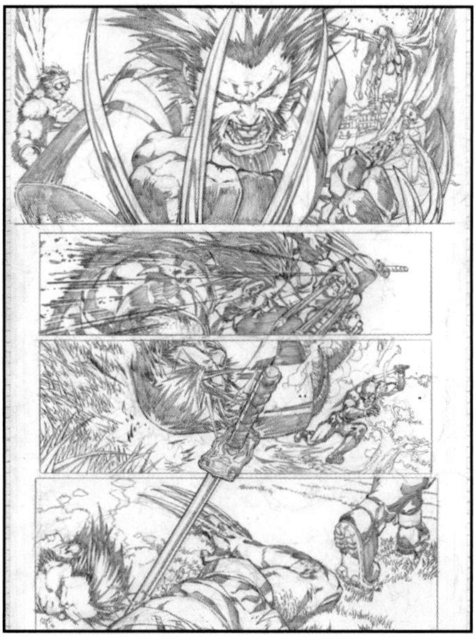

"Killing Wolverine Made Simple" Pencils by Koi Turnbull

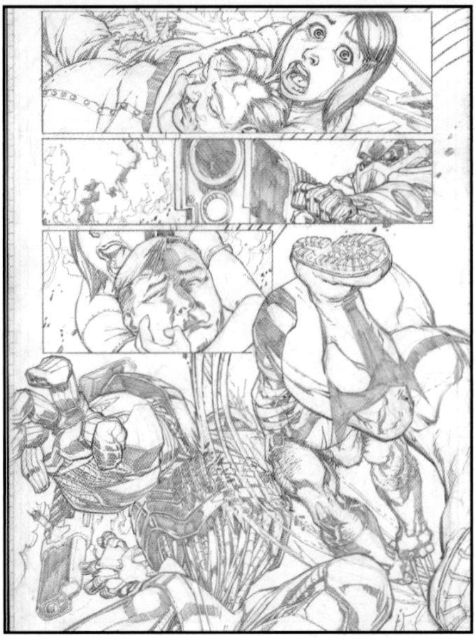
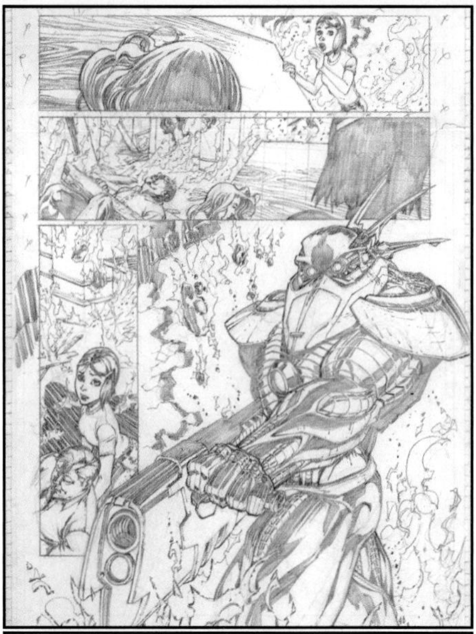
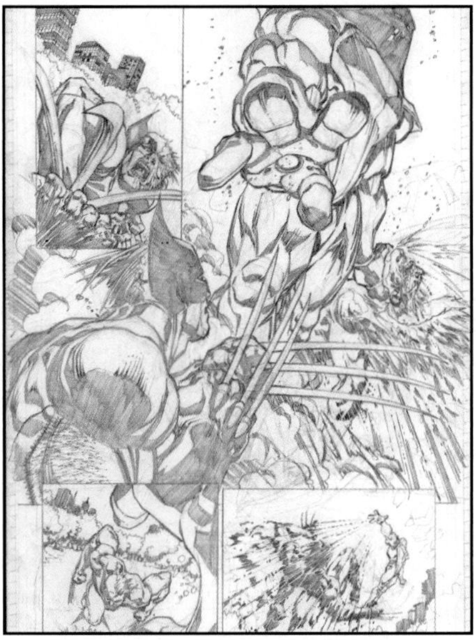
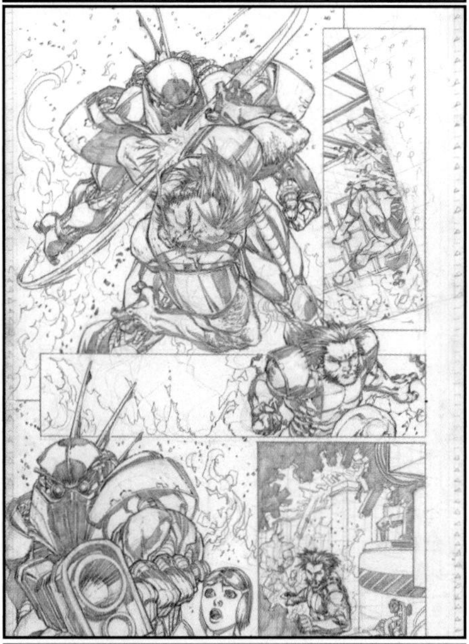
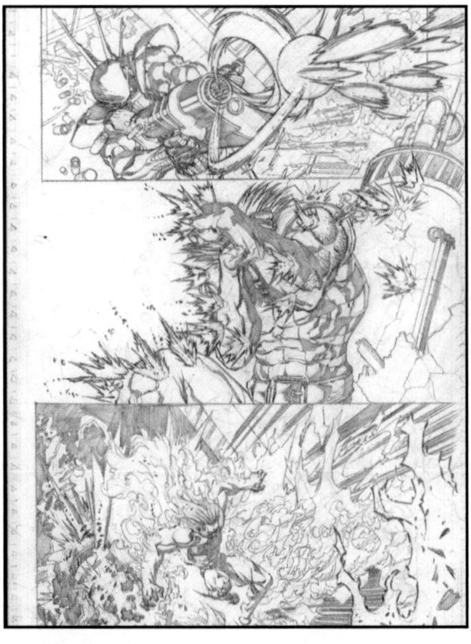
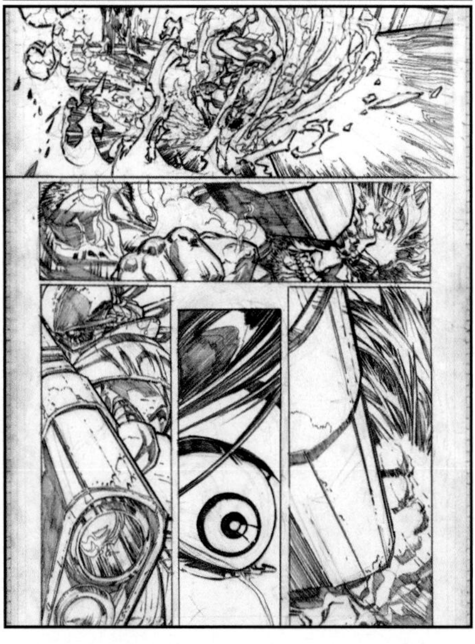

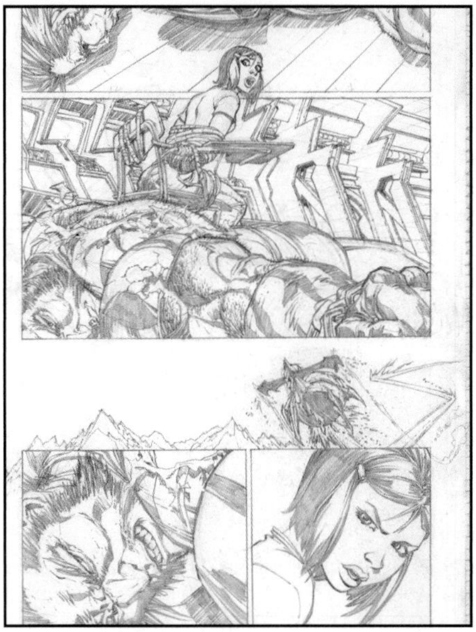
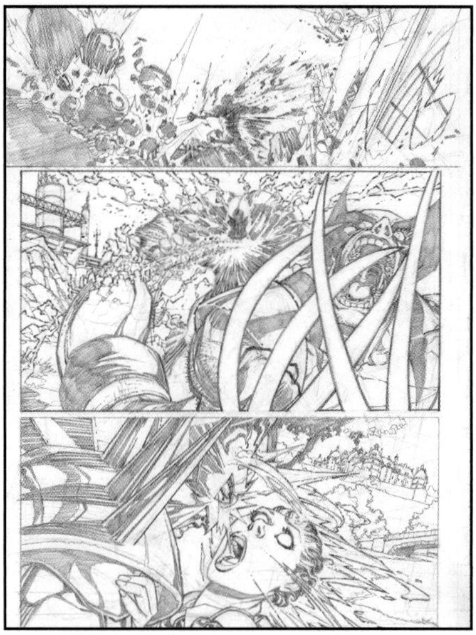
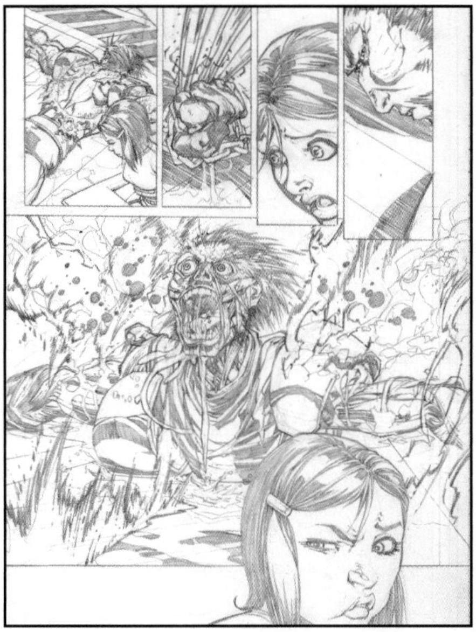
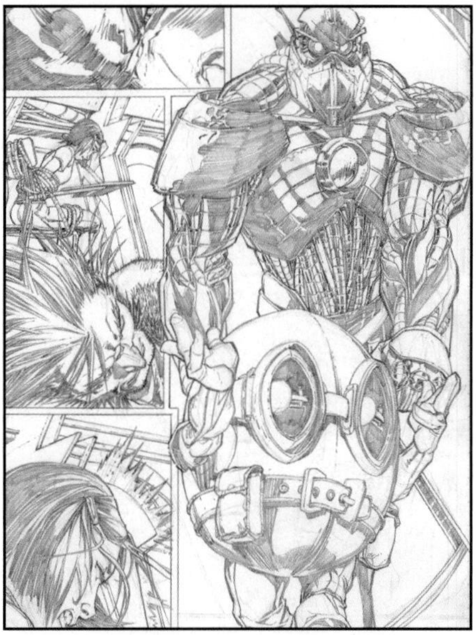
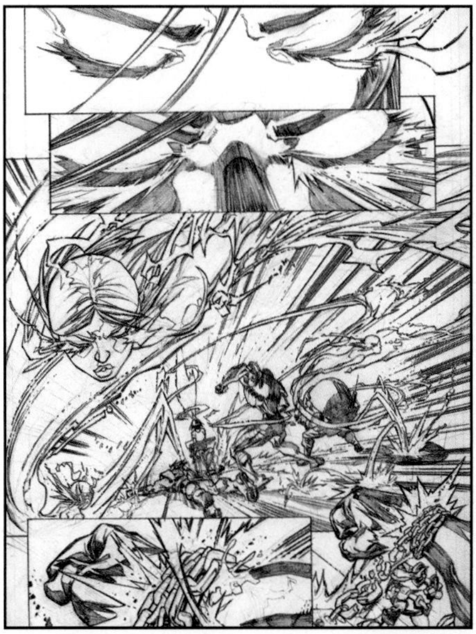
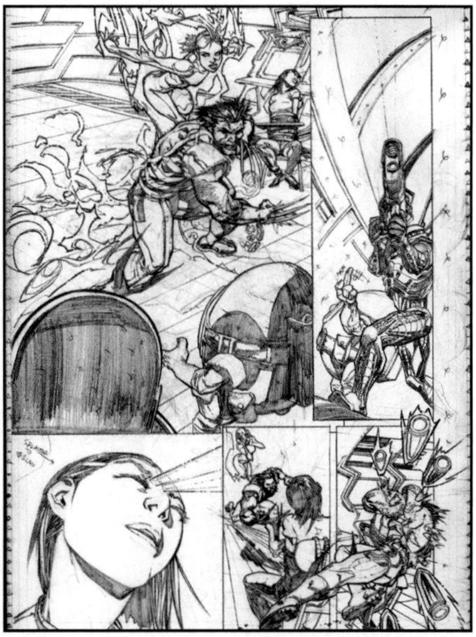

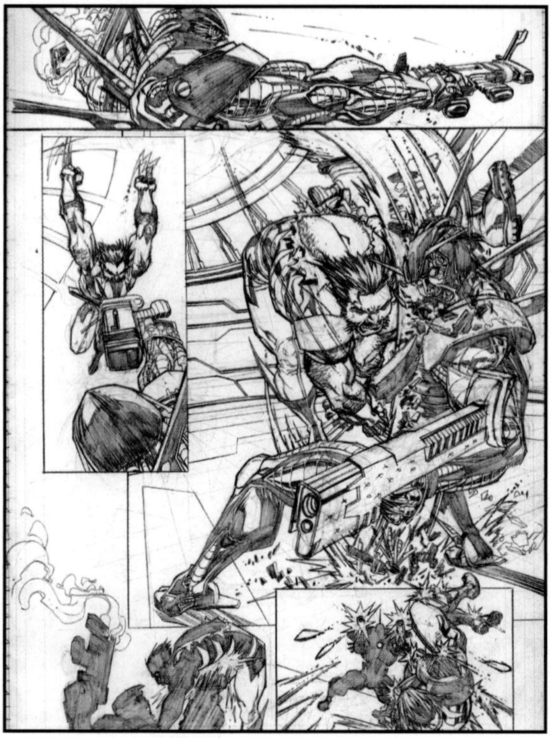
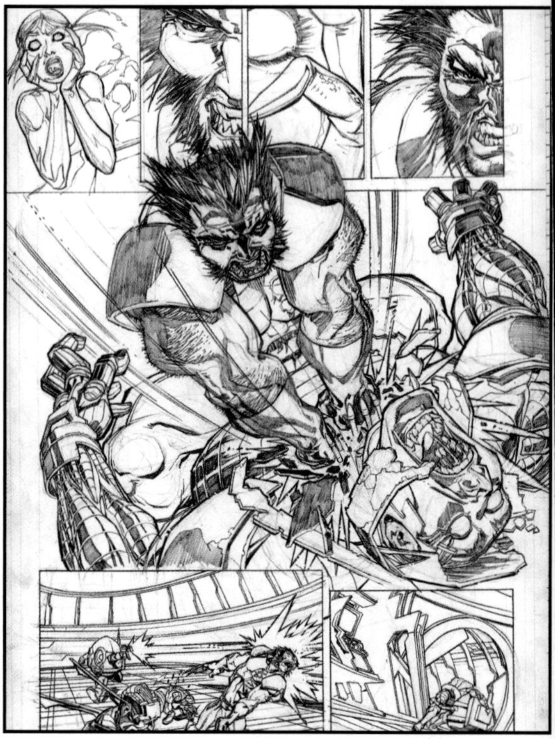
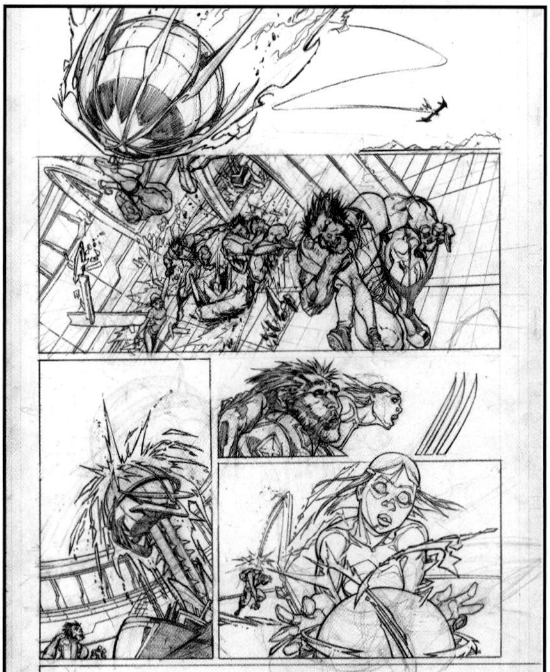
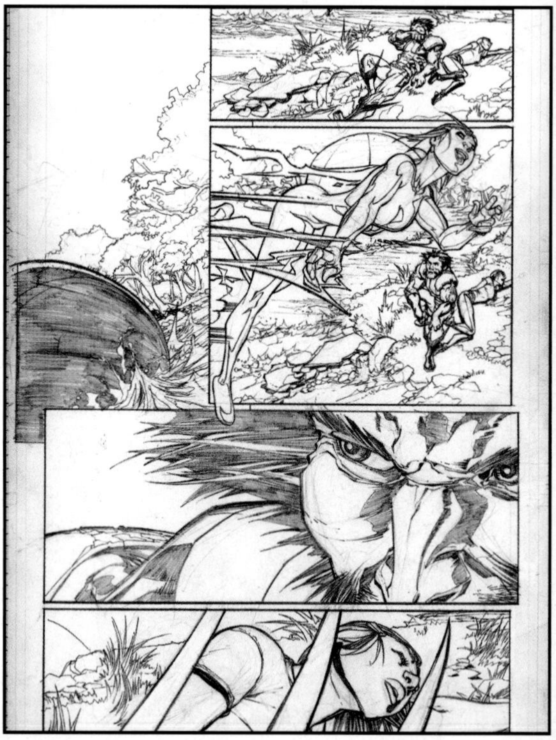